JOHN MAJOR

An Unsuccessful Prime Minister?

JOHN MAJOR

An Unsuccessful Prime Minister?

—REAPPRAISING JOHN MAJOR—

Edited by Kevin Hickson & Ben Williams

First published in Great Britain in 2017 by
Biteback Publishing Ltd
Westminster Tower
3 Albert Embankment
London SE1 7SP

ISBN 978-1-78590-067-9

10 9 8 7 6 5 4 3 2 1

A CIP catalogue record for this book is available from the British Library.

Set in Bulmer

Printed and bound in Great Britain by
CPI Group (UK) Ltd, Croydon CR0 4YY

CONTENTS

NOTES ON CONTRIBUTORS

Paul Anderson was editor of *Tribune* (1991–93) and deputy editor of the *New Statesman* (1993–96). He was co-author of *Safety First: The Making of New Labour* (1997, with Nyta Mann) and is currently a lecturer in journalism at the University of Essex.

Lord (Paddy) Ashdown was the founding Leader of the Liberal Democrats between 1988 and 1999 and the international communities' High Representative and European Union Special Representative to Bosnia and Herzegovina between 2002 and 2006. He is now a Liberal Democrat peer. His autobiography, *A Fortunate Life*, appeared in 2010 and he has also published two volumes of diaries and six other books.

Arthur Aughey is Emeritus Professor of Politics at Ulster University. He has published extensively on the Conservative Party, British national identity and the politics of Northern Ireland.

Charles Clarke was MP for Norwich South (1997–2010), during which time he held various Cabinet posts including Home Secretary. Since 2010 he has been Visiting Professor to the School of Political, Social and International Studies at the University of East Anglia.

Mark Davies holds a Masters degree in History from Cambridge University, and a Masters degree in Law from University College London. He specialises in twentieth-century British history, European Union law and British constitutional law.

David Denver is Emeritus Professor of Politics at the University of Lancaster and is widely recognised as one of the leading experts on electoral studies. He has written extensively on British elections.

Sonia Exley is Assistant Professor in the Department of Social Policy at the London School of Economics. She has written extensively on education policy in Britain.

Mark Garnett is Senior Lecturer in Politics at the University of Lancaster, and is widely recognised as a leading scholar of the Conservative Party having published numerous biographies and histories.

Cathy Gormley-Heenan is Professor of Politics and Pro-Vice Chancellor for Research and Impact at Ulster University.

Kevin Hickson is Senior Lecturer in Politics at the University of Liverpool, where he has taught since 2003. He specialises in British political ideologies and has published on the political thought of the Conservatives, Labour and the Liberals/Liberal Democrats.

Wyn Grant is Emeritus Professor of Politics at the University of Warwick. He has written extensively on economic policy, agricultural policy and pressure groups.

Kevin Jefferys was formerly Professor of Contemporary History at Plymouth University and has written major studies of post-war British politics, the Labour Party, electoral politics and sport policy.

Shaun McDaid is Lecturer in Politics at the University of Huddersfield. His book, *Template for Peace: Northern Ireland, 1972–75*, was published in paperback in 2016.

Catherine McGlynn is Senior Lecturer in Politics at the University of Huddersfield, where she teaches and researches on conflict resolution and identity politics. She has published widely on the politics of Northern Ireland.

Lord (Philip) Norton is Professor of Government and Director of the Centre for Legislative Studies at the University of Hull and a Conservative peer. He is widely recognised as a leading authority on the British constitution, having published thirty-one books and many articles.

Peter Oborne is the former chief political commentator of the *Daily Telegraph*. He writes a weekly column for *Middle East Eye* and the *Daily Mail*. He has written a number of books, including *The Triumph of the Political Class* (2007) and *The Rise of Political Lying* (2005). He appears on BBC programmes *Any Questions?* and *Question Time* and often presents *Week in Westminster*. He was voted Columnist of the Year at the Press Awards in 2017.

Gillian Peele is an Emeritus Fellow of Lady Margaret Hall, Oxford. Her most recent publications are *The Regulation of Standards in British Public Life* (with David Hine) and *David Cameron and Conservative Renewal* (edited with John Francis).

Bruce Pilbeam is Senior Lecturer in Politics at London Metropolitan University. He is the author of *Conservatism in Crisis* (2003) as well as numerous journal articles and chapters in edited books.

John Redwood is Conservative MP for Wokingham, where he has sat since 1987, having previously been Head of the No. 10 Policy Unit. He served in John Major's Cabinet prior to his resignation and leadership challenge in

1995. He has published numerous books on various aspects of politics and public policy.

Anthony Seldon is Vice Chancellor of the University of Buckingham, having previously been Master of Wellington and Brighton Colleges. He has produced many books on British politics, including biographies of John Major, Tony Blair and David Cameron.

Andrew Taylor is Professor of Politics at the University of Sheffield. He has published widely on British politics. Currently he is completing a study, *What About the Workers?* (Manchester University Press), examining the Conservative Party's relations with the organised working class.

Tony Travers is a professor in the Department of Government at LSE and has published extensively on British local government and London politics.

Alwyn W. Turner is an author who has published extensively on British politics and popular culture. His books include *Rejoice, Rejoice: Britain in the 1980s* (2010) and *A Classless Society: Britain in the 1990s* (2013). He lectures at Chichester University.

Ben Williams is a politics tutor at the University of Salford. He completed his PhD at the University of Liverpool between 2009 and 2013 and has written for a range of books, magazines, blogs and journals covering British politics.

Christian Wolmar is a writer and broadcaster who is the author of more than a dozen books on transport policy and railways, including, most recently, *Are Trams Socialist? Why Britain Has Never Had a Transport Policy* (2016) and *To the Edge of the World: The Story of the Trans-Siberian Railway* (2013). *Railways and the Raj: The Story of Indian Railways* is due to be published in the autumn of 2017. www.christianwolmar.co.uk @christianwolmar

FOREWORD

Peter Oborne

I NOW REGRET MY REPORTING of John Major in the 1990s. In partial mitigation I was a junior political reporter, and others were more twisted and biased than me. The press corps refused to give Mr Major a chance. We were out to destroy him and this we duly did when his Conservative Party was obliterated at the 1997 general election.

We collectively created a narrative which defined John Major as weak, sleazy, incompetent and out of his depth. We told a story of failure, and went on telling it. Towards the end it was almost impossible to get a story into any paper which was not framed in this way.

The leader of the pack was, at first, Alastair Campbell. Campbell later became press secretary for Tony Blair but he was political editor of the *Daily Mirror*, and one of Westminster's most powerful and charismatic journalists, when John Major became Prime Minister in 1990.

He refused to give John Major any of the respect to which a Prime Minister is entitled. On one occasion he called him 'the piece of lettuce who passes for a Prime Minister'. He also called John Major 'simply a second-rate, shallow, lying little toad of a man'.

Mr Campbell was abusive to the Prime Minister in person. On one official journey, on the Downing Street VC10, John Major wandered back to the press seats. He was full of ebullience, eager to talk. Campbell glared at him: 'Oh, sod off Prime Minister, I'm trying to do my expenses.' Campbell boasted about this in a column.

It was Campbell who spread the urban myth that John Major tucked his shirt into his underpants (although it was Ian Aitken, former political editor for *The Guardian*, who actually first wrote that this was the case). This was an especially vicious barb because it preyed so precisely on John Major's social insecurity about his urban, lower middle-class background. Some politicians, such as Bill Clinton, have turned a disadvantaged background into a political asset. One of John Major's weaknesses was an evident embarrassment about unfashionable origins.

Certain journalists – Matthew Parris of *The Times*, Bruce Anderson (who arguably veered too far in the opposite direction) and Charles Reiss as political editor of the *Evening Standard* – reported the Major government fairly and gave full credit to its achievements.

Most of the rest of us emerge poorly from this lamentable period of Fleet Street history. It was not merely that we were grossly unfair to Major. We also lost all sense of reality when it came to the rising new Labour leader, Tony Blair. Just as Major could do nothing right, Blair could do nothing wrong.

Political reporters don't like to admit this, but they are in essence courtiers. They gravitate to power. They crave access. In order to do this they turn a blind eye to the failings of the most powerful men and women, and they exaggerate their virtues.

Worse still, they scapegoat those who are seen to be losers. By the mid-1990s it was obvious to even the dimmest intelligence that Tony Blair was destined to be the next Prime Minister. The lobby fawned to him. It begged for favours. It squabbled for access. It became impossible to write a negative story about Mr Blair.

It wasn't just journalists who behaved in this undignified fashion. Proprietors did the same. Rupert Murdoch switched allegiance to Blair. Express Newspapers, for which I went to work on 1996, realised that it would be going too far to urge our elderly readership to vote Labour, but we were polite about Mr Blair.

Fleet Street collectively portrayed Mr Blair as the saviour of the nation and Major as a disaster. Both versions were false. It is today obvious, especially with the benefit of hindsight, that Mr Blair had few of the attributes we attributed to him, while John Major has substantial achievements to his credit.

But the narrative of John Major's hopelessness was so strong that for many years it was impossible to make the case in his favour. For example, Tony Blair, abetted by the client press, claimed all the credit for the Northern Irish peace process. Actually it was John Major who launched the peace process in 1993 with the Downing Street Declaration, which led to the IRA ceasefire. Politically this was brave, not least because it meant jeopardising the support of Ulster Unionist MPs at a time when the Conservative majority was wafer-thin. Yet his very distinguished role in ending the Troubles was airbrushed from history.

Let's now examine John Major's economic achievement. He became Prime Minister at the height of a recession, yet he and his Chancellor of the Exchequer, Ken Clarke, handed over the economy to New Labour in 1997 in near faultless condition. Unemployment was 1.6 million and falling, national finances were sound and growth steady. Yet New Labour and its acolytes in the press never once acknowledged this inheritance – and indeed they often went out of their way to deny or distort it.

Tories were at fault here too. They too started to grovel to Blair. After Labour had been in power a few years Michael Portillo stated in a *Sunday Times* column that Gordon Brown 'has single-handedly delivered the longest period of economic growth in Britain's industrial history'.

At the time Portillo was writing there had been fifty consecutive quarters of growth. This was indeed a record, but twenty of those quarters (and a further eight under inherited Tory spending plans) had occurred under John Major's government – of which Michael Portillo had been a member. Furthermore, John Major's growth was solid, whereas we now know that Brown's was an illusion, fuelled by borrowed money and imported labour.

Nor was John Major given credit for stopping the euro. It is reasonable to praise Gordon Brown for keeping Britain out of the single currency – even though he never once uttered a word against it, so far as I can discover. But Brown as Chancellor would never have been able to prevent Tony Blair taking us in but for John Major's very brave stand at Maastricht in arranging a British opt-out from European Monetary Union. But for that opt-out, we would today have been unable to use any of the weapons which the government has used to fend off recession: quantitative easing, dramatic currency easing and demand management. We never praised him for it.

Major was slammed for that Maastricht Treaty, both at the time and ever since. John Major's most enduring achievement, however, concerns public services. The press parroted the Labour myth that traffic cone hotlines and the Citizen's Charter were the limit of his achievement.

However, it is easy to show that his government was stunningly radical when it came to education, health and the welfare state. His educational reforms gave schools autonomy from local authority control, encouraged parents' right to choose and set head teachers free to run their own schools. In health, John Major introduced the internal market, the purchaser-provider split and GP fund-holding.

All of these changes were denounced by Tony Blair and his media chorus. Labour's 1997 manifesto pledged to 'restore the NHS as a public service working co-operatively for patients'. Frank Dobson, Labour's new Health Secretary, immediately scrapped patient choice and GP fund-holding. Likewise David Blunkett sabotaged grant-maintained schools, ended their financial independence and imposed an array of centrally imposed targets, few of which worked.

After Tony Blair won the 2001 election he finally realised that John Major's view of the public services had actually been rather visionary after all. So he set about restoring patient choice, brought back GP fund-holding and recreated the internal market. It was too embarrassing to restore grant-maintained schools so they were reincarnated under a new name as 'trust schools'. John Major's derided city technology colleges, which he had personally rescued in July 1991, were re-launched as city academies.

So the so-called 'radicalism' of Tony Blair's final few years in office was actually a laborious recreation of the John Major reforms that had been reversed by New Labour in 1997. These 'Blairite' reforms were put on hold by Gordon Brown, then implemented in a truly thoroughgoing way by the coalition government after the 2010 election.

Then there were the minor triumphs like the National Lottery, which has raised £25 billion for good causes. The reason why John Major was able to achieve so much was because – in sharp contrast to Tony Blair – he believed in Cabinet government. He left decision-making in the hands of a highly competent collection of ministers – Ken Clarke, Douglas Hurd, Michael Howard, Peter Lilley, Michael Heseltine and the young William Hague. There was no sofa government and no attempt to establish control from the centre, the misconception that turned New Labour into such a disaster.

Major's government gathered a reputation for division and there was indeed a (rather honourable) split over Europe. But there was very little of the hatred, the plotting and distrust between the most senior figures of government over narrow personal matters that subsequently damaged New Labour in power. Indeed the most senior members of the Cabinet – Major, Clarke, Heseltine, Hurd, Howard – got on pretty well.

The John Major government is remembered as sleazy. But this idea was mainly the creation of the brilliant New Labour propaganda machine in alliance with the press. So-called Tory sleaze was dwarfed by the systemic New Labour corruption and deceit which disfigured the first decade of the twenty-first century. And consider the Gulf War in 1990. Under Major it was well-planned, with limited objectives, a considered exit strategy, and no lying. What a contrast to the Iraq invasion in 2003!

John Major will not go down in history as a great Prime Minister. He lacked the language and the inner poise and made one reputation-destroying howler – Black Wednesday in 1992, with sterling's forced eviction from the Exchange Rate Mechanism.

After that he faced a two-pronged attack. On the one hand he was hated by the Thatcherites. On the other hand, New Labour ran a brilliant, though unprincipled, operation to discredit him. It became fashionable to mock John Major by imitating his voice and mannerisms, the trend started by Alastair Campbell when he was political editor of the *Daily Mirror*.

Snobbery was part of it. As a youngish and relatively inexperienced political reporter on the *Evening Standard* at the time, I am afraid that I swallowed this vindictive analysis and feel remorseful about it today.

Something strange happened to the press in the 1990s. It had been dragooned behind Maggie Thatcher and against Neil Kinnock (who as leader of the opposition received almost as unfair a press as Major) in the previous decade.

Then Thatcher fell. She went at a moment when the media class was on the rise and the age of deference was ending. Superior interviewers like Paxman and Humphrys, who behaved as if they were more virtuous than politicians, were greatly admired. Politicians were despised. The press and media cut loose. Tony Blair brought the press back into heel when he became Prime Minister in 1997.

John Major was good at substance, but wretched at spin. New Labour was the opposite. For many years this public relations expertise worked for New Labour. However, over time I believe that John Major will come to be regarded as a more honest, decent and competent Prime Minister than either Tony Blair, Gordon Brown or, for that matter, David Cameron. He left Britain, as he might himself have remarked, a not-inconsiderably better place than he found it. He has an honourable place in our island story.

INTRODUCTION

Kevin Hickson and Ben Williams

JOHN MAJOR'S TIME AS Prime Minister is often overlooked; a stop gap between the much more eventful governments of Margaret Thatcher and Tony Blair. For the final years of his premiership his government appeared to be living on borrowed time. Beset by sleaze, divisions over European integration and apparent policy failures, it is easy to dismiss Major's premiership. Certainly this was the way it was viewed by many contemporaries including many right-wing journalists, his own rebels and even his immediate predecessor, who undoubtedly made life difficult for the person she had once endorsed as her successor.

However, the passage of time allows for deeper reflection and historians often reach different perceptions. This is so with a number of Prime Ministers who were deemed by contemporaries to have 'failed', not least in the Labour Party, where successive administrations have failed to live up to the aspirations of its more radical supporters. With a clearer understanding of the historical context it is possible to reach more positive, or at least more balanced, verdicts on the likes of Harold Wilson and James Callaghan.

This study follows the model of *Harold Wilson: An Unprincipled Prime Minister?* published by Biteback in 2016. Unfortunately, some reviewers missed the all-important question mark! Doing so, they thought it was another attack on Wilson, when in fact the aim of the book had been to challenge the widely held belief that he was an 'unprincipled' Prime Minister. In the same way, this book seeks to challenge the widely held view that Major was an 'unsuccessful' Prime Minister.

Obviously this requires us to set out criteria for assessing the success and failure of Prime Ministers. Clearly one such measurement is the ability to win elections. Major's success in 1992 – against the prediction of the pollsters – should not be overlooked. Arguably, his instinct to go back to old-fashioned campaigning with his 'soap box' swung the result and thereby achieved a fourth consecutive term in office, which was unprecedented in the democratic era. But, of course, he also went down to a crushing defeat in 1997 at the hands of New Labour. He was one of the longer-serving Prime Ministers of the twentieth century, but he was less successful in terms of elections than a number of his predecessors or his immediate successor.

In our teaching we regularly ask our students who were the most successful Prime Ministers in modern times (since 1945) and the answers are usually Thatcher and Blair. Some with more historical knowledge will say Clement Attlee. Few others ever get a mention. Thatcher and Blair were clearly more successful electorally; Attlee recast the political agenda as did Thatcher, though it is arguable whether Blair did in the same way. However, more advanced analysis would suggest that some of those frequently regarded as unsuccessful do in fact deserve more credit than they are usually given. Factors such as the unity of the Prime Minister's Cabinet and parliamentary party, the size of the majority in the Commons, the strength of the opposition, the presence of strong rivals, the economic context, and other domestic and international issues all affect the ability of a Prime Minister to appear in control of events. As Sir Anthony Seldon has written (see the concluding chapter, for example), ideas, personalities, circumstances and interests interplay in any given historical context.

For Attlee, Thatcher and Blair there were clear advantages in terms of their parliamentary majorities, the relative unity of their parties and the contexts within which they governed (Attlee's inheritance of a war-torn economy imposed very serious constraints, but also opportunities). Thatcher, and to a lesser extent Blair, very often defined themselves by what they were against. Thatcher's tenure was defined by her fight against the 'enemies within' and the 'enemies without', and for much of that time the enemies were easily identifiable: the trades unions and the USSR primarily, but increasingly as her premiership continued 'Europe' also. By 1990, the Soviet Union had all but ceased to exist and the trade unions were a much-reduced force. It simply was not clear who the enemies were in the '90s apart from the European Economic Community/European Union, and the Conservatives ripped themselves apart over this issue.

Major faced a fundamentally divided party for all of his time in power, which began with the nature of Thatcher's removal from office. She endorsed him as her successor, but very soon afterwards said that she felt betrayed by him and said she would be a good 'back-seat driver'. Although Major won the 1992 election, his majority was greatly reduced and the passing of the Maastricht Treaty effectively wiped out even that. The right of the party were in open rebellion, encouraged by Thatcher and her key ally Norman Tebbit. Major had won the 1992 election in part, if not mainly, on the basis of perceived economic competence. But this was shattered later in the same year when the pound was forced out of the European Exchange Rate Mechanism (ERM), which Major had signed up to as Chancellor three years earlier. Not only did this immediately shatter the Conservative's reputation for economic competence, it also encouraged the rebels in his own party in their opposition to European integration.

Finally, the government faced a stronger opposition than Thatcher had for most of her premiership. Neil Kinnock had led the recovery of the Labour Party since 1983, making it more popular, but was ultimately unable to win the election. John Smith proved a popular, if cautious, leader from 1992 until his untimely death two years later. The creation of New Labour under Blair led to the landslide three years after that. Blair appeared dynamic and fresh, certainly when compared to the tired and stale Tories, increasingly faced with scandals of both a financial and a sexual nature. Finally, part of the reason for Major's troubled tenure was the fracturing of the dominant New Right ideology.

So a full examination of the context within which Major governed allows us to reappraise his record. He simply faced a more difficult set of circumstances than either Thatcher or Blair.

It is possible to set out a number of successes and failures of the Major years in a more objective way once this context is understood. His personal contribution to winning an unprecedented fourth successive general election should not be underestimated. By most objective standards the economy did well once it began to recover from recession (and, some would say, once outside the ERM). By 1997 there had been several years of steady economic growth which Gordon Brown inherited and subsequently built upon. There were a number of key reforms at home which have stood the test of time, including the creation of the National Lottery. Although Blair took the credit for the Northern Ireland peace process much of the groundwork had been done on Major's watch. He did manage to ratify the Maastricht Treaty, eventually, as he intended. His ability to keep the party together should not be forgotten. Finally, he took the inevitable defeat in 1997 with good grace and has acted with dignity as an ex-Prime Minister, unlike – it could be said – Edward Heath and Margaret Thatcher (who openly resented their removal from the leadership of their party), and Tony Blair (for different reasons). Hence, Major's personal stock has increased since he stood down from frontline politics. Of course, this does not mean that there were not clear policy failures. Each contributor has been allowed to make their own assessment of Major's premiership. Some are clearly more sympathetic, others openly critical and many more balanced in their assessments. Ultimately it is for the reader to give their own answer to the question posed in the title of this book.

STRUCTURE OF THE BOOK

In addition to the Foreword by leading political author and journalist Peter Oborne and this Introduction, the book is split into four main sections. The first section analyses the political and intellectual context of Major's premiership. In terms of the political context David Denver evaluates Major's electoral record and Paul Anderson examines the rise of New Labour. In looking at the intellectual climate, Kevin Hickson explores Major's contribution to British Conservatism as an ideology, while Arthur Aughey explores the nature of Major's understanding of Britishness.

The second section explores the governance of the UK under John Major. Lord (Philip) Norton examines Major's approach to the constitution. Some of the issues he identifies are explored further in terms of Major's views on devolution (Shaun McDaid and Catherine McGlynn), Major's administration's reforms to local government (Tony Travers) and his important contribution to the Northern Ireland peace process (Cathy Gormley-Heenan).

The third – and largest – section examines all of the key policy areas in which Major's government was active including economic policy (Wyn Grant), industrial relations (Andrew Taylor), transport (Christian Wolmar), social policy (Ben Williams), social morality (Bruce Pilbeam), education reform (Sonia Exley), sport and the arts (Kevin Jefferys), foreign and defence policy (Mark Garnett) and European integration (Gillian Peele).

The final section provides a range of perspectives on John Major's premiership. Three of Major's leading contemporaries offer perspectives from across the party political spectrum. John Redwood MP, who challenged Major for the leadership in 1995, offers a perspective from the right. Lord (Paddy) Ashdown, who led the Liberal Democrats throughout Major's time as Prime Minister, offers a view from the centre. And Charles Clarke, a leading figure in the Labour Party throughout the Major years, offers a view from the left. Major famously said at the start of his premiership that he wished to create a 'classless society'. What exactly he meant by that, and how far he succeeded is explored by political author Alwyn Turner. Finally, Major's official biographer Sir Anthony Seldon and political researcher Mark Davies offer an overall assessment of Major as Prime Minister.

The editors are very grateful to Biteback, who readily agreed to publish this book, and to the contributors who very generously gave their time. As always, we would like to thank our family and friends for their support. Sometimes in life things happen which are unexpected and unpleasant. It is at those times when we realise who our true friends are.

PART ONE

CONTEXT

1

FROM HEGEMONY TO IGNOMINY: ELECTIONS AND PUBLIC OPINION UNDER JOHN MAJOR

David Denver

When John Major succeeded Margaret Thatcher as Conservative leader and Prime Minister in November 1990, the party was in the electoral doldrums and its third successive triumph in the 1987 general election long forgotten. Labour had taken the lead on voting intentions in the opinion polls by the middle of 1989 and the gap steadily widened thereafter. During the first ten months of 1990 the Conservative deficit remained well into double figures, peaking at twenty-two points in March and April (Figure 1). Unfortunately for the government, there was a by-election in the Mid-Staffordshire constituency in March and the Tories duly lost the seat to Labour on a swing of more than 21 per cent. A Conservative majority of almost 15,000 in the general election was converted into a Labour majority of almost 10,000 votes. Further electoral embarrassment followed in the local elections in May. Although the Conservatives held up relatively well in London, elsewhere in England they had their worst performance since the reformed local government system was instituted in 1973. In the metropolitan districts the party's vote share (24.6 per cent) was less than half that won by Labour (54.6 per cent), while even in the 116 shire districts where elections were taking place the Tories were trounced, winning less than a third of votes (30.7 per cent) and only 452 seats out of 1,854 at stake. Perhaps less surprisingly, in the Scottish regional council elections – despite fielding a record number of candidates – the Conservatives remained in third place with less than a fifth of the votes and just fifty-two councillors out of 445 elected.

In part, the increasing unpopularity of the government reflected weak economic performance. In particular, inflation was on the increase and to deal with this the government had progressively raised interest rates. These were below 10 per cent to mid-1988 but then increased steadily to reach 15 per cent at the end of 1989 which, to say the least, was not good news for households repaying mortgages. In addition, however, in the spring of 1990 the government's new method for financing local government – labelled the 'community charge' by proponents and the 'poll tax' by opponents – was extended from Scotland to the rest of the UK. Having provoked a campaign of civil disobedience and increased support for the Scottish National Party during the trial run in Scotland, the unlikely subject of local government finance now led to violent disturbances in London and elsewhere. It was little wonder, then, that in the autumn of 1990 the electoral prospects of the Conservatives appeared gloomy. Their parlous position was brought home to them in dramatic fashion in a by-election in Eastbourne in mid-October, when this formerly safe seat was lost to the Liberal Democrats on a swing of just over 20 per cent. In these circumstances it is perhaps not surprising that enough Tory backbenchers, nervous about their prospects in the next general election, plucked up the courage to end the reign of Mrs Thatcher, who the public strongly identified with the unpopular poll tax.

The impact on public opinion of her demise was immediate. In October 1990, the Conservatives trailed Labour by twelve points in voting intentions; in November the deficit was cut to six points and the party then went into a four-point lead in December. Although the impact of the change in leadership faded somewhat after a few months, Labour was never able to open up the kind of lead over its rivals that had been seen during Mrs Thatcher's last year in office. This improvement in the Tories' position was reflected in the 1991 local elections. These involved all shire and metropolitan districts in England and Wales and, although the Conservatives still sustained seat losses, their overall performance was clearly better than in the previous year. The 'national equivalent vote' in the 1990 contests had put the Conservatives at 33 per cent, compared with 44 per cent for Labour and 17 per cent for the Liberal Democrats. In 1991 the respective figures were 35, 38 and 22 per cent.[1]

Figure 1: Voting intentions January1990 to March 1992

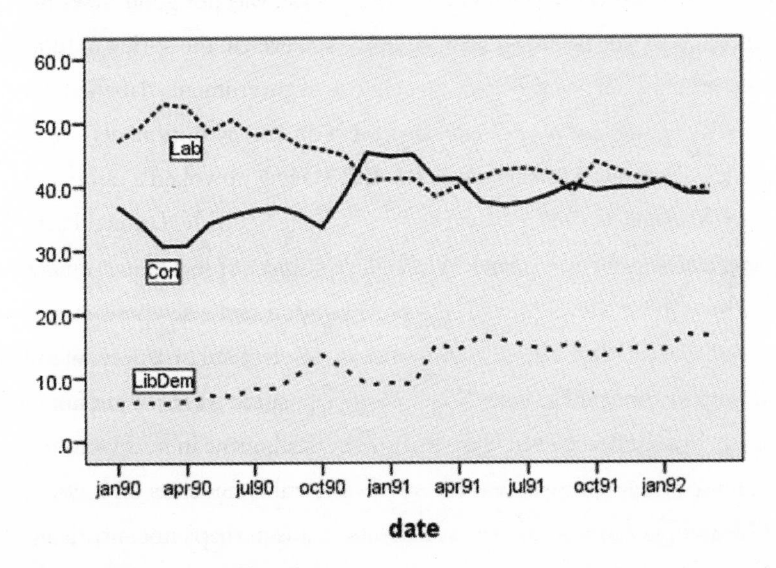

Note: here and in subsequent figures showing trends in voting intentions the data used are the monthly means for all published polls.

There is little doubt that it was the change of leadership which brightened the Conservatives' prospects. From January to October 1990 Mrs Thatcher's personal ratings (percentage satisfied with her performance minus percentage dissatisfied) averaged -37.5, according to Gallup. On John Major's accession, he immediately registered +22 in December and remained in positive territory throughout 1991. At this stage, he was seen by the public as more flexible than Mrs Thatcher, more honest, more down to earth, more in touch with ordinary voters and less likely to talk down to them. In short, he simply seemed a nicer person than his predecessor.

Nonetheless, the Tories were not out of troubled waters. During 1991 they defended four seats in parliamentary by-elections and lost all of them – two to Labour and two to the Liberal Democrats. The latter were at last pulling out of the lengthy slump which followed the creation of the new party in 1988 (as also evidenced in the local elections). On the positive side for the Conservatives, however, the swings in the by-elections held in November were much smaller than in previous ones and during the first three months of 1992, as the next general election approached, the major parties were running almost neck and neck in voting intentions.

THE 1992 ELECTION

In electoral terms, the 1992 general election represented John Major's finest hour. Throughout the campaign, the polls consistently indicated that the outcome would be very close, with most suggesting that Labour would be the largest party. The latter's campaign managers were so confident that they organised a highly stage-managed rally in Sheffield, during the penultimate campaign week, which was widely viewed on television news and featured the Labour leader, Neil Kinnock, predicting victory in a triumphalist address. John Major, meanwhile, was plodding doggedly around the country. He had started the campaign with a series of 'Ask John Major' events at which the Prime Minister sat on a stool and answered unscripted questions from the (usually quite polite) audience. This approach was soon abandoned, however, and Major took to standing on a soapbox in the open air and addressing (sometimes hostile) crowds through a megaphone.

Never the most inspiring of orators, Major's efforts were criticised as being wooden and dull. He was also clearly resolute and sincere, however, and his old-fashioned campaigning style appealed to voters turned off by Labour's carefully choreographed and glitzy approach. Even so, on election night itself, exit polls for the broadcasters pointed to the Conservatives being in a minority in the House of Commons.

As results began to be declared, however, it quickly became clear that John Major would be returning to Downing Street. Across the UK, the Conservatives led with 41.9 per cent of the votes compared with 34.4 per cent for Labour and 17.8 per cent for the Liberal Democrats. This gave the Tories 336 seats out of 651 – an overall majority of twenty-one – which should have been large enough to enable the party to govern effectively.

Media commentators struggled to explain such an unexpected outcome, and even academic electoral analysts appeared nonplussed. Some of the former suggested that the Sheffield rally was a turning point but, in fact, Labour's average lead in the first seven opinion polls taken after it (2.5 points) was exactly the same as in the seven immediately preceding it. For academics who expected the election to be decided by the electorate's views on key issues, the problem was that on the most frequently nominated issues affecting party choice – health, unemployment and education – Labour had large leads as the party best able to deal with them. Even on what had long been a trump card for the Conservatives – economic competence – they had a relatively narrow lead of just five points over Labour in the last campaign poll on the topic by Ipsos MORI.

It was clear, however, that throughout the 1992 campaign, John Major maintained a significant lead over Neil Kinnock as the best person to be Prime Minister. As Table 1 shows, the proportions viewing him as most capable slipped slightly over the campaign but, even so, on the eve of polling he was by some margin the preferred Prime Minister. Contemporary analysts tended to play down the importance of this evidence.[2] One reason for this was that traditional theories of voting suggested that evaluations of party leaders had minimal effects on voters' choices. It was more a case of the voters' party determining their evaluations of leaders than of leadership evaluations determining party choice. This was becoming an increasingly difficult position to sustain, however, and by the start of the twenty-first century it had been consigned to the psephological dustbin.

Table 1: Most capable Prime Minister, 1992 (%)

	Major	Kinnock	Ashdown
March 11–12	40	27	22
March 16	42	28	20
March 30	38	29	21
April 7–8	38	27	20

Source: Ipsos MORI

In their study of the 2001 British general election, Harold Clarke and colleagues developed a theory of 'valence politics' as a more adequate framework for understanding voting behaviour in modern conditions than older theories dating from the 1960s and 1970s.[3] From this perspective, voters' evaluations of party leaders play a crucial role, acting as shortcuts helping them to evaluate the competence of the parties in handling the important issues of the day. Clarke *et al.* (Chapter 20) re-analysed British Election Study (BES) survey data and showed that, in 1992, the electorate's preference for Major over Kinnock was actually a significant element in delivering victory for the Conservatives. As suggested above, it was indeed Major's finest hour.

THE FALL FROM GRACE: 1992–97

Following a fourth successive win for the Conservatives, it is not difficult to understand why people began to talk about the party having established an electoral hegemony in Britain. The BES study of the 1992 election was entitled *Labour's Last Chance?*[4] And after the election, Anthony King ruminated about 'the implications of One-Party Government'.[5] The argument that the Conservatives enjoyed an electoral hegemony in Britain was always over-simple, however.

For one thing, at the end of 1991 the party controlled no local authorities in Wales; three out of fifty-three districts and no regions in Scotland; one of thirty-six metropolitan boroughs and just seventy-four of 296 shire districts in England. In any event, however, the apparent impregnability of the Conservatives in general elections evaporated very rapidly after the 1992 election.

Initially, John Major's new government enjoyed a brief honeymoon with the electorate and during this period – just four weeks after the general election – the Conservatives benefited in local elections. With Labour supporters deflated by their unexpected defeat, and the Conservatives cock-a-hoop, the latter outpolled the former in the metropolitan boroughs for the first time since 1978, while in the shire districts the Tories again had their best results since the 1970s. Even in Scotland, the bleeding away of Conservative support was certainly stemmed in 1992 and there was, indeed, a partial recovery in the party's performance. Commenting on the local election results overall, *The Economist* summed up: 'soaked in the general election, Labour has now been drenched at the local polls'.[6] Any euphoria in Conservative ranks was soon to be blown away, however.

In October 1990 the then Chancellor of the Exchequer, Nigel Lawson, had finally persuaded Margaret Thatcher that the UK should become part of the European Exchange Rate Mechanism (ERM). Rather than being allowed to 'float' against other currencies, the pound was now tied to the value of the German mark and could 'float' only within narrow limits. It was widely suspected that the pound was actually overvalued, however, and during the summer it came under intense pressure in the currency markets. As late as 10 September, John Major was insisting that 'it's a cold world outside the ERM … There is going to be no revaluation, no realignment'.[7] On 16 September ('Black Wednesday'), however, the value of sterling plummeted despite the Bank of England spending massive amounts in buying pounds and successive hikes in interest rates from 10 to 12 and then 15 per cent in the space of a few hours. Nonetheless, in the evening the Chancellor, Norman Lamont, appeared outside the Treasury to announce that sterling's membership of the ERM had been suspended. Effectively, the pound had been devalued.

These events involved the complete collapse of a central plank of the government's economic policy. They also had important consequences for the future of John Major and his party. First, the Eurosceptics in the party were emboldened and they continued to be a thorn in the government's flesh for the rest of the parliament. The image conveyed to the voters was of a party deeply divided over Europe. Second, the Conservatives lost the support of most of the Tory press. With *The Sun* in the vanguard, Major was now portrayed as a weak and indecisive muddler and he never regained even lukewarm support. Third, the Conservatives lost their long-standing reputation for economic competence. This had always given the party a distinct advantage over Labour in general elections, but it now drained away like the millions of pounds that had been poured down the drain in a vain effort to shore up the pound. Finally – and as a consequence of the previous points – the popularity of the Conservatives among the electorate nose-dived (Figure 2). A Labour lead of one point just before the crisis was transformed into one of seventeen points just ten weeks later.

Figure 2: Voting intentions, 1992 – 1997

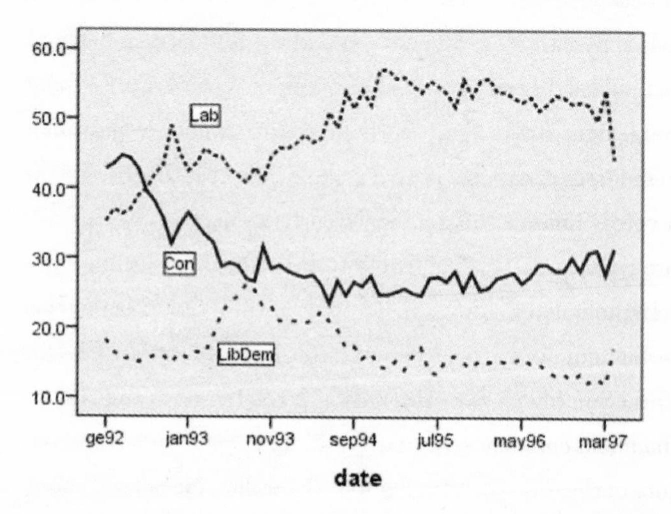

Note: the results of the 1992 and 1997 general elections form the starting and ending points for the graph.

As Figure 2 shows, the Conservatives were never within hailing distance of Labour in the opinion polls from late 1992 through to the general election in 1997. Since regular polling in Britain began, no party had maintained so large a lead for so long as did Labour from October 1992. Unsurprisingly, this yawning gap in popularity was reflected in various mid-term elections.

Table 2: Conservative losses in by-elections 1992–97

Date	Constituency	Change in Con Vote Share	Winner
May 1993	Newbury	-29.0	Lib Dem
July 1983	Christchurch	-32.1	Lib Dem
June 1994	Eastleigh	-26.6	Lib Dem
Dec. 1994	Dudley West	-30.1	Labour
May 1995	Perth & Kinross	-18.8	SNP
July 1995	Littleboro & Saddleworth	-20.6	Lib Dem
April 1996	Staffs South East	-22.2	Labour
Feb. 1997	Wirral South	-16.4	Labour

Table 2 summarises the Conservative performance in the eight seats that the party defended between 1992 and 1997. All were lost. It is not unusual for governments to lose by-elections, of course, but it was the sheer scale of the defeats that was unusual. In every case the decline in the Conservative vote share was in double figures and reached around thirty points in three cases. The scale of these losses can perhaps be better appreciated if expressed in terms of actual votes. Thus, in Christchurch, for example, a Conservative majority of more than 23,000 at the general election was turned into one for the Liberal Democrats of more than 16,000 votes. Even with the next general election looming, in February 1997, the Labour candidate cruised to victory in Wirral South with a majority of almost 8,000 in a seat that the Conservatives had held comfortably in 1992 with a majority of over 11,000.

The same story of electoral disaster was repeated in local elections. Table 3 shows, firstly, the national equivalent vote estimates in each round of local elections from 1992. As indicated above, the Conservatives had something of a triumph in that year but by 1993 had fallen well behind Labour. Things went from bad to worse in 1994 and 1995 before a slight recovery in 1996.

Table 3: 'National equivalent vote' in local elections and total number of Conservative Councillors, 1992–96

	Con	Lab	Lib Dem	Con Councillors
	%	%	%	
1992	46	30	20	8,288
1993	31	39	25	7,802
1994	28	40	27	7,286
1995	25	47	23	4,883
1996	29	43	24	4,276

Source: Rallings and Thrasher, 2012[8]

The nadir was reached in 1995, when there were elections for all the newly created unitary councils in Scotland and Wales, as well as in all English shire districts and metropolitan boroughs and fourteen new English unitary authorities. Although no one would have expected the Conservatives to do well, few could have anticipated the severity of the drubbing visited on the party by the voters. In Scotland, the Tories had their worst-ever share of votes in a Scottish election (11.3 per cent) and won only eighty-two seats (out of 1,161) on the new councils. Only 'others' won fewer seats and in only one council (Edinburgh) did the number of Conservative councillors reach double figures. In Wales, the outcome of the elections for twenty-two new unitary authorities was similar. The Conservatives won less than 10 per cent of the votes and just forty-two (out of 1,272) seats – with none at all on nine councils.

These very poor results could be shrugged off to some extent, since Scotland and Wales had proved difficult territory for the Conservatives in local government elections from the 1970s. In England, however, the 1995 results were also disastrous. In the metropolitan boroughs a new low was reached, with just 20 per cent of votes and only forty-nine seats won, while in the shire districts – the very bedrock of their support – the Conservatives attracted just over a quarter of the votes cast (26.4 per cent) – by far their worst-ever performance in 'all in' shire districts. They came third in terms of seats won with 1,867 – only about half the number won by Labour (3,743) and well behind the Liberal Democrats (2,321). In the inaugural elections for fourteen unitary authorities, it was the same story. Labour won heavily while the Conservatives came third, in both votes and seats, behind the Liberal Democrats. Having insisted on setting up unitaries, the Tories found themselves largely rejected by the voters and virtually frozen out of influence in council affairs

The effect of the dramatic losses of support for the Conservatives among voters was a collapse in local influence and power. As the final column of Table 3 shows, the number of Conservative councillors in Britain as a whole almost halved in the four years after 1996. By 1996 the party controlled just thirteen local authorities across the country, compared with 207 run by Labour and fifty-five by the Liberal Democrats. Even in the English shires, where they had previously dominated, the Conservatives were reduced almost to the position of a minor party. The effect on the morale of local Conservative associations and their ability to campaign effectively must have been shattering.

The third electoral test for John Major's government during these years came in the shape of the European Parliament elections of 1994. Again the Conservatives plumbed new depths. Their share of votes (27.8 per cent) was the worst performance by the party in a nationwide election during the twentieth century and lagged far behind that of Labour on 44.2 per cent.

Explaining the inability of the Conservatives to rally support among the voters after 1992 is not difficult. As already indicated, withdrawal from the ERM had lost the Tories their reputation for economic competence and support in the press while also exacerbating divisions in the party over Europe. This was bad enough for the government, but in various ways they managed to make things worse for themselves.[9] The Conservatives had pilloried Labour as the party of high taxation during the 1992 election campaign but, in the March 1993 Budget, the Chancellor increased taxes on alcohol and tobacco by more than inflation, raised national insurance contributions, reduced tax allowances for married couples and mortgage holders, froze other allowances (an effective cut in real terms) and extended value-added tax (VAT) to domestic fuel and power. The latter, in particular, was a direct betrayal of a campaign promise. In the aftermath, polling by Gallup found that the Budget was thought to be unfair by 75 per cent to 19 per cent of voters – a record margin. Labour was now viewed as the party best on taxation by 42 per cent compared with 33 per cent choosing the Conservatives and the latter never regained the lead on this issue before the 1997 election.

The Major government also came to be associated with 'sleaze'. This came in two forms – sex and money. Between September 1992 and June 1996 no fewer than nine members of the government resigned (and another died) in the context of assorted sex scandals. Most of those involved were relatively minor figures, but the Conservatives had cast themselves as the champions of family values and, in 1993, Major had launched a 'Back to Basics' initiative – interpreted by the media as a sort of moral crusade. In this context, the ensuing sexual scandals could be taken as evidence of breath-taking hypocrisy within the governing party.

Financial sleaze was probably even more damaging to the government's reputation. In some cases, this involved revelations concerning MPs who were willing to take cash from lobbyists in return for asking specific questions in the House of Commons. In others, ministers were discovered to be accepting hospitality and cash payments from prominent businessmen and were forced to resign their positions. A different sort of financial sleaze related to the so-called 'revolving door', through which leading Conservatives were whisked from the Cabinet to city boardrooms. Many of these lucrative positions were offered by firms that had featured in the privatisation programme carried through by these self-same ministers.

Partly as a consequence, the programme of privatisation, which had been a central and apparently successful element of Thatcherism during the

1980s, itself became unpopular. The people running the newly privatised utilities were paid vastly more than those who had managed them when they were publicly owned, yet did not seem to perform very differently; indeed, they were often the same individuals. Despite the change in public sentiment, the government pressed ahead, against strong opposition, with the privatisation of British Rail. This was completed in 1996, and was followed by hundreds of train cancellations by one company which had sacked too many drivers. For a significant body of opinion, this was a privatisation too far.

Divisions over Europe came to a head in November 1994 when eight backbench rebels abstained in a Commons vote on the European Finance Bill (which had been made an issue of confidence). Major deprived them of the Conservative whip (and another MP resigned the whip to join them). These nine proceeded to embarrass the government at every opportunity. The following April, however, in a humiliating climb-down by Major, the whip was restored unconditionally. The sniping on Europe continued to frustrate the Prime Minister, however, and in June 1995 he dramatically resigned as Conservative leader in order to force a leadership contest, challenging his critics to 'put up or shut up'. He was challenged by the Eurosceptic John Redwood and was duly re-elected by his MPs, with 218 votes to eighty-nine for Redwood and twenty-two abstentions. Given that one-third of the parliamentary party had withheld support from the Prime Minister, Major's manoeuvre had served to highlight rather than mitigate the extent of party divisions.

For the most part, the public was well aware of strains within the Conservative Party. Figure 3 charts the proportions of Gallup's respondents saying that the Conservatives were united or divided over the period. By the autumn of 1992 the gap was enormous and that situation did not change significantly thereafter. Overall, these were the worst figures recorded for the Conservatives since Gallup started asking electors their views on party unity in the 1960s, and there seems little doubt that the evident disunity made the party and the government look shambolic.

Figure 3: Proportions seeing the Conservatives as united or divided, 1992–97

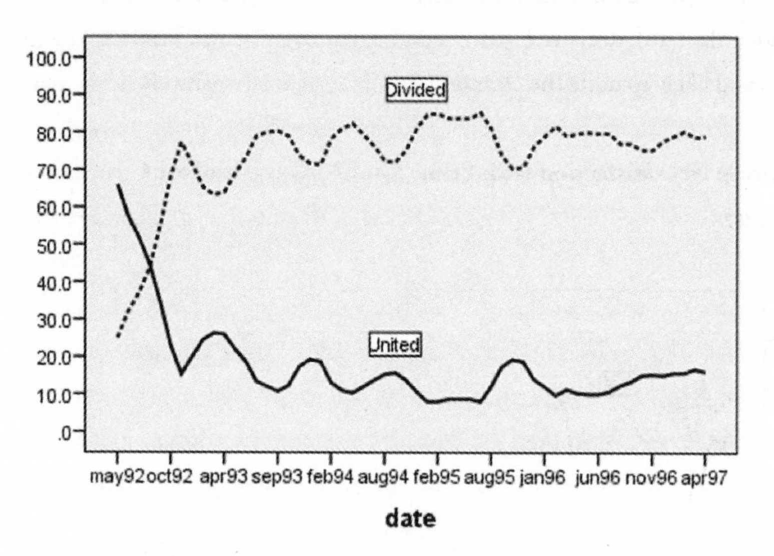

Note: the data shown are three-monthly moving averages.
Source: Gallup

In July 1994, the already rather dim electoral prospects of John Major's government were dealt a veritable hammer blow. In that month Tony Blair became leader of the Labour Party. As previously discussed, at the 1992 election Major had been personally more popular than the then Labour leader, Neil Kinnock. The latter announced his resignation immediately after the election and was succeeded by John Smith. Smith's personal ratings were much better than those for Kinnock had been but he died in May 1994. Blair proved to be even more popular and proceeded to transform the Labour Party and its electoral appeal. At the same time Major's appeal among the electorate sank like a stone. Over his second term Major recorded the worst average satisfaction ratings for any Prime Minister since 1945. The contrast in the popularity of the two leaders is illustrated in Figure 4. Although Smith's ratings were well ahead of those for the Prime Minister after the ERM disaster, the gap became truly enormous when Blair became

Labour leader. Major's image – in contrast to that of Blair – was almost entirely negative. When asked to rate him on a variety of qualities, respondents in a 1996 Gallup poll, for example, gave him negative scores on being trustworthy (-18), decisive (-36), effective (-46), tough (-49), firmly in charge (-60) and likely to unite the country (-67). Blair scored positively in all cases.

Figure 4: Net satisfaction with Prime Minister/Leader of the Opposition, 1992–97

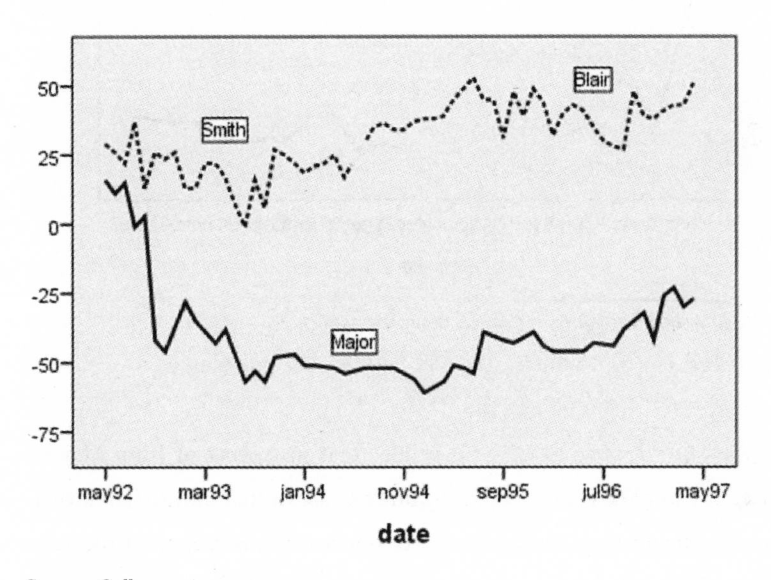

Source: Gallup

Given this background it is no surprise to note that when Gallup's respondents were asked which leader would make the best Prime Minister, Major lagged well behind his Labour rivals from 1993 onwards. Table 4 shows the relevant average annual figures. For the first few months after the 1992 election, Major remained the nation's choice as best person to be Prime Minister. Along with much else, however, this advantage collapsed in the last three months of the year. John Smith then led the field on this question for every month of 1993 and his lead extended in the first five months of 1994. When Tony Blair entered the lists, however, he proved an immediate hit with the voters and quickly established himself as the clearly preferred aspirant for the job. Although the gap narrowed in the first three months of 1997, as the next general election approached, Blair nonetheless retained a very clear advantage over Major.

Table 4: Best person for Prime Minister, 1992–97 (%)

	1992	1993	1994		1994	1995	1996	1997
Major	32	20	17		16	17	20	27
Smith	33	32	35	**Blair**	40	42	38	40
Ashdown	17	21	20		15	13	14	13

Note: the figures for 'Don't Know' are not shown.
Source: Gallup

THE 1997 ELECTION

At no point after September 1992 was the Prime Minister in a position to call a general election which his party had any serious chance of winning. Not unexpectedly, therefore, the Tories clung on until the last possible minute and the election date was fixed for 1 May 1997. Even so, the electoral outlook for John Major and his government could hardly have been bleaker. As a result, the national campaign was almost a matter of going through the motions. Although the Conservatives inched forwards in voting intention polls, and Labour declined a little from the high point at which the party began the campaign, the gap between the two major parties remained huge throughout.

It came as little surprise, then, that the Conservatives maintained their string of 'worst-ever' records when the election results came in. Their share of the UK vote (30.7 per cent) was their worst since the first election after the passage of the Great Reform Act of 1832; the number of seats won (165) was the smallest since 1906; the swing from Conservatives to Labour (10.0 per cent) was the biggest since 1945. In Scotland (for the first time ever) and Wales (for the first time since 1906) the Conservatives won no seats at all.

There is little difficulty in understanding why the Conservatives met with such an electoral disaster.[10] Although the economy was improving and economic optimism on the part of the public was growing in the year leading up to the election, this failed to deliver any significant improvement in the government's position. The Tories were perceived as sleazy, divided and incompetent and were up against a revitalised Labour Party which now not only had a highly professional campaigning machine but also led its opponents as the 'best party' on a whole string of key issues, including the NHS, education, law and order, unemployment and the cost of living, as well as less salient topics such as pensions and public transport. The only issue on which the Conservatives retained a significant advantage was defence, and that was well down the electorate's list of priorities. To cap it all, John Major continued to lag well behind Tony Blair as the nation's preferred Prime Minister. In the last week of the campaign just 23 per cent of MORI's respondents thought Major the best person for the job, compared with 40 per cent opting for Blair.

As the latter prepared to enter Downing Street amidst triumphal scenes orchestrated by his media advisers, Major reportedly took himself off to watch some cricket. One cannot help but think that he must have felt some relief that almost five years of torture at the hands of the British electorate was over at last. A premiership that had started surprisingly well, in terms of electoral performance and standing among the electorate, had ended in ignominy for him and his party.

ENDNOTES

1 C. Rallings and M. Thrasher, *British Electoral Facts 1832–2012* (London: Biteback, 2012), p. 238

2 I. Crewe and A. King, 'Did Major Win? Did Kinnock Lose? Leadership effects in the 1992 election' in A. Heath, R. Jowell and J. Curtice with B. Taylor (eds), *Labour's Last Chance? The 1992 Election and Beyond* (Aldershot: Dartmouth, 1994)

3 H. Clarke, D. Sanders, M. Stewart and P. Whiteley, *Political Choice in Britain* (Oxford: Oxford University Press, 2004)

4 Heath, Jowell and Curtice with Taylor (eds), *Labour's Last Chance?*
5 A. King, 'The Implications of One-party Government', in A. King (ed.), *Britain at the Polls 1992* (Chatham, NJ: Chatham House, 1993), pp. 223–48
6 *The Economist*, 16 May 1992, p. 80
7 *The Times*, 11 September 1992
8 Rallings and Thrasher, *British Electoral Facts 1832–2012*, p. 238
9 D. Denver, 'The Government That Could Do No Right' in A. King (ed.), *New Labour Triumphs: Britain At The Polls 1992* (Chatham NJ: Chatham House, 1998), pp. 15–48
10 A. King, 'Why Labour Won – At Last' in King (ed.), *New Labour Triumphs*, pp. 177–207

2

MAJOR AND THE LABOUR PARTY

Paul Anderson

John Major's governments of 1990–97 are not often discussed in terms of their impact on Labour – except insofar as Major's travails with his party from summer 1992, particularly over Europe, provided the backdrop against which first John Smith and then Tony Blair built commanding opinion poll leads for Labour, culminating in Blair's general election victory of May 1997.

Even two decades after that triumph, protagonists, commentators and historians typically assign only a minor role to Major in the making of New Labour. As in the dog days of his administration and in Blair's first years in office, he is still considered primarily as the inept grey man who happened to be at the helm of the doomed Tory ship as Labour rode a tide of popular enthusiasm to win an inevitable landslide.

The keepers of the Blairite flame – and there are a few of them yet – insist that the New Labour victory marked a decisive breach in British politics. There are plenty of David Cameron Tories who agree. Left-wing critics of New Labour emphasise the continuities between Blair and Margaret

Thatcher, not Blair and Major. And Eurosceptic Tories dismiss the Major years as the time when the Tory leadership sold the pass on Europe and paid dearly for its apostasy.

So – nothing to see here, move along. Except that it's just a little too easy to dismiss Major's impact on Labour quite so summarily. Of course, Major's second term was a catalogue of disasters, from Black Wednesday in September 1992 until the very end. You name it, it went wrong: the bitter Tory row over Europe, Michael Heseltine's pit-closures programme, the arms-to-Iraq fiasco, the shocking complacency of the government over the crisis in former Yugoslavia, back to basics, cash-for-questions ... But Major became Prime Minister in 1990, not in 1992. And his first – very short – term was a quite stunning success, not least in forcing Labour into a fundamental rethink of its political positioning, particularly on the economy.

LABOUR IN 1990

The defenestration of Thatcher in autumn 1990 was of course traumatic for the Conservative Party, and the wounds remain sensitive today. But when it happened, to all but the Thatcherite faithful, it seemed less of a problem for the Tories than it was for Labour. Under the leadership of Neil Kinnock, particularly since 1987, Labour had made great strides towards electoral credibility after the debacle of the 1983 general election, which it lost under Michael Foot. Labour lost again in 1987 – and lost badly, winning only a handful more seats than in 1983 – but its campaign had been competent. The party saw off the threat of the Liberal-SDP Alliance. And in the wake of defeat, Kinnock had not only launched a major policy review to bury his party's unpopular commitments to nationalisation, unilateral nuclear disarmament and anti-Europeanism, but had also got serious about expelling Trotskyist infiltrators from the Labour Party.[1] Meanwhile, the Thatcher government had embarked on an extraordinarily inept reform of local taxation, the introduction of the community charge, the poll tax, which was hated by voters.[2] The economy boomed through 1987, 1988 and early 1989, but the housing price bubble it created began to deflate in spring 1989, and with it went the feel-good factor that had won Thatcher her third term. Simultaneously, Tory divisions on Europe became glaringly visible – particularly over whether sterling should join the Exchange Rate Mechanism (ERM) of the European Monetary System, but also over how Britain should respond to the disintegration of communism in east-central Europe.

Labour's opinion poll standings improved steadily, and in the European elections of spring 1989 the party won a convincing victory. The Tories' troubles reached a first crisis point in autumn 1989, just before the Berlin Wall came down, when Nigel Lawson resigned as Chancellor of the Exchequer because he felt his pro-ERM position was being undermined by Thatcher's anti-ERM economic adviser, Sir Alan Walters. The new Chancellor was Major, previously a rather lacklustre Foreign Secretary, whose views on the ERM were considered by just about everyone as rather more conciliatory than Lawson's. But still it went wrong for Thatcher. By spring 1990, when the poll tax came in – greeted with a giant riot after a demonstration in central London – Labour enjoyed double-digit leads in all the polls, and Kinnock looked set for No. 10.

Labour's poll ratings declined slowly over the summer of 1990, but the Tories remained in turmoil. The row about the ERM continued, exacerbated by government divisions over German reunification (which Thatcher, unlike most of her Cabinet, opposed).[3] Then Saddam Hussein invaded Kuwait, adding an international security crisis to the government's troubles – one that required anything but a bunker mentality in No. 10. There followed a period of high political drama in which, in rapid succession, sterling joining the ERM, the Tories lost the Eastbourne by-election to the Lib Dems, Geoffrey Howe resigned as Deputy Prime Minister, Heseltine challenged Thatcher for the Tory leadership and Major came through the middle as the compromise candidate after Thatcher was persuaded by her colleagues that she had lost their support.[4]

THE MAJOR EFFECT

The transformation in the Tories' fortunes brought about by the arrival of Major was dramatic – and a massive shock to Labour, which had watched transfixed, unable to get any kind of media hearing as the Tories sharpened their knives to remove Thatcher. Kinnock's political strategy since 1987 had been to reposition Labour as centrist and responsible. But he had worked on the assumption that he would be fighting a strident, tired and unpopular Thatcher at the next election – not a youngish, inoffensive, classless moderate who was a fresh face to most voters. Major had spent just two and a half years as a senior Cabinet member before he became Prime Minister, and he came to power promising reconciliation and inclusivity, with an end to the poll tax the keynote policy. The 'Major effect', boosted by the success of the war to remove Saddam from Kuwait, shifted the opinion polls emphatically in the Tories' favour through late 1990 and early 1991. From spring 1991 until the election in April 1992, the two main parties were neck-and-neck, with the Tories on average marginally in front.

Labour's response to the Major succession was, *faut de mieux*, to stick to the game plan it had devised after 1987: a vague broadly pro-European policy, no significant dissent from the government (or the US) in defence and foreign affairs – Labour supported military action to remove Saddam from Iraq – and a moderately redistributive line on tax and spend. Above all, it did its best to project a professional and respectable public image. The expulsion of Trotskyists from Labour continued apace. There were no concessions either to the left-wingers and pacifists who opposed military action against Saddam or to the campaign for non-payment of the poll tax. There were a few rumblings of discontent, with suggestions from the party right that Kinnock should give way as leader to John Smith, the shadow Chancellor, but there was never any serious momentum behind the rumblings (let alone any articulation from Kinnock's critics of a different strategy) because the perceived problem wasn't for the most part policy but Kinnock's personality and demeanour.

Although his minders had put him into sharp suits and he had developed a tone of gravitas for his TV and platform appearances, he was still the Welsh windbag to readers of *Private Eye* and viewers of the popular TV satirical show *Spitting Image*. It wasn't obvious, however, that replacing him as leader with a Scottish bank manager would make a great deal of difference before a general election. The hard left was out in the cold with nothing by way of a programme beyond what it had been pushing for twenty years, and it was compromised by its association with the 'anti-imperialists' of the Trotskyist left who thought Saddam was quite right to invade Kuwait. The soft left wanted to give Kinnock a chance, even though part of it harboured doubts about the Gulf War and worried he had given up too much to the right, while another part thought that he hadn't gone far enough in modernising Labour's message.[5] And the old right, whatever its gripes, really didn't want too much disruption: it was sitting comfortably after seeing off the left insurgencies of the 1980s and was in control of a string of shadow Cabinet portfolios as well as the Labour policy-making process. The unions were all on board but for a handful of leftist Scargillites. Labour adopted an outward stance of disciplined unity – every journalist disparaged the Labour conference of 1991 in Brighton as the dullest in memory – and set about creating a modern electoral machine, all phone banks and targeted direct mail, presided over by Larry Whitty as General Secretary, an affable but intellectually razor-sharp operator, with Jack Cunningham as campaign co-ordinator.

LABOUR'S 1992 DISASTER

What could go wrong? As it turned out, everything. Labour's 1992 campaign was well organised and efficient. But it was completely unable to counter the Tories' message, relentless from late 1991, that Labour would tax and spend recklessly. The line was most memorably relayed in the Conservative 'Labour's tax bombshell' poster, plastered over billboards the length and breadth of the country, declaring that 'You'd pay £1,250 more tax a year under Labour'. The claim was untrue for all but top earners – but Labour had set itself up to be attacked on tax with long-standing proposals for small increases in top income-tax rates to pay for modest increases in pensions and child benefits. The details were haggled over, semi-publicly, for months in late 1991 and early 1992 – with Kinnock favouring a phased introduction of the tax increases and Smith resisting – and the plan was eventually released by Smith in a 'shadow Budget' on 16 March 1992, nearly a week after Norman Lamont had kick-started the election campaign by delivering a real Budget that included big reductions in the basic rate of income tax. The shadow Budget was a public relations' disaster. The next day's stories in the press about Labour tax hikes might have been expected, but they were given a helping hand by Labour's failure to supply journalists with 'what this will mean for typical voters' factsheets on its proposals.[6]

The shadow Budget wasn't all that went pear-shaped in Labour's campaign. The party was wrong-footed on the NHS, when its party-political broadcast about a little girl whose ear surgery had been delayed by spending cuts was shown by gleeful Tory campaigners to have been at odds with some of the facts – a spat dubbed 'the war of Jennifer's ear' by the press. And on 1 April, a week before polling day, Labour overdid the glitz by hosting a giant rally at the Sheffield Arena. Kinnock arrived by helicopter and, emboldened by what turned out to be a couple of outlier opinion polls showing Labour would win, took the stage like a wannabe Mick Jagger: 'Well, all right!' he shouted at the audience, to wild applause. But Jennifer's ear and the Sheffield rally were not what lost it for Labour (and nor was *The Sun*, despite its claims that 'It was *The Sun* wot won it').[7] It was tax and spend – economic policy.

It is difficult to exaggerate the impact of the 1992 general election defeat on Labour. It was closer than 1987, but still a massive humiliation when it had expected at least a hung parliament. With 34.4 per cent of the popular vote, up from 30.8 per cent in 1987, Labour took 271 seats, up 42. Yet the

Tories won 41.9 per cent, just 0.3 percentage points down on 1987, and 336 seats, down forty but still enough for a narrow majority in the Commons.

Labour's performance was particularly poor in the affluent south and east of England, where it failed to win target seat after target seat. (The failure that hurt most was in Basildon in Essex, where the Tories' David Amess, a populist right-winger, held on with a safe majority at just the moment TV viewers were tiring of election coverage.) Kinnock announced his resignation the weekend after polling day, and the major trade unions moved fast to endorse Smith as their chosen 'safe-pair-of-hands' candidate. They pointedly refused to opt for Bryan Gould, the shadow Environment Secretary and a longstanding Eurosceptic, or skip a generation for Gordon Brown, Kinnock's shadow chief secretary to the Treasury. Brown rejected appeals to enter the leadership contest, pleading loyalty to Smith. Gould stood anyway and lost to Smith by a landslide, after a lacklustre campaign that Gould wanted to be about Europe, but which turned into a dull wrangle about how Labour's internal structures should be reformed to ensure the union bosses could not anoint a Labour leader again.

THE POST-MORTEM

The leadership election was mercifully brief – Smith was crowned in mid-July – and as it came to its close the first party post-mortem on the election appeared. The Shadow Communications Agency, the ad hoc advisory body Kinnock had set up to supplement the Labour HQ campaign team (which had worked closely with it, with only minor bust-ups), produced a report in late June that made it clear that Labour was seen by voters much as it had been in 1987 – as the party of high tax and irresponsible state spending, favouring benefit claimants rather than hard workers, over-reliant on the trade unions, soft on crime.

The analysis was backed up by the centre-right Labour MP and intellectual Giles Radice, whose Fabian pamphlet *Southern Discomfort*, published in September 1992, was one of the talking points of Labour's conference in Brighton. Radice was clear: Major had had a better reading of the politics of class in late 1980s and early 1990s Britain. The Tories won in 1992 because they recognised that lower-middle-class and skilled-working-class voters with mortgages didn't see why they should pay more tax – and that Labour was vulnerable because it had not yet worked this out. 'With respect to tax and spending,' he wrote, 'it is vital that spending commitments, if they have to be made at all, are made very cautiously indeed.'[8]

The academics David Butler and Dennis Kavanagh, in their Nuffield election survey of the election, *The British General Election of 1992*, published a few weeks later, supplied a vast amount of data to support the conclusions of the SCA and Radice.[9] Mood music came from the veteran American political economist John Kenneth Galbraith, whose jeremiad on the failure of the US liberal left to respond to Reaganism and its creation of a 'two-thirds, one-third' society in which the poor were ignored, *The Culture of Contentment*, was a must-read paperback in British Labour circles in summer 1992.[10] 'Two-thirds of the people are not doing too badly thank you, but there's one-third knocked out,' Smith told me. 'The Labour Party cannot in good conscience turn away from that. But I want to get a wider consensus: there are decent people who don't vote Labour yet who are troubled about it too. I want to reach out to them.'[11]

DAYS OF HOPE

Labour's post-mortem on the 1992 election was, however, only one running story in the six months afterwards, and it was by no means the most spectacular. In domestic politics, the Tory civil war over Europe – suspended for the election campaign – resumed within weeks at full intensity.

After Denmark voted in a referendum in June to reject the Maastricht treaty, anti-European Tory MPs went into all-out parliamentary rebellion against Major, who had delayed British ratification of Maastricht until after the election. Labour did its utmost to cause the government embarrassment in the Commons by siding with the Eurosceptic Tory rebels, on the grounds that the government's opt-out from the Social Chapter was unacceptable (though the opt-out on the single currency was fine and there really was no need for a referendum on Maastricht). To add fuel to the fire, over the summer of 1992 it became increasingly obvious that Britain would not be able to sustain the valuation of sterling in the ERM to which the government was committed – to which Labour responded by saying as little as possible that deviated from the government line until well after sterling crashed out of the ERM on 16 September 1992, 'Black Wednesday' as it was immediately described by the media. Little more than six weeks after that, Bill Clinton shocked every British Labour supporter who had imbibed Galbraith's pessimism in *The Culture of Contentment* by winning the American presidency.

This sequence of events had profound and lasting effects on Labour. Labour's stance on Maastricht, adopted in the last days of Kinnock's leadership but continued by Smith, was in part a means to neutralise left Eurosceptic support for Gould. And the refusal by Labour to endorse any realignment of currencies within the ERM, doggedly reiterated by Gordon Brown as Smith's shadow Chancellor, was orthodox safety-first politics.

Both positions made tactical political sense. In opposition, you do your best to undermine not only the government but the critics on your own side; and you don't advocate devaluation even if you think it is inevitable or a good idea. And in their own terms the tactics worked. The hard-line Eurosceptic left became a marginal rump in Labour politics on Smith's victory (and remained so until Jeremy Corbyn was elected Labour leader in 2015); and Brown's refusal to talk currency realignment until after the event gave Labour easy pickings after Black Wednesday forced devaluation on a panic-stricken Major government (though at the cost of Brown's popularity among soft-left MPs).[12] Labour's opinion poll ratings rocketed, and the lead established in autumn 1992 remained until the Labour victory of 1997.

But if the tactics worked, there wasn't a great deal of strategic thinking behind them – which became clear very soon.[13] Labour was playing Europe for party-political advantage with little sense of what it wanted for or from Europe. Partly because the tactics were effective against a riven Tory party, partly because opening up a debate about the future of Europe would have exposed rifts inside Labour, the Labour leadership was content to leave long-term thinking about Europe until later.

It is difficult to discern any coherent Labour line on Europe under either Smith or Blair as leaders of the opposition beyond enthusiasm for the Social Chapter and 'wait and see' on joining the single currency. Brown and Blair stamped on attempts by dissident soft-left Labour MPs and MEPs to raise the idea of modifying the Maastricht criteria for monetary union to make growth and employment as important for the new European Central Bank as low inflation; and no one in Labour's upper echelons had anything coherent to say about how the EU should develop political union, the great unfinished business of the Maastricht process.

Blair promised a referendum on joining the single currency in 1996, after Major had made the same pledge. But that was it. When Labour came to power in 1997, it was all over the place on European policy: completely at odds over whether Britain should join the single currency; in favour of enlargement of the EU to the east, in part because it would give succour to countries only recently under the Soviet yoke but also because enlargement would scupper plans for a federalist, rather than intergovernmentalist, Europe; at once proclaiming its enthusiasm for the European project and parroting the Major government's antipathy to European red tape.

Despite its professed pro-Europeanism under Kinnock, Smith and Blair, Labour never dared to become more European than Major or Kenneth Clarke except on the single issue of the Social Chapter. The Tories set the agenda, and no one more effectively than Major. And in the end it was Brown in 1992–93, Labour's keenest Europhile, who in 1997 effectively ruled out British membership of the single currency, setting the Major settlement on Europe in mud until the 2016 Europe referendum.

IT'S THE ECONOMY, STUPID

But in 1992 Europe was complicated for British politicians – not least because it was not clear how events would pan out. The single currency was a relatively distant prospect on which crucial detail had still to be negotiated, and it was by no means obvious that it would even come about (let alone what a Tory UK government's attitude would be if and when it did).

The election of Clinton was a lot easier to grasp for Labour than anything happening in Britain's own back yard. The British left had been fascinated by American politics for more than a century, and after John Kennedy became president in 1960 the fascination turned obsessional, fuelled by TV coverage and a constant traffic of politicians and academics across the pond. Britain's position in the world in the early 1990s might have been rather more tied up with Europe than with the US, but it was the US presidential election of 1992 that became Labour's big talking point, with 'modernisers', as they called themselves – essentially the part of the soft left that felt Smith should move faster to ditch Labour's 1992 baggage – insisting that Clinton's campaign was the model for Labour in the UK. Particularly influential here was the pollster Philip Gould, a key figure in Labour's 1987 and 1992 campaigns, who worked on the Clinton campaign and returned to Britain an evangelist for Clinton's centrist politics and electioneering style.[14]

Blair and Brown were the most prominent moderniser MPs – and they visited the US with Gould to meet Clinton's campaign team in early 1993. But they were backed by the major trade unions whose bosses had shooed in Smith, including the Transport and General Workers Union, led by Bill Morris, and by the GMB, led by John Edmonds. And Smith more-or-less demurred – even though one subtext of the modernisers' message was that Labour needed a generational shift in leadership of the kind Clinton had given the Democrats. From early 1993, everything from the Clinton Democrats' playbook that could be adapted for use in the UK was embraced by Labour: a relentless emphasis on economic policy (business-friendly and no tax hikes), a hard line on criminality – 'tough on crime, tough on the causes of crime', as Blair put it in the *New Statesman* in early 1993 – and (later, after Blair became leader) heavy investment in spin-doctors and the paraphernalia of electioneering, from focus groups to databases designed to give Labour the opportunity of 'instant rebuttal'.

It was economic policy that was most important, however. As shadow Chancellor under Smith, Brown enforced a strict line on his shadow Cabinet colleagues: no spending commitments that might require tax increases, no interventionist promises that might scare big business. His stance won him few friends in the parliamentary Labour Party – which was one of the reasons that Blair was able to supplant him as leader of the moderniser faction and become its candidate for the party leadership on Smith's sudden death in spring 1994. But his single-mindedness was effective. By the time he promised, shortly before the 1997 general election, that a Labour government would stick to Clarke's spending plans for two years, he had all but eliminated Labour's popular reputation for profligacy and high taxation.

AND IN THE END...

Labour's economic policy was transformed by its response to its defeat to Major in the 1992 election; and on Europe, Labour copied Major without a great deal of thought. Those were fundamental influences – but they weren't all that Labour took from Major. Despite his administration's deserved reputation for crisis-management, incompetence and tinkering reform, there were plenty of Major's policies which Labour continued. Labour stuck with rail privatisation (horribly botched but too expensive to reverse), the council tax (too politically sensitive to reform), the Northern Ireland peace process, polytechnics becoming universities, the private finance initiative (supposedly a cunning scheme to keep public spending off the books, which the Blair government embraced enthusiastically and at great cost) and various market reforms aimed to make the welfare state more efficient: student loans, tougher qualifications for benefit claimants and so on. Which is not to claim that Labour made no difference. In several areas, the Blair government marked a radical break with the Major years: devolution, the minimum wage, the signing of the Social Chapter, the Human Rights Act, the Freedom of Information Act, the Sure Start programme, tax credits and so on. But twenty years after Blair came to office – and in the wake of Jeremy Corbyn's election to the Labour leadership and the Brexit vote – it is the continuities between Major and Blair that are most striking.

ENDNOTES

1 On the policy review, see C. Hughes and P. Wintour, *Labour Rebuilt: The New Model Labour Party* (London: Fourth Estate, 1990); R. Heffernan and M. Marqusee, *Defeat From the Jaws of Victory: Inside Kinnock's Labour Party* (London: Verso, 1992); and P. Anderson and N. Mann, *Safety First: The Making of New Labour* (London: Granta, 1997). On the Leninists, see M. Crick, *Militant* (London: Biteback, 2016)

2 The best account of the poll tax fiasco is D. Butler, A. Adonis and T. Travers, *Failure in British Government: Politics of the Poll Tax* (Oxford: Oxford University Press, 1994)

3 One Cabinet member who agreed with Thatcher on Germany was Nicholas Ridley, who was forced to resign as trade secretary in July 1990 after telling *The Spectator* in an interview (14 July 1990) that economic and monetary union was 'a German racket designed to take over the whole of Europe'.

4 On the Major succession, see D. Kavanagh and A. Seldon (eds), *The Major Effect* (Basingstoke: Macmillan, 1994)

5 At this point, the soft left in the Parliamentary Labour Party – as reflected in membership of the Tribune Group – included Tony Blair, Gordon Brown and many others who redefined themselves as 'modernisers' after 1992.

6 'I can't believe this,' said Meghan Desai, one of Labour's key economic advisers, as we walked around the room at the shadow Budget launch. 'There's nothing at all here.' Private conversation, 1992

7 See H. Semetko, M. Scammel and T. Nossiter, 'The Media's Coverage of the Campaign', in Heath, Jowell and Curtice, *Labour's Last Chance? The 1992 Election and Beyond* (Aldershot: Dartmouth, 1994) and M. Linton, *Was It The Sun Wot Won It?* (Oxford, Oxford University Press, 1994)

8 G. Radice, *Southern Discomfort* (London: Fabian Society, 1992), p. 24

9 D. Butler and D. Kavanagh, *The British General Election of 1992* (Basingstoke: Macmillan, 1992). The Butler–Kavanagh analysis was broadly backed by Heath, Jowell and Curtice in *Labour's Last Chance?*

10 J. K. Galbraith, *The Culture of Contentment* (Harmondsworth: Penguin, 1992)

11 P. Anderson, 'Easy Does It? Interview with John Smith', *Tribune*, 19 June 1992

12 Brown eventually accepted that Labour would have supported a realignment. See P. Anderson, 'New Economics: Interview with Gordon Brown', *Tribune*, 1 January 1993

13 P. Anderson, 'A Fine Mess over Maastricht', *Tribune*, 10 July 1992

14 See P. Gould and P. Hewitt, 'Lessons from America', *Renewal*, January 1993, and P. Gould, *The Unfinished Revolution: How the Modernisers Saved the Labour Party* (London: Little, Brown, 1998)

3

JOHN MAJOR AND THE EVOLUTION OF BRITISH CONSERVATISM

Kevin Hickson

THE CONTEXT OF JOHN MAJOR'S ADMINISTRATION

JOHN MAJOR, SO IT is widely held, travelled light in terms of political ideology. This was in stark contrast to Margaret Thatcher, who was openly ideological and missionary in her politics, championing the ideology of the New Right. The contrast could not have been starker. For those who argue that the Conservative Party is concerned only with the defence of the status quo, Major is closer to the authentic tradition of British Conservatism; for those who believe that the Conservative Party has a more ambitious agenda, Thatcher comes closer to being an 'authentic' Tory.

However, it is a central assertion of this chapter that politics is always ideological. Some political leaders will seek to usher in a new ideological agenda and create a policy legacy. Others will seek to operate within the existing ideological paradigm. The former are relatively rare in British politics. Since 1945 there have only been two such administrations. The first was the immediate post-war Attlee government, which ushered in the Keynesian welfare state, which lasted until the election of Thatcher in 1979 who sought to replace it with free-market liberalism and a more socially conservative agenda. This brings out the contrast between Thatcher and Major much more clearly. Thatcher was clearly an agenda setter; her successor had to work within the new ideological paradigm she had created.

The Keynesian welfare state was a coherent ideological framework which accepted a larger role of the state in the pursuit of clearly defined economic and social objectives. The economic objectives included a belief in higher rates of economic growth and full employment. The social objectives consisted of the provision of universal welfare, free at the point of use, the elimination of poverty and the fostering of greater equality. The extent to which governments – even Labour governments – achieved these objectives is debatable, but in broad terms this was the basis of the post-war consensus. Arguably the parties retained their distinctive ideological perspectives, and debate between the parties often focused on the merits of greater equality versus a more selective welfare state designed to improve the absolute position of the worst off. But the means (or policies) of the Keynesian welfare state were more or less continuous between 1945 and 1979.[1]

Criticism of the post-war consensus was limited to those on the left and the right of the political spectrum. The Labour left would reassert itself in opposition. The Conservative right was marginalised until the rise of 'Powellism' in the 1960s, when the case for economic liberalism was heard once more in mainstream politics. Before that the economic liberals had been pushed to the fringes of politics with think tanks such as the Institute of Economic Affairs (IEA). The new economic circumstances of the 1970s changed all that as the optimism of the post-war years was shattered. Rising inflation and unemployment – 'stagflation' as it became known – appeared to contradict the Keynesian belief that full employment could be maintained without inflating prices. Mounting government debt and the weakness of the currency were recurring issues throughout the 1970s, as was trade union militancy. Commentators talked of Britain becoming 'ungovernable' and the state 'overloaded'.

It was within this context that Thatcherism emerged. Thatcher offered to combine the free economy with the strong state.[2] In place of Keynesian economics there would be monetarism, privatisation, deregulation of markets, and free movement of labour. The welfare state would be cut back in order to reduce 'dependency' and the 'cycle of deprivation'. The powers of the central state would be increased in order to defeat the 'enemies within' and 'without' who threatened the nation state. This would include a more powerful military alliance with the USA to defeat the Soviet Union, more powers for the police and restrictions on organised interests such as the trade unions and left-wing local authorities. In short, the ideology of the New Right. However, the ideology which underpinned Thatcherism was divided between those who drew from the wellspring of classical liberalism and those who claimed inspiration from Traditional Toryism. In philosophical terms, there were clear differences between these ideological traditions though Thatcher effectively held them together for the course of her premiership, partly through the strength of her personality and also because they shared the same targets; for example, the trade unions were viewed as being both a barrier to economic freedom and a challenge to the authority of the democratic state.

By the 1990s this had begun to change. John Major's political style was clearly distinct from Thatcher's – part of the reason he was elected – and he had less dominance over his party than Thatcher appeared to have. But also, the enemies of Thatcherism had largely been defeated by 1990. The Soviet Union had collapsed and the trade unions had been beaten. Major continued with trade union reform though it was not clear to many why this was by the 1990s. Thatcher had started to tackle the welfare state more decisively in her third and final term but much was left for Major to do. As successive governments have discovered, the welfare state is difficult to reform. Tony Blair famously said that he wore the scars on his back of trying to reform the welfare state. But, beyond welfare 'scroungers', it is difficult to see who the enemies of the nation are. Certainly not the professionals and 'managers' any much more faceless than flying pickets. An understanding of the complexities of John Major's governing strategy is only really appreciated in the light of the limitations of New Right ideology.

A secondary issue is the extent to which Major sought to reposition the Conservative Party as a return to the earlier One Nation tradition. This chapter will go on to explore these issues in more detail. In doing so it will utilise the ideological framework outlined in an earlier book on the political thought of the Conservative Party edited by the current author.[3] In that book, four ideological positions are identified within the Conservative Party: Traditional Toryism, New Right, Centrism and One Nation. We will look at the extent to which John Major fitted into each of these ideological traditions during his time as Prime Minister and examine how his contemporaries viewed his premiership from each of these four perspectives. In short, the aim of the chapter is to answer the question: what kind of Tory was John Major?

TRADITIONAL TORYISM

The essential features of traditionalism are a pessimistic view of human nature stemming from the Christian doctrine of original sin, the idea of 'Hobbesian man' or a more empirical foundation, the maintenance of social order and defence of traditional social morality, the maintenance of the authority and sovereignty of the central state, and a defensive nationalism.[4] Historically, these notions were bound up with the British Empire but by the 1950s that was in terminal decline. Although some traditionalists such as Julian Amery sought measures to preserve the Empire, others led by Enoch Powell from the mid-1950s sought to fashion a post-Imperial nationalism which accepted the reality of the loss of the Empire and recognised the illusion of the Commonwealth. For Powell, the decline of the nation state had occurred during, and indeed been caused by, the Keynesian welfare state. The restoration of national power required a free-market counter-revolution and an acceptance that Britain must live within its means. Powell held to an absolutist view of sovereignty which led him to believe that the idea of 'pooling' sovereignty in the form of the Commonwealth or European integration was a falsehood, and similarly attempts to share sovereignty within the territory of the UK, in the form of devolution to Scotland and Wales or power sharing in Northern Ireland, were also an illusion. Sovereignty resided at Westminster. This led Powell to increasingly stronger opinions on these issues until he effectively told people to vote Labour in the February 1974 election in an attempt to restore national sovereignty through Labour's promise of a referendum on continued EEC membership. Powell also came to regard the rise of a more multicultural society as a threat to the nation state. Many of Powell's natural supporters ignored the fact that on other issues he was progressive, including homosexuality and the death penalty. For others on the traditional right, the 1960s were an era of 'permissive' social legislation with disastrous consequences for the moral fabric of society.

By the 1970s, traditionalists argued that the economic and moral decline of the nation was readily apparent and they largely supported Thatcher, who despite her rhetoric of wanting to 'set the people free', was really a traditionalist who shared their concerns they claimed. Some traditionalists, such as the journalist T. E. Utley and the academic Shirley Letwin, supported Thatcher throughout, believing that she was restoring the moral, as well as the economic, strength of the nation. Others were initially sceptical of Thatcher, believing that she had borrowed too much from economic liberalism and lacked a sufficiently robust sense of patriotism, but recognised their own views in Thatcher during the Falklands War and the miners' strike. Others remained, or became more, sceptical of Thatcherism with her unrelenting support for free-market economics which led to radical social change and undermined traditional morality. Whereas traditionalists sought to defend much-cherished institutions, capitalism had no such respect for them. Karl Marx had pointed out in the *Communist Manifesto* that 'all that is solid melts into air'.[5] Far from restoring Victorian values, Peregrine Worsthorne accused her of championing vulgar bourgeois materialism.[6]

It was in this context that traditionalists viewed the Major government in differing ways. His statement shortly after coming to power that his aim was to be 'at the heart of Europe' was deeply troubling for them. Thatcher, for sure, had not been a consistent Eurosceptic. She had, after all, been active in the 'Yes' campaign in the 1975 referendum and subsequently signed the Single European Act (SEA), claiming later and somewhat implausibly that she had not realised what she was signing up to. But by the end of her time in office she claimed to have realised that the European project was indeed federalist and was opposed to the creation of a European superstate. It was this issue that led to the resignation of the sole surviving member of her 1979 Cabinet, Geoffrey Howe, and her removal from office. Her position by this stage was strongly Eurosceptic, but Major not only wanted to usher in a new, more friendly relationship with Europe, but had led Britain into the Exchange Rate Mechanism and wanted to sign up to the Maastricht Treaty (albeit with opt-outs from the single currency and social policy aspects of the treaty), which his critics argued was far more integrationist than the SEA. Hence, on issues of national sovereignty, Major's critics were closer to the traditionalist perspective.

However, on other constitutional issues Major appeared closer to the traditionalist perspective. The dominance of the Conservatives in the 1980s had led to demands for constitutional reform. Charter 88 was established and the Labour Party increasingly supported constitutional reform, including establishing a review into proportional representation and John Smith's wish to complete the devolution measures he had tried to implement in the 1970s. Major opposed all of these measures. He stated his opposition to electoral reform in the 1992 and 1997 elections, and said in 1997 that the real danger posed by New Labour was the disintegration of the United Kingdom through their devolution proposals, a view echoed by Powell who said that the result of that election was to abolish the United Kingdom. The creation of the Scottish Parliament and the Welsh Assembly posed dilemmas for Conservatives. In principle many were opposed to devolution, but after being wiped out in the 1997 election, they recognised pragmatically that devolution offered a way back for their party in Scotland and Wales. Moreover, Conservatives were divided between those who wished to see the maintenance of a Unionist position and those who favoured a more English nationalist stance. Major was pragmatic on both of these issues, whereas others who had opposed devolution later came to embrace an English nationalist position.[7]

John Major's decision to call for the UK to go 'back to basics' also posed interesting issues for traditionalists. It was far from clear what Major meant by the term and, as Geoffrey Wheatcroft argues, he left much to the remit of individual members of the Cabinet.[8] His Home Secretary, Michael Howard, took it to mean a tougher approach to law and order, introducing stronger sentences and increasing police powers for the first time since talk in the early years of Thatcher's government of wanting to bring in a 'short, sharp, shock' to stop offending and reoffending. His Social Security Minister, Peter Lilley, wanted tougher sanctions on benefits, leading to the introduction of Jobseeker's Allowance. These policy developments are addressed in more detail in subsequent chapters. The salient point here is the extent to which they revived traditional moral concerns. While many on the right supported tougher sanctions on welfare claimants and law and order measures, others would point out that the fact that these things were needed at all was a sign of the moral decline which had engulfed Britain for decades, and especially with the so-called 'permissive' reforms of the 1960s.[9] If people had a clear sense of moral purpose in the first place they would not transgress and so would not need to be coerced in this way.

NEW RIGHT

As stated above, the New Right consisted of socially conservative and economic liberal elements. For some, including Thatcher, these two strands of thought were entirely compatible whereas for others we have seen that they were not. While traditionalists wished to defend institutions, economic liberals wanted to press on with their free-market crusade. These tensions occasionally erupted in the 1980s as for instance when John Biffen, who had been an early monetarist, believed that a period of consolidation was needed by the middle of the decade, and when Peter Thorneycroft, who Thatcher had brought back into frontline politics as party chairman, said that in the debate between 'wets' and 'dries' he increasingly detected 'rising damp' in his political beliefs! By the 1990s these divisions were still greater.

Major recognised the socially divisive unrest that free-market policies had brought about. Early in Thatcher's tenure there had been the urban riots in major cities and at the end there were riots in central London in reaction to the community charge (or poll tax). Major said that he wished to create a 'nation at ease' with itself, thus recognising the social divisions which Thatcherite policy had created. He scrapped the poll tax and developed a softer tone designed to reassure voters.

However, in many ways his government marked a continuation of economic liberal policies. The privatisation agenda continued, with the selling off of what remained of the coal industry, while the sale of British Rail was perhaps the most controversial privatisation measure. There was a continuation of the trade union measures introduced by Thatcher, albeit with a softer tone and the abandonment of rhetoric such as the 'enemy within' which had defined her approach. The Thatcher governments had not really begun to address the reform of the welfare state until the third term and Major pushed on with much of this agenda. A key reform here was the Citizen's Charter, which regarded users of public services as consumers, a quintessential theme of the New Right. Competition between schools, GP practices and hospitals was further encouraged through the use of new funding models and league tables. By allowing polytechnics to become universities from 1994 onwards the Major government was encouraging more competition and choice in higher education. There were further attempts to reform the civil service, through the importation of private sector management practices and economy drives, and Jobseeker's Allowance was defended in terms of reducing the burden on the taxpayer.

Once again, many of these reforms survived the change of government in 1997 as New Labour not only accepted many of the measures as irreversible but also sought to build on them. The Major years can be regarded, therefore, as the development of New Right policy measures, albeit with a different tone and rhetoric when compared to his predecessor.

This creates an intellectual difficulty in understanding the Major years since his strongest critics were very often from the free-market right of the party. His leadership challenger in 1995 was one of the leading exponents of economic liberalism. John Redwood campaigned on the basis of defending the Thatcherite agenda. Apart from the obvious difference of Europe – where Major rather than Redwood could be said to have been closer to the view Thatcher herself held for much of her political life – Major did not deviate from the economic liberal agenda significantly, notwithstanding the increase in public expenditure in the early to mid-1990s which was largely caused by the recession, with falling tax revenue and higher social security expenditure. Of course, the economic liberals wanted to see a leader more in keeping with Thatcher's more combative style, but it was the nature of economic liberalism to constantly seek reform. The differences between Biffen and the younger Thatcherites in the mid-1980s could also be applied to the divisions between Major and his critics from the right on domestic policy. Whereas Major wanted to build on the economic liberal agenda more cautiously, his critics believed that there was a need for ever deeper and faster reform. Established free-market think tanks such as the IEA continued to demand ever more reforms, but were now joined by newer groupings of MPs such as the No Turning Back Group, which sought to maintain parliamentary pressure for economic liberal measures. Consolidation of the Thatcher reforms was therefore tantamount to treachery and perpetual revolution seen as 'true Thatcherism'.

THE CENTRISTS

The third broad position within the Conservative Party is that of the party centrists, those who stress the need for party unity and loyalty to the leader. Although often the subject of less academic attention, this position is ordinarily held by the majority of MPs in the party. In an article towards the end of Thatcher's premiership, Philip Norton argued that the Conservative Party had not become 'Thatcherised' to anywhere near the extent that appeared to observers of the party.[10] Certainly Thatcher was closer to the instinctive position of many party members and activists. She received rapturous applause at the annual party conference and she was held in higher regard that many of her predecessors or successor there. Normally leaders were tolerated at the party conference, albeit with the natural instinct to appear united showing in set piece events such as the leader's speech. However, this did not feed through into the parliamentary party. Selections at successive elections did not lead to a dramatic rise in the number of Thatcherite MPs. Despite appearances, her Cabinet was never fully 'Thatcherised', hence the inability to find a fully committed heir in 1990. Most MPs remained what Norton called 'party loyalists'. Hence Thatcher was tolerated for as long as she won elections. By 1990 she was regarded as an electoral liability and was removed accordingly.

Major himself could lay claim to be a party loyalist under Thatcher. Indeed, Mark Garnett has argued that Major could be regarded as the epitome of the party centrist, as he tended to give the appearance that he agreed with whoever he happened to be talking to.[11] For some of his later right-wing critics this showed his lack of principle and justified the Thatcherite allegation of 'betrayal', whereas for his supporters it was simply his nature not to be confrontational and he had never been a solid Thatcherite. He was first elected in 1979 and had risen almost without trace to be first Foreign Secretary and then Chancellor of the Exchequer. His style was very different from Thatcher's and he would hold the broad centre of the party who wanted to calm things down. It was felt that Michael Heseltine would be divisive. Douglas Hurd could lay reasonable claim to be a man of the centre as someone who had served loyally under both Heath and Thatcher, but he would not have the support of the right. So Major emerged, ironically as it proved to be, as the candidate who could best unite the party. His ability to win the 1992 general election appeared to support the decision to remove Thatcher from office two years earlier but he could not then hold the party together.

According to the political scientist Jim Bulpitt, the Conservative Party is best understood by its commitment to 'statecraft', defined as the art of winning elections and maintaining the appearance of governing competence in order to win subsequent elections.[12] Hence, for Bulpitt, Thatcherism should not be considered primarily in terms of an economic or moral crusade so much as reviving the electoral fortunes of the Conservative Party. Heath had lost three out of the four elections he had contested and Harold Wilson was boasting of Labour now being the 'natural party of government'. Given that three of Wilson's four election wins had been by a very narrow margin this claim was somewhat hyperbolic but Conservatives worried about their apparent electoral decline, made worse by the revival in the Liberal vote in the 1970s. Thatcher claimed to offer a new way of restoring the electoral health of the Conservatives and to the extent that she won three successive elections appeared to have amply justified her claim. By 1990 the electoral fortunes of the party were again in doubt, hence Major's election.

However, the period after 1992 was uncharted territory for any party in the democratic era and could be understood as the squeezing of the party centre. It is doubtful that any leader could have done better than Major at holding the party together given that it now contained serious fault lines, not least over Europe. The party had become more overtly ideological and with ideology comes fragmentation. This was true of the Labour Party in the 1950s and 1980s but now was also true of the Conservatives after 1992, something which long outlasted Major's premiership. Arguably, the centre of the party did not recover until after the third successive election defeat in 2005, by which time even those not instinctively in tune with the idea came to recognise the importance of 'modernisation' under David Cameron.

ONE NATION

The final broad position identified is that of One Nation Conservatism. One Nation dates back to Benjamin Disraeli in the nineteenth century, who argued that Britain was on the verge of social unrest unless it more effectively bridged the gap between rich and poor. Social unity would be fostered though invoking a stronger sense of patriotism and through social reform. His successors sought to build on this tradition, including progressives after 1945 who accepted the larger role for the state with Keynesian economics and universal welfare.

Some would argue that Major marked a return to the One Nation tradition which had been abandoned by Thatcher. His call to create a 'nation at ease with itself' could be regarded as evoking the One Nation concern for social unity. He also stated that his political hero was Iain Macleod, who had been a prominent Tory reformer in the post-war era. Brought into politics as one of the bright young men cultivated by R. A. Butler after the 1945 general election defeat, Macleod was a founding member of the One Nation Group of MPs. He rose in the Conservative governments of the 1951–64 period to become the minister responsible for decolonisation, much to the frustration of the right, who established the Monday Club in response. He then refused to serve after Alec Douglas-Home became Prime Minister in 1963 before becoming Chancellor under Edward Heath, dying in office only months after the 1970 general election. Despite his association with Powell, Macleod was widely seen as a moderate, saying that he travelled on the same train as Powell but got off several stations ahead of him, who would remain until it crashed into the barriers. In claiming to be in the tradition of Macleod, Major could be seen as laying claim to the One Nation tradition, and certainly his style of leadership was more in keeping with that tradition.

At times his rhetoric also had echoes of the One Nation Conservatives. In the 1920s, at times of industrial unrest, Stanley Baldwin had invoked a medieval view of Englishness:

> The sounds of England, the tinkle of the hammer on the anvil in the country smithy, the corncrake on a dewy morning, the sound of the scythe against the whetstone, and the sight of the plough team coming over the brow of the hill, the sight that has been in England since England was a land, and may be seen

> in England long after the Empire has perished and every works in England has ceased to function, for centuries the one eternal sight of England.[13]

That this image was irrelevant to most people at the time he said it – who lived in urban areas or had seen the mechanisation of agriculture – did not take away from Baldwin's attempts to heal class divides. Major's invocation of such rhetoric was arguably further evidence of his recognition of the social divisions that free-market economics had created.

> Fifty years from now Britain will still be the country of long shadows on county grounds, warm beer, invincible green suburbs, dog lovers and pools fillers and – as George Orwell said – "old maids bicycling to Holy Communion through the morning mist" and if we get our way – Shakespeare still read even in school. Britain will survive unamendable in all essentials.[14]

It also fitted into Major's expressed desire of creating a classless society. What exactly he meant by this is open to debate. As David Cannadine has pointed out, a vision of a classless society was offered by Marx once all productive capital had come under collective ownership.[15] Any society with private property ownership would be a class-based society, with a class owning wealth and a larger class excluded from private property ownership and therefore having to sell its labour. Clearly Major did not have such a view of a classless society in mind, quite the reverse where the wider dispersal of private property ownership would create a classless society, a meritocracy in which family background, accent, manners, schooling and so forth would no longer matter. No doubt Major felt this sincerely as he had failed to leave school with good qualifications, had not been to university and had an unusual family background which had defied easy classifications of social gradation. He had felt patronised by those in his own party who had looked down on him. The Conservatives had boasted of their wish to create a 'property-owning democracy' since Anthony Eden in the late 1940s, and certainly it was an aim of Macleod, which is why Major felt an affinity towards him.

However, advocates of One Nation Conservatism believed that Major was not one of them. Ian Gilmour, perhaps the most intellectually distinguished of the Tory wets from the early 1980s, argued that Major had an opportunity to throw off Thatcherism in the very early days of his premiership and move decisively back to One Nation ideals.[16] However, he failed to achieve this, or indeed to even attempt it. Major's Conservative Party was therefore destined to remain on the right, looking more and more irrelevant and harsh compared to the resurgent Labour Party. This view is problematic, however. Firstly, it assumes that Major had significant room for manoeuvre. But for reasons already articulated this was not so. The nature of the succession, and then the reduced majority after 1992, meant that he could not simply discard Thatcherism. Moreover, it is difficult to see that there was room for the Conservatives as a moderate party of the centre ground given the success of New Labour in dominating that area of political opinion. Therefore, although Gilmour may have been right in arguing that Major was not an authentic One Nation Tory, he fails to see the limited scope for the kind of Conservatism he preferred by the 1990s. It is doubtful that Heseltine or Hurd could have been any more successful in recasting the Conservative Party in the mould of the Tory wets.

THE DEATH OF CONSERVATISM?

John Major can therefore be seen as representing elements of all four of the above traditions. In policy terms his government marked the continuation of Thatcherism, in some ways a radicalisation of the Thatcher agenda. Privatisation, marketisation, consumerism and so forth were the hallmarks of Thatcher's programme. Constitutionally Major was a traditionalist though in other ways he was not and the traditionalists were directly opposed to Major's position on Europe and social morality, with the National Lottery viewed by social conservatives as the state's encouragement of gambling. In terms of party management and style of leadership Major was closest to the centrists, although his calls for unity went largely unheeded, especially over the ratification of the Maastricht Treaty. He was initially Thatcher's preferred candidate, though this was more to do with the fact that she was never able to promote a true believer and he was the nearest thing to it in 1990. She and her followers soon distanced themselves from the new regime even though, as we have seen, in domestic policy the agenda was marked more by continuity than change. For the first two years Major lacked a personal mandate; by the time he secured an unprecedented fourth term in office, the right of his party were already in mutiny and with his majority greatly reduced his parliamentary position was weakened and at times precarious. Hence, Major came to rely increasingly on the moderates in his party, from Chris Patten as the organiser of the 1992 election campaign to Michael Heseltine and Kenneth Clarke. His rhetoric had echoes of Disraeli and Baldwin. Yet as Gilmour contested he could not be seen as a return to the One Nation tradition in policy terms.

At the end of Major's seven years as Prime Minister a debate erupted between the Conservative minister David Willetts and his former tutor Professor John Gray over the 'death of conservatism'.[17] Both Willetts and Gray had been supporters of Thatcherism, the latter one of the leading exponents of Hayekian neo-liberalism. However, by 1997 he had abandoned his old cause and argued that Thatcherism contained the seeds of the destruction of Conservatism. In pursuing free markets and constant change, her governments had destroyed the traditional institutions (physical and ethical) which held conservative society together. This was something traditionalist critics of Thatcherism had been saying since at least the 1980s. By 1997 it was too late. Conservatism was dead, argued Gray, not just in terms of being an electoral force following the New Labour landslide in 1997, but also ideologically. Willetts contradicted his old tutor, saying that free markets and the institutions of civil society were fully compatible. Instead the social democratic state and the pursuit of equality were the enemies of both markets and community. His idea, which he termed 'civic conservatism', would evolve into David Cameron's 'Big Society' where he would argue that there is such a thing as society but it was not the same thing as the state, thus in an act of political triangulation distinguishing his ideology from both Thatcherism and New Labour. His thesis had much to commend it as an attempt to revive conservatism but it was flawed in that there were all too obvious tensions between free markets and the institutions of civil society. The closure of uncompetitive coalmines in the early 1990s could be justified on free-market grounds but destroyed communities which depended on their continued operation. The closure of uneconomic rural post offices was justified on neo-liberal grounds but took the heart out of many rural communities.

By the late 1990s some traditionalists were talking openly of the death of England. The political journalist Peter Hitchens and the academic philosopher Roger Scruton wrote at length on this theme.[18] The economic and social policy framework ushered in by the Conservatives between 1979 and 1997 was more or less maintained by the Blair governments (albeit with considerably higher levels of public expenditure) but the areas where New Labour was more radical were in constitutional reform and social morality. Liberalism triumphed writ large and in the Conservative Party the so-called 'mods' such as Michael Portillo and Francis Maude called for the party to embrace social liberalism alongside economic liberalism. The Conservatives were finally returned to office in 2010 as part of a coalition with the Liberal Democrats and accepted much of the New Labour reform agenda. David Cameron had already said that he would be a 'liberal conservative' and introduced such liberal reforms as gay marriage.[19] For traditionalists this was a fundamentally 'unconservative' approach, showing once again that 'Old England' had passed away. Perhaps Major was the last authentic Conservative Prime Minister, and those traditionalists who opposed him at the time may one day look back nostalgically on his tenure as Prime Minister, if not quite as a golden age then at least as a last hurrah.

ENDNOTES

1 See K. Hickson, 'The Post-war Consensus Revisited', *Political Quarterly*, Vol. 75, Issue 2 (April 2004), pp. 142–54
2 A. Gamble, *The Free Economy and the Strong State* (Basingstoke: Palgrave, 1988 and 1994)
3 K. Hickson (ed.), *The Political Thought of the Conservative Party since 1945* (Basingstoke: Palgrave, 2005)
4 I intend to explore traditional Toryism in the period since 1945 understood in these terms in a further book for publication in 2018.
5 K. Marx, *The Communist Manifesto* (London: Penguin, 2002), p. 223
6 See M. Garnett and K. Hickson, *Conservative Thinkers* (Manchester: Manchester University Press, 2009) for a discussion of Worsthorne's thought
7 See, S. Heffer, *Nor Shall My Sword: The Reinvention of England* (London: Weidenfeld & Nicolson, 1999)
8 G. Wheatcroft, *The Strange Death of Tory England* (London: Penguin, 2005)
9 B. Pilbeam, 'Social Morality' in Hickson (ed.), *The Political Thought of the Conservative Party since 1945*
10 P. Norton, 'The Lady's Not For Turning but What About the Rest? Margaret Thatcher and the Conservative Party 1979–89', *Parliamentary Affairs*, Vol. 43, No. 1 (1990) pp. 41–58
11 M. Garnett, 'The Centre' in Hickson (ed.), *The Political Thought of the Conservative Party since 1945*
12 J. Bulpitt, 'The Discipline of the New Democracy: Mrs Thatcher's Domestic Statecraft', *Political Studies*, Vol. 34, No. 1 (1986), pp. 19–39
13 S. Baldwin, *On England and Other Addresses* (London: Philip Allan, 1926), p. 7
14 J. Major, speech to the Conservative Group for Europe, 22 April 1993 available at http://www.johnmajor.co.uk/page1086.html, although as Arthur Aughey points out in the next chapter this speech was primarily about committing to closer European integration rather than a nostalgia for old England.
15 D. Cannadine, *Class In Britain* (New Haven and London: Yale University Press, 1998)
16 I. Gilmour and M. Garnett, *Whatever Happened to the Tories? The Conservatives since 1945* (London: Fourth Estate, 1998)
17 J. Gray and D. Willetts, *The Death of Conservatism* (London: Profile, 1997)
18 P. Hitchens, *The Abolition of Britain* (London: Quartet, 1999) and R. Scruton *England: An Elegy* (London: Continuum, 2001)
19 See Matt Beech's essay 'A Tale of Two Liberalisms' in S. Lee and M. Beech, *The Cameron–Clegg Government: Coalition Politics in an Age of Austerity* (Basingstoke; Palgrave, 2011) for further articulation of Cameron's liberalism

4

JOHN MAJOR AND BRITISHNESS

Arthur Aughey

WINSTON CHURCHILL ONCE REMARKED that an empty taxi drew up at 10 Downing Street and Mr Attlee got out. The former Director of the Conservative Research Department, Robin Harris, made a similar judgement about the political stature of John Major. In his 527-page history of the Conservative Party, Major – who was Prime Minister for seven years and who, in the general election of 1992, achieved more votes for his party than any previous or subsequent leader (of any party) – has no chapter devoted to him, is passingly referred to in the text and has only four separate entries to his name in the index. Like the famous mention for Wales in the 1888 edition of *Encyclopedia Britannica* – 'For Wales, See England' – the reference to Major in Harris's book is essentially: 'For Major, see Thatcher'. The association is described simply as the 'unevenly virtuoso Thatcher performance, and its downbeat Major coda'.[1] To paraphrase and invert Churchill's remark, it is as though, when Mrs Thatcher's car left Downing Street on 28 November 1990, No. 10 remained empty of a competent successor. It is a view that has become part of the common, if cruel, wisdom about the Major years, and one also shared by a substantial proportion of the Conservative Party. That this view misrepresents his achievements and that his reputation requires some reassessment has been recognised recently by a number of commentators. For example, the journalist Bruce Anderson, who has been a consistent advocate of Major's virtues as Conservative leader, thought that he had nothing to fear from history and was confident that his standing as a politician could only rise now and in the future.[2] This sort of claim is based mainly on two related considerations. The first is context. As the virtuosity of his predecessor is revised and the performance of his successors is reckoned, it is believed that Major will emerge as a much more substantial historical figure. The second is Europe. Major's premiership was distorted to caricature by the gravitational pull of the European black hole, one which absorbed into its political darkness much of his energy as well as his reputation. As that particular distortion is reviewed from a longer historical perspective – especially from a post-Brexit Britain, where Europe's capacity to wreck the Conservative Party remains a potent threat – it becomes possible to appreciate in a new light other aspects of his legacy. Taking both considerations into account, one can reconsider in general Major's view of Britishness and the relationship between a predominantly English Conservatism and a multi-national Union.

MISUNDERSTANDING MAJOR

On this complex question of identity and constitutional politics, Major is not well served by enduring folk wisdom. It is common, when the matter of Britishness is discussed, to refer to the speech in which he argued that Britain would 'survive unamendable in all essentials'. It would remain, thought Major, 'the country of long shadows on county grounds, warm beer, invincible green suburbs, dog lovers and pools fillers and – as George Orwell said – "old maids bicycling to Holy Communion through the morning mist" and if we get our way – Shakespeare still read even in school'.[3] These thoughts have been taken to confirm not only how out of touch Major was with modern times but also how incapable he was to distinguish his English references and British experience. In truth, this judgement is a caricature. The passage was neither the emotional core of a thesis on British character nor was it a sentimental rhetorical indulgence. It came at the conclusion of a speech proclaiming, ironically, that after twenty years of membership the country had 'come of age in Europe' and, trusting in their own integrity, the British people had nothing to fear from European cooperation. It was an invitation to be open to the future and not a nostalgic yearning for the past, as relevant today as it was then. Even passing attention to Major's speeches on the Union, as well as to reflections on the subject in his autobiography, reveals someone acutely sensitive to its contemporary challenges as well as to charges of Conservative Anglocentricity. One accusation thrown at Major is of choosing the wrong side of history and, like Mrs Thatcher before him, failing to take ownership of devolution to Scotland and Wales, consequently putting the Conservatives at a serious disadvantage in both places. This accusation has substance but abstracts that choice from a complex historical inheritance. If there was nostalgia in Major's Britishness, then it was for a certain idea of Britain – albeit a venerable Conservative idea. Indeed, one can argue that Major's premiership was that idea's Indian summer.

Major was not insensitive to the moment, for there is a devolution paradox in his autobiography and one that is quite telling about his style of leadership. One can detect a fatalistic assumption about constitutional change at odds with his commitment to resist it. Thus, while Major believed that the devolved institutions proposed by the Labour Party would be a danger to the integrity of the Union, he nevertheless conceded that they were 'inexorable'.[4] This particular paradox is a recognised part of the Tory tradition, perhaps best captured by the Prince of Salina in Lampedusa's novel *The Leopard*: 'delay is life' – if only because delay is freighted with the faint possibility of avoidance. For one authority on the Conservative Party this was very much in character, observing how on many issues Major preferred to put off decisions when consensus was elusive.[5] It was a style which, though collegial, suggested lack of resolve and resolution, if only – and unfairly – by comparison with Mrs Thatcher. However, on the British question Major was the opposite: he was resolved and resolute. During the 1992 general election campaign he summoned up all the authority of his office into a single warning – Britain in danger – and called on his fellow countrymen to wake up to that danger before it was too late.[6] And that single warning echoed the uncompromising message of Conservatives during the Home Rule crisis of 1912: there is no halfway house between unity and separation. Here, familiar celebration of the Union as the great vocation of the Conservative Party was mixed with an equally familiar Jeremiad – the sounding trumpet – of its possible dissolution. It was a passionate wager on continuity and in 1992 it appeared to be a successful one in Scotland, if not in Wales (where the party lost two seats). As Major told the Scottish Conservative Party conference a year later, they had 'proved faint hearts wrong'.[7] Standing by the principles of British Unionism against devolution, the party had increased its votes and seats in Scotland. That the Prime Minister would maintain that commitment was understandable, especially if there was no clear consensus for change.

In sum, it is tempting to argue that Major naively came to believe his own press releases: that opposition to devolution had turned around Conservative fortunes in Scotland and that it would continue to do so. Again, this is a caricature. The evidence suggests otherwise and that Major was well aware of the fragility of the party's support. The negative interpretation is that he missed the opportunity to reposition the party and to take advantage, as he conceded, of the slow but inexorable shift of public opinion, especially in Scotland, towards devolution. The positive interpretation is that he put conviction first. The great master of Conservative statecraft, the third Marquess of Salisbury, speaking about the Queen Victoria's Diamond Jubilee in 1897, had opined that a dangerous temptation of statesmanship is to consider 'rhapsody an adequate compensation for calculation'.[8] There was certainly rhapsody in Major's defence of Britishness, but there was also party political calculation. After all, Major *was* a Conservative leading a party – the members of which shared overwhelmingly his idea of Britishness.

A CERTAIN IDEA OF BRITAIN

Historians attribute the division in British politics over Irish Home Rule to have consisted in a question of identity: very starkly, was Britain composed of a single people, albeit one with distinctive national and regional cultures; or was it composed of separate nations whose identities demanded acknowledgement in distinctive political institutions? A similar question of identity informed the debate about devolution in the very different circumstances of the 1990s and the position adopted by Major was rooted firmly in the former, traditionally Conservative, camp. As the Conservative Political Centre's National Policy Group on the Constitution reported, this position assumed the existence of a British *constitutional people*, defining Britishness as a unitary synthesis of patriotic identity and political belonging.[9] It was an identity expressed, equally singularly, by the sovereignty of Parliament. The idea of the constitutional people stressed the value of the whole, one which involved, to use that resonant – if ambiguous – Scottish phrase, a partnership for good. British, as the identity of the whole, is 'second nature' in the manner which Edmund Burke understood it, what political theorists used to call 'national character', an identity formed by political custom, convention and a common history. In sum, if Britishness is an artifice, a Union 'forged' – to use Linda Colley's equally ambiguous word – through long association, conquest and external threat, it should not be confused with being *artificial*.[10] It is far from artificial and remains an enduring identity bound up with, and not distinct from, its component regional and national differences. It was this territorial version of One Nation Conservatism to which Major re-dedicated the party during his premiership. And the reason, according to the CPC report, is that the second idea of Britain reverses these propositions and assumes the priority of *sovereign peoples* – English, Scottish, Welsh and Irish – for whom the nation forms the basis of identity. Therefore, by contrast with the first, this idea implicitly (devolution) or explicitly (nationalism) asserts that the nation and not Parliament is, or ought to be, sovereign. Moreover, indirectly (devolution) or directly (nationalism) it assumes the right to dissolve the Union, even if those who support devolution understand it as the way to *avoid* that outcome. Hence the political logic, if not necessarily the political wisdom, of the 'no halfway house' argument. Major's defence of that first, 'certain idea' of Britain involved three inter-related notions of identity, constitution and international standing. In traditional Conservative fashion, their inter-relationship was held to compose the historical fabric of the country which, if unpicked, would unravel the Union. It is possible to trace these connected arguments in keynote speeches which Major made throughout his time as Prime Minister.

At a press conference in Edinburgh on 11 September 1992, Major stated the key proposition of this territorial one nation.[11] The cultural uniqueness of each part of the country was recognised but it was axiomatic that the whole is far greater than the sum of its parts. This was the very language of the 1992 party manifesto, which also declared that the Union preserved the historic and cultural diversity of those parts. In response to journalists' questions, Major welcomed the fact that the Scots are distinctively Scots, the English distinctively English, the Welsh distinctively Welsh, and the Northern Irish distinctively Northern Irish. 'I don't wish,' he said, 'to do anything that would damage the distinctive cultures, natures, traditions and instincts of the component parts of the United Kingdom.' What Major expressed was a very British elective affinity, a term one can adapt from Max Weber. Elective suggests agency and deliberate choice; affinity implies that individuals and nations are related by something other than choice. In short, component national identities elect to stay in relationship with one another but this relationship exhibits deep affinities which make Britain more than a mere formal, instrumental or external association. In that enigmatic phrase of Michael Oakeshott, it presupposes a 'flow of sympathy' between identities, past, present and future which gives substance to Britishness. It captures the intersection of active democratic choice – representation at Westminster as the sovereign key to being British – but also emotional identification – feeling sympathy with most, if not all, things British. In short,

Britishness can be understood as a choice and yet, paradoxically, as natural. To be British, Major accepted, admits the right to leave – 'no nation can be held irrevocably in a union against its will' – but it is an article of faith that there is no good reason for any nation to do so.[12] The consequence of separation can be only to diminish all members of the Union, individually and collectively. Devolution is a threat because, to adapt an Irish expression, it would establish elected factories of grievance in Edinburgh and Cardiff, inevitably disrupting the flow of sympathy with Westminster, only to the advantage of separatists. Ultimately, the logic of the constitutional people is incompatible with the idea of sovereign national peoples. Devolution is an attempt to square the circle by accommodating both, and Major's argument was that this accommodation could only be temporary.

CONSERVATIVE CONSTITUTIONALISM

These matters of British identity were intimately linked, of course, to the constitution, and Major also re-dedicated himself and his party to its maintenance. In doing so, he was confirming the Conservative apostolic succession and restating a venerable political liturgy. As it has been argued consistently, the Conservative adheres to established institutions 'not merely as a beachcomber, or as an antiquarian, or as a fool, but as in some sense a political being', for those institutions deserve allegiance and have authority.[13] Change, if it should be necessary, ought to be reform in the manner which Hailsham described as 'natural', that is change according to the acquired and inherited character of a society.[14] To which one can add the enduring conceit that only the Conservative Party understands that institutional inheritance sufficiently to be trusted with its reform. In a keynote speech on the British constitution, Major defined the sovereignty of Parliament as the very soul of the British constitutional people.[15] Parliament 'is, and should be, at the centre of that democratic, political process'. That had been Disraeli's view: the great wisdom of the constitution had been to remove supreme power from the sphere of human passions (by which he meant the *demos*). Disraeli's biographer Lord Blake believed that the party's appropriation of the patriotic card – at least when it could be played with any relevance – certainly was a winner.[16] It had enabled the Conservative Party to assume its own 'halo' of political virtue such that, in modern democratic politics, the 'national' cry and the 'constitutional' cry were 'assets hard to challenge'. It was those assets which Major recognised in the hope that they would remain winners. He could not be so dismissive of democracy, of course, but he certainly wore the patriotic halo as he deployed the national and constitutional 'cries'.

Major modified Disraeli's formula and argued that 'Parliament is supreme, because the people are supreme'. It was 'where things happen', but happen publicly. 'It is the focus of the nation's unity at times of national grief or outrage. And it is the theatre for the great convulsions of political history.'[17] However, it was more than a political forum for the national drama. Parliament was and remains the cement that holds together Britain and the British, linking politics and identity. It represents countries with distinct traditions, culture, history and language. 'But countries which have remained one nation because it was in their interests to do so. Unity brought stability. And stability bought prosperity.' If that central, integrative, elective role is threatened, then the unity, cohesion and affinity of the country are also threatened. Labour's proposals for devolution, then, could only recognise Parliament, depriving the British people of a single focus for democracy. 'Set up rival parliaments or assemblies, and they will grow hungry for more power', a process which would begin 'to unstitch our way of life'. Major concluded with the accustomed association of the Conservative Party with the good of the nation, committing to 'defend our tradition, our heritage' and guarding 'against any needless change which threatens the institutions that make us one nation. It is that which makes me a Conservative and Unionist.'

One month later, speaking to Welsh Conservatives, Major described Labour's constitutional proposals 'to carve up Britain' as 'an act of constitutional vandalism'.[18] Britishness 'depends on unity' and, once broken up, 'it would be difficult – probably impossible – to put it together'. Fiddling with the constitution would ultimately destroy the Union; or to put that more accurately, fiddling with the constitution in a non-Conservative way would destroy the Union. For the Prime Minister was not ruling out any and every alteration. Almost in a direct reprise of Hailsham's rule, Major's theme was not whether the constitution should change – he thought it was a living, adaptable set of practices – but how and at what pace. Certainly it should not be change for change's sake, the result of some technocratic plan, or to serve the interests of the institutions themselves.[19] Reform should be practical, respecting the existing order of parliamentary sovereignty and the identity of one nation. In other words, modification of the procedures at Westminster was appropriate but the radical constitutionalism proposed by other parties was reckless. The modifications that were implemented under Major's premiership were proudly identified in the Conservative Party manifesto for the 1997 general election. Parliament's role at the centre of the Union had been preserved, but new powers also had been given to the Scottish and Welsh Grand Committees, enabling greater democratic debate and accountability to take place at Westminster, something, it was claimed, that would be impossible under devolved institutions. That was the ground upon which the institutional flag of Britishness was planted, as a rallying symbol for the Union, the whole Union and nothing but the Union. It was a position which could not be held after 1997. The reason for failure was attributed to the victory of partisan self-interest over Tory patriotism.

RHAPSODY MISCALCULATED

According to Malcolm Rifkind, the Labour Party in Scotland had not only coat-tailed on the nationalism of the SNP but also added that the Conservative Party had no mandate for its policies north of the border.[20] Though

Rifkind expected this of nationalists, Labour aspired to be a *British* government. 'To use the "no mandate" argument was wholly unprincipled. It has left a legacy from which it, and we all, suffer – that a British government can lack legitimacy' in Scotland (and by extension, Wales). Rifkind, of course, had been a longstanding Conservative advocate of devolution and so his criticism carries weight. And it was a criticism which can be found – as one would expect – in Major's speeches, often expressed in a tone of selfless political martyrdom. In short, while Labour displayed electoral cynicism on matters of identity and the constitution, the Conservatives committed to principle hoping, *contra* Salisbury, that rhapsody would be an adequate compensation for such devious calculation. Conservative opponents, claimed Major, calculated a 'short-term advantage in seeking to appease, not to wrestle with, this demon of nationalism, imperiling the Union for party benefit.[21] By contrast, Major continued to rhapsodise: 'why do I feel so strongly about the Union? In many ways, the cynics would say I shouldn't. After all, a purely English Westminster would be to the advantage of the Conservative Party. But the unity of the nation, all parts of it, is so crucial to our future that our duty is to stand up to protect it.'[22]

Of course there was a massive hint here about what really might be Conservative self-interest. If viewed from 'one aspect', Blake had thought, the Conservative Party 'could be regarded as the party of English nationalism'.[23] And it is 'England's structure' which takes the central role in Robert Tombs's recent history, a book detailing England's long administrative unity; its powerful central government; its tradition of representation; its common law; and, above all, its sovereign Parliament.[24] It is an English inheritance which had become British, and Major was conscious of the possible difficulties – both of its rejection by Scottish nationalists and of its re-appropriation by an English nationalist tendency within (and without) his own party. Though he recognised the English temptation, Major would not forsake the British vocation.[25] He was not interested in the business of 'trading easy [English] votes today for constitutional chaos tomorrow'. He was not only an English Conservative but also a British Unionist, articulating the broad consensus within his party: that the Union secured the welfare and prosperity of all parts of the Kingdom and, as a whole greater than its parts, gave Britain a powerful voice globally, a special role internationally and made it a force for good in the world. In 1997, the Indian summer of that idea of Britain came to an end. The general election – which Major, characteristically, had delayed as long as possible in the hope of a revival in Conservative fortunes – resulted in a Labour landslide. The Conservatives lost 178 seats and had no MPs in either Scotland or Wales. Major's wager on Britishness had lost. As Ian Gilmour put it rather unkindly, Major's strategy meant that the Conservative Party 'became in the worst sense a "One Nation" party – of England'.[26] Following his defeat, this very English ex-Prime Minister did a very English thing. He went to the Oval to watch cricket.

A DEADLY LEGACY?

The fading light of Major's Indian summer was replaced by Tony Blair's glad, confident morning, one promising to make Britain anew. It involved a considered rejection of the prevailing Conservative idea, for the renewal required would not tolerate what was thought to be the exclusive and unitary British identity of the past.[27] The new government expressed its conviction that devolution would accommodate popular sovereign claims and thus contain separatist tendencies, especially in Scotland. In short, constitutional change was designed to guarantee – by democratic, institutional recognition – the rights of the nations within the Union. It was a conviction which the Conservative Party very swiftly after 1997 – with a sure pragmatic acceptance of necessity – claimed for itself, ditching in the process the arguments of its former leader. However certain the governing (and opposition) wisdom – that devolution would strengthen rather than weaken the United Kingdom – this was yet another wager on the future. There was no certainty that the consequence would not be the attenuation of Britishness as Major had argued. Nor could there be any assurance that it would not boost moves towards separatism. Once again, here was a contemporary replay of that old divide over Irish Home Rule and another test of the belief that there could – or could not – be a halfway house between unity and separation. Even Blair was uncertain privately, later acknowledging devolution to be a dangerous game.[28] He accepted that there was no guarantee that nationalist sentiment might not become separatist politics. His judgement was simply that it was 'inevitable' – ironically repeating Major's own autobiographical conclusion. In the two decades subsequently, one can argue that the old certainties of the constitution and faith in the British nation which, in their very different ways informed the thinking of both former Prime Ministers, have taken a battering. It is also possible to argue that there has been a crisis of belief – as well as self-belief – in the institutions of Britishness, confirming the prophetic wisdom of the warning in 1992 of Britain in danger. Major is convinced that he read the times correctly.

For instance, speaking to journalists in Edinburgh during the Scottish independence referendum campaign, Major reminded them that he had opposed devolution consistently because he believed it would provoke a politics of grievance between Scotland and Westminster.[29] He repeated his then prediction that it would likely be a stepping stone to separation. He did not spell it out in so many words but the implication was clear: events have proved me right about its threat to British identity. Of course, that actually put him in a logically difficult position. If devolution really is the high road to separation, surely opposition to independence just delays the inevitable? Surely the 'is' of devolution can only 'become' eventually what one always feared? Politics, however, is not logic and that was not the conclusion drawn. Major simply repeated the mantras of the No campaign: 'we are safer together. Stronger together. More prosperous together. More influential together. We have more opportunities together'. The elective affinities, though significantly modified by devolution, remain and are worth sustaining. Essentially, Major was reminding his audience and the country of the continued existence of the constitutional people: that despite devolution it endures as a political community, and that Britishness remains a 'flow of sympathy'. He did concede that the Scots had the ultimate say – the principle of consent he had acknowledged as Prime Minister – but that their choice would affect everyone else in the United Kingdom. There was a *British* interest. Moreover, he returned to that Unionist conviction which he accepted as fundamental to his party. Why should an English Conservative care, especially if, without Scotland, the Conservative Party would become electorally dominant in Westminster? The reason was conviction and not selfish interest. The old halo of British patriotism, which had served the party well in the past, may not be as burnished as it once was, yet Major could see no good reason to discard it.

ENGLISH TEMPTATIONS

Nevertheless, it was noticeable how an edgy sense of English identity and reciprocal political grievance had come to inform some of his public pronouncements. When, during the general election campaign in 2015 it appeared that no party would have an absolute majority, it became possible to imagine a situation reminiscent of the early years of the twentieth century when Irish nationalists had held the balance of power. Only in this case, it would be Scottish nationalists who would have strategic advantage in a Labour–SNP coalition. Here was the potential to provoke an English backlash, one informed by party interests – Conservatives challenged in England by the UK Independence Party (UKIP) – and fuelled by popular grievance – the sense that while the Scots, the Welsh and the Irish get self-determination, it is the English who subsidise it financially. Already, Prime Minister David Cameron had announced after the Scottish referendum that the voices of England must be heard – Major had always worried that those voices might speak in a manner fatal to Britishness. Thus he argued that any Labour–SNP coalition would 'pick the pockets of the Tory Shires' as well as privileging Scotland at the expense of everyone else.[30] Since Labour in Scotland had already proposed to raise the Mansion Tax in England to boost Scottish spending, this would only encourage the SNP to press for further appeasement. Slowly but surely, Major argued, the nations of Britain would be split apart. Though he expressed this threat as 'the alienation of the Scots from the English', his argument was really the reverse: he was intimating the very real possibility that the English 'Sod Off School of Anglo-Scottish relations' – as the academic Jim Bulpitt once put it – would drown out other voices.[31] The English have taken a lot of abuse lately 'and – tolerant and slow to take offence as the English are – this is beginning to have an effect'. That the Conservative Party unexpectedly won a majority in 2015 does not diminish the substance of Major's concern. The politics of Englishness, as all parties now acknowledge, has become a separate key battleground.

If Conservatives are sometimes, in the circumstances, compelled to be radical, then there is evidence that, when linking identity and constitution, Major has been prepared to rethink radically on the constitution. One is reminded of the old tale of Sir John Cutler's stockings. In the story, Sir John had a pair of silk stockings which his housekeeper darned regularly with wool. After years of such darning all the silk had disappeared and his stockings were now entirely unrecognisable. This tale raises all sorts of interesting questions about identity but it confronted Conservatives with one particular question. Do they continue to keep on darning the old constitution or has a new one come into being already which needs to be recognised – and that their response should adjust accordingly? For example, in his Ditchley Lecture (2011) Major claimed that the 'quasi-federalist' constitution with Scotland was unsustainable. 'Scottish ambition', he argued, 'is fraying English tolerance' and the politics of grievance and appeasement was damaging sentimental affinities and political relationships throughout the country. It was time to move to a form of Home Rule which devolved 'all responsibilities except foreign policy, defence and management of the economy'.[32] Though his comments were addressed directly to the Scots as a way to relieve the 'aggravation' of the English, the federalist kite floated by Major in 2011 has drifted into the party political mainstream.[33]

CONCLUSION

When challenged to defend the Conservative Party's legitimacy to govern the whole country when its support was overwhelmingly English, Mrs Thatcher restated the right of the constitutional people: 'we are a party of the whole United Kingdom. We are the Conservative and Unionist Party. And we will always be a Unionist party.'[34] Major restated that right as the hyphen which joined and the buckle which fastened together national identities and parliamentary sovereignty in the shape of Britishness. Major's Britain is a world now gone, yet the Conservative commitment to Britishness remains. Mrs May began her first speech as Prime Minister in Downing Street with a rededication to the Union. Of course, its content has changed because the party has adjusted to devolution – most pragmatically and others absent-mindedly – and Westminster business remains relatively undisturbed. Major may take some comfort from the recent Conservative revival in Scotland and Wales. It is now the Labour Party which finds itself on an electorally sticky wicket, an irony which he would appreciate.

ENDNOTES

1 R. Harris, *The Conservatives: A History* (London: Bantam Press, 2011) p. 498

2 B. Anderson, 'The Conservative Party's treatment of John Major marked the most shameful period in its history', Conservative Home, 9 April 2012, http://www.conservativehome.com/thecolumnists/2012/04/bruce-anderson-the-conservative-partys-treatment-of-john-major-marked-the-most-shameful-period-in-it.html

3 J. Major, 'The text of Mr Major's speech to the Conservative Group for Europe on 22 April 1993', http://www.johnmajor.co.uk/page1086.html

4 J. Major, *The Autobiography* (London: Harper Collins, 1999), p. 415

5 T. Bale, *The Conservative Party from Thatcher to Cameron* 2nd edn (London: Polity, 2016), p. 418

6 J. Major, 'The text of Mr Major's speech: "The Threat to the Integrity of Britain" made at a Conservative Party Rally at Wembley on 5 April 1992', http://www.johnmajor.co.uk/page2437.html

7 J. Major, 'The text of Mr Major's speech to the 1993 Scottish Conservative Party

Conference, held on 14 May 1993 in Edinburgh', http://www.johnmajor.co.uk/page1093.html

8 A. Roberts, *Salisbury: Victorian Titan* (London: Weidenfeld & Nicolson, 1999) p. 2

9 CPC National Policy Group on the Constitution, *Strengthening the Union* (London: Conservative Political Centre, 1996)

10 L. Colley, *Britons: Forging the Nation, 1707–1837* (New Haven: Yale University Press, 1992)

11 J. Major, 'The text of Mr Major's press conference in Edinburgh, held on 11 September 1992', http://www.johnmajor.co.uk/page1413.html

12 J. Major, 'The text of the press release issued after Mr Major's speech to Scottish Conservative candidates, made at the Moat House Hotel in Glasgow on 22 February 1992', http://www.johnmajor.co.uk/page1267.html

13 J. Casey, 'Tradition and Authority', in M. Cowling (ed.), *Conservative Essays* (London: Cassell, 1978), p. 85

14 Hailsham, Lord *The Conservative Case* (Harmondsworth: Penguin Books, 1959), pp. 15–16

15 J. Major, 'The text of Mr Major's speech on the British Constitution, made on 26 June 1996', http://www.johnmajor.co.uk/page846.html

16 R. Blake, *The Conservative Party from Peel to Thatcher* (London: Methuen, 1985), pp. 362–3

17 J. Major, 'The text of Mr Major's speech on the British Constitution, made on 26 June 1996', http://www.johnmajor.co.uk/page846.html

18 J. Major, 'The text of Mr Major's speech to the Welsh Conservative Party Conference in Porthcawl on 14 June 1996', http://www.johnmajor.co.uk/page842.html

19 J. Major, 'The text of Mr Major's speech on the British Constitution, made on 26 June 1996'

20 J. Lloyd, 'Britain's four nations', *Financial Times*, 1 November 2008

21 J. Major, 'The text of Mr Major's speech: "The Threat to the Integrity of Britain" made at a Conservative Party Rally at Wembley on 5 April 1992', http://www.johnmajor.co.uk/page2437.html

22 Major, 'The text of Mr Major's speech on the British Constitution, made on 26 June 1996'

23 Blake, *The Conservative Party from Peel to Thatcher*, p. 361

24 R. Tombs, *The English and their History* (London: Allen Lane, 2014)

25 J. Major, 'Speech to the 1995 Conservative Party Conference, Blackpool 13 October, http://www.johnmajor.co.uk/page1269.html

26 I. Gilmour and M. Garnett, *Whatever Happened to the Tories: The Conservatives since 1945*, p. 382

27 See for example M. Leonard, *Britain TM: Renewing Our Identity* (London: Demos, 1997)

28 T. Blair, *A Journey* (London: Hutchinson 2010), p. 702

29 J. Major 'Text of Sir John Major's speech at the Scottish Parliamentary Journalists' Association', Edinburgh 17 June 2014, http://www.johnmajor.co.uk/page4374.html

30 J. Major 'It is shameful that Labour hasn't ruled out a pact with the SNP', *Daily Telegraph*, 5 March 2015, http://www.telegraph.co.uk/news/general-election-2015/11452938/John-Major-It-is-shameful-that-Labour-hasnt-ruled-out-a-pact-with-the-SNP.html

31 J. Bulpitt, 'Conservative leaders and the "Euro-Ratchett": Five doses of scepticism', *Political Quarterly* (1992) 63:3, p. 271

32 J. Major, 'Ditchley Annual Lecture', 9 July 2011, http://www.johnmajor.co.uk/page2282.html

33 Constitutional Reform Group, *Towards a New Act of Union* (2015), available at www.constitutionreformgroup.co.uk

34 M. Thatcher, *The Downing Street Years* (London: Harper Collins, 1993), p. 244

PART TWO

GOVERNANCE

5

THE CONSTITUTION

Lord (Philip) Norton

JOHN MAJOR WAS THE last Conservative Party leader to address, on any systematic and reflective basis, the UK constitution as a constitution and to pursue policies designed to preserve that constitution.

Major's style of leadership was different to that of his predecessor, Margaret Thatcher – he was a healer rather than a warrior – but his approach to constitutional issues was not that dissimilar. 'John Major has frequently been contrasted with Mrs Thatcher; she being a conviction politician and he not. This is far too facile a comparison. On constitutional matters, he was very much a conviction politician, believing in traditional Conservative constitutional values, pre-eminent among them the supremacy of Parliament.'[1] Like Thatcher, he was committed to the constitution, but much more wedded to the Westminster model – the traditional approach to constitutional change[2] – than she was.

Thatcher's commitment was instinctive and at times in conflict with her desire to get rid of institutional barriers to achieving a market economy. It was also in time to conflict with her stance on European integration. Although persuadable to adapt her position when in office – as one of her Cabinet colleagues put it, 'she recognised a brick wall when she saw one' – the exile to the backbenches left her free to express criticisms without responsibility for delivering on policy. She was able to express criticisms unconstrained by office – the brick walls were no longer barriers, but obstacles to be overcome.

STRENGTH THROUGH UNITY

Major's stance was more reflective than Thatcher's and one that he recognised he had to adapt to the reality of the situation he inherited. He had a clear objective and that was to defend the integrity of the extant constitution. He developed this theme in speeches throughout his premiership. It was to form part of the party's stance in both the 1992 and 1997 general elections. The 1997 party manifesto articulated his philosophy. The constitution was core to political stability and security. 'We owe much of that to the strength and stability of our constitution – the institutions, laws and traditions that bind us together as a nation.'[3]

The binding together as a nation was central to his belief system. The United Kingdom was held together under one Crown and Parliament. The Crown, he declared, 'is one of the great features of the nation, binding us together as a people, and ensuring that political debate … leaves our Head of State untouched and untarnished.'[4] The Crown helped unify the people. Parliament gave effect to their will. 'Parliament is supreme', Major said in 1996, 'because the people are supreme.'[5]

In the words of the 1997 manifesto, 'the supremacy of parliament is fundamental to our democracy, and the guarantee of our freedoms.'[6] Parliament was the body through which the people spoke. It bound together the peoples of the United Kingdom and helped facilitate that which made the nation strong. Parliament, he declared, 'is the cement that holds together the countries of the United Kingdom … Unity brought stability. And stability brought prosperity. Threaten the central role of our national Parliament, and you threaten that unity and stability.'[7]

The theme of binding together the people of the United Kingdom was a consistent theme. The United Kingdom was greater than the sum of its parts. 'The Union is, I believe, the rock on which this Kingdom's authority rests. Standing together, we have moulded the history of much of the world. Separating or separated we would be tossed on its tides.'[8] He recognised that the Union rested on consent. The different parts of the UK could not be forced to remain within the Kingdom. They had to be convinced of its merits. He saw his task as making the case for the Union.

The emphasis was very much on the United Kingdom as a nation state. This also informed his stance on European integration. He embraced what he termed 'a flexible Europe, a Europe of nation states; not a federalist State.'[9] This formed the basis of his approach to negotiations, especially of the Maastricht Treaty. He would have preferred no negotiations. 'I thought it was a negotiation before its time, and was frustrated that a new treaty was still on the agenda.'[10] Given the reality that negotiations on a new treaty were unavoidable, his task was to avoid UK entanglement with economic and monetary union and a social chapter. He achieved both in the negotiations. The principle of subsidiarity – that decisions were only taken at community level when they could not be taken at a lower level – was also agreed. The authorship of the principle is disputed, but the outcome was very much in line with Major's goals.

Although stressing that he adopted a pragmatic approach in dealing with negotiations, he couched his approach in terms of his overarching commitment to the nation state and Parliament. As he said in a speech in 1996 on the constitution:

> I have often set out my view of a flexible Europe, a Europe of nation states. Not a federalist state. Not a Europe of regions that would effectively by-pass national governments and weaken our strong national voice. I will not reiterate these points again this evening, except to say that they rest on my belief that our national Parliament must remain the primary focus for our democracy.[11]

This theme was reiterated in the party's 1997 manifesto, emphasising the vision of the European Union as a 'partnership of nations'. Foreshadowing the negotiations for the Amsterdam Treaty, it advocated, *inter alia*, a strengthening of the role of national parliaments. 'We will defend the right of national parliaments and oppose more powers being given to the European Parliament at the expense of national parliaments.'

CONSTITUTION UNDER THREAT

Major not only articulated his stance, but took the lead in ensuring that it was heard and that it formed the basis of his government's approach to constitutional change. He took office at a time when there were increasingly vocal demands for change to the nation's constitutional arrangements. By the 1980s, the consensus on the Westminster model of government had dissolved, and advocates of different approaches were making a mark in debate.[12] A constitutional reform movement, Charter 88, had been formed in 1988 on the tercentenary of the Glorious Revolution and Declaration of Rights, demanding a new constitutional settlement. It embraced a liberal approach to constitutional change. It thus favoured a fragmentation of power, with a new electoral system for the House of Commons, an elected second chamber, a Bill of Rights, and devolution (or, in the pure form of the liberal approach, federalism), all to be embodied in a codified constitution. It was an approach that was to influence Labour leader, John Smith, who developed a scheme of constitutional reform as Labour policy. Other than electoral reform, he essentially embraced Charter 88's proposals.[13] Advocates of change, especially those embracing the liberal approach, were making much of the running in debate.[14]

The initial response of supporters of the existing system was to keep their heads below the parapet and not engage, but Major's approach was to be proactive and to ensure that his ministers followed suit. Various pamphlets were written by Cabinet ministers, including Foreign Secretary Douglas

Hurd, Party Chairman Brian Mawhinney and Education Secretary John Patten, making the case for the existing constitutional framework. As Patten was later to write, the debate was seen not as one between necessary change and no change, but between advocates of grand schemes, imposed from above, and 'a philosophy that emphasises common sense and continuity'.[15] In his 1996 speech on the constitution, Major made clear that there was a concerted effort by ministers to make the case for the existing, evolutionary constitution. 'I intend to make sure that the issues at stake in the constitutional debate are properly understood. So over the coming weeks, a number of ministers will directly address current constitutional issues.'[16] Ministers made speeches covering the judiciary, the electoral system, Parliament, local government, public services, and devolution.

EMPOWERING CITIZENS

Major emphasised that the opposition was not to change, but to proposals that would undermine the existing constitution. He wanted to strengthen the citizen within the existing framework. He pursued a policy of constitutional change focused on open and accessible government. There was a stress on giving more powers to local organisations and to empowering citizens through access to information. A code of access on government information was introduced, as was a civil service code. However, the most prominent feature of the reforms was the Citizen's Charter. The emphasis was on citizens as consumers, or customers, of public services. The scheme was embodied in a 1991 White Paper, *Citizen's Charter*, which stressed that it was designed as a toolkit, rather than a blueprint, to help raise standards in a way that was appropriate to each service. Individual charters were introduced for public services, each essentially forming an agreement between service users and providers. The intention was that citizens would know what they were entitled to and the service would know the level of delivery it was expected to achieve.

The emphasis on openness remained a feature of Major's programme throughout the parliament. There was a 1993 White Paper on Open Government, developing the government's plans, and the 1997 manifesto embodied a commitment, derived from the White Paper, to legislate for a right of access by citizens to personal records held by government and other public authorities.

The manifesto also brought together the twin themes developed by Major. In rejecting the case for regional government, it emphasised the case for pushing power further down to the citizen. Regional government, it declared, would be a dangerously centralising measure. 'We wish to go in the opposite direction, shifting power to the local neighbourhood – for example, by giving more power to parish councils.'

The approach to the constitution was very much driven by Major. He appointed ministers in tune with his thinking to deliver what he sought to achieve, but he was central not only to articulating the case for defending the constitution, but also to delivering the policies.

In terms of the unifying, or binding, features of the nation – Crown and Parliament – Major was the key actor. On dealing with demands for change in respect of devolution, Northern Ireland and Europe, he worked in partnership with his senior ministers.

CROWN AND PARLIAMENT

The Major premiership was marked by problems for the royal family. The Queen famously described 1992 as her *annus horribilis*. There were tensions in the marriages of three of her four children, including that of the Prince of Wales. St George's Hall at Windsor was destroyed by fire. There was a dispute over the future of the Royal Yacht Britannia. The costs of the monarchy also caused controversy, as did the government's decision to fund the rebuilding of St George's and the decision, announced in 1997, to commission a replacement for the Royal Yacht. It fell to Major to announce the decision of the Prince and Princess of Wales to separate. He also announced, as part of a damage-limitation exercise, the decision of the Queen to pay income tax. Though other ministers were involved in decisions affecting funding – the Chancellor, Kenneth Clarke, apparently initially blocking funding for replacing Britannia – Major, as the Queen's first minister, was responsible for advising his sovereign. He had to steer a difficult path to protect the institution of monarchy at a time when it was attracting unwanted headlines.

The same applied to Parliament. There was the 'cash for questions' scandal in 1994, with two MPs accused of accepting money for tabling parliamentary questions, which fuelled public perceptions that MPs were in office to benefit themselves rather than the public interest. Recognising the reputational damage to the House of Commons, Major appointed a Committee on Standards in Public Life, under retired law lord, Lord Nolan, to investigate and report. The committee made several recommendations, including the appointment of a parliamentary commissioner for standards, a code of conduct for MPs, and a tightening of the rules over lobbying and the publication of any consultancy agreements entered into by MPs. The recommendations proved controversial, especially among Conservative MPs – one publicly berated Lord Nolan outside the Palace of Westminster – and Major responded by setting up a Cabinet committee. The committee supported most but not all of the Nolan proposals. Major took the decision to support the committee's recommendations and these were accepted, albeit with many Conservative MPs thinking they went too far and the opposition arguing that they did not go far enough.

At the Scottish Office, Ian Lang, a Scot in tune with Major's thinking on the Union, worked with Major to make the case against devolution. 'If devolution had to happen,' recalled Lang, 'as sooner or later it probably did, it could not credibly come from us: better to stand on principle and conviction and, if necessary, lose.'[17] It was Lang who decided to make the issue of devolution central to the Conservative campaign in Scotland in the 1992 general election campaign, putting the case for the Union. He also persuaded Major to include Scotland more often in UK events. The PM made speeches in defence of the Union, including in Edinburgh in March. 'I speak as I do because I believe – and believe with a passion – that we must fight for what is right ... We are the Unionist Party. And we will fight for the Union.'[18]

THE UNION AND EUROPE

Major and Lang pursued a policy of seeking to give Scotland a greater voice within Westminster. Foremost among these was expanding the role of the Scottish Grand Committee at Westminster, enabling the committee to discuss the second reading of Scottish Bills, and utilising evidence-taking special standing committees. Various UK responsibilities were also devolved to the Scottish Office. It was essentially a holding exercise, designed to stave off demands for devolution.

It was a similar joint effort in respect of Northern Ireland, where Major invested considerable energy and political capital in seeking agreement. Peter Brooke authorised the reopening of an intelligence channel through which Major received messages from the Provisional IRA and began developing a new political initiative. As Major recalled, 'it was from this base that Peter and I slowly built up our joint approach during my first year and a quarter in office.'[19] Patrick Mayhew – who Major had served as PPS (Parliamentary Private Secretary) after he became an MP – continued in Brooke's footsteps.

On Europe, Major was necessarily central to the Maastricht negotiations. Much preparatory work had been done by Douglas Hurd at the Foreign Office and by Norman Lamont at the Treasury, but it was the heads of government that were ultimately crucial. As Hurd recalled, 'once the meeting began and he was in harness again, John Major pulled steadily for agreement all day, sustained by Norman Lamont and myself.'[20] Lamont conceded that Major 'indeed deserved the credit. He had negotiated skilfully and patiently and achieved his objectives.'[21] Afterwards, the majority view in the Commons, recalled Lamont, was that Major had succeeded where Thatcher had failed, 'both in safeguarding British interests and in maintaining good relations with our Continental neighbours'.

Major not only worked hard to produce agreement in Maastricht, but also had to work hard in Parliament to deliver the legislation to give effect in UK law to the agreement. The bruising battle to get the Maastricht Bill enacted was politically fraught, but also constitutionally significant, not just for the content of the measure, but also for the steps Major was prepared to take to get it through. This applied also to the European Union (Finance) Bill in 1994 to increase the UK's contribution to the EU Budget. The period was remarkable for the extent to which the Prime Minister employed votes of confidence to get the government's legislation through and the use, on an unprecedented scale, of withdrawing the whip from Conservative MPs.

Following the defeat on the Social Chapter motion – needed in order for the Maastricht Act to take effect – another motion was put before the House the following day and a motion of confidence made (the first time such a motion had been taken on a Friday); Major was making it clear that the government would resign if defeated. Downing Street had already checked with Buckingham Palace that dissolution would be granted in the event of the vote being lost. In order to ensure passage the following year of the EU (Finance) Bill, Major announced that the Bill 'in all its essentials' was to be an issue of confidence. The phraseology was unusual, appearing to embrace not only the vote on second reading, but also other votes on the Bill. Opponents in the party claimed his action was 'a constitutional outrage'.

Withdrawing the whip from an MP is especially unusual on the Conservative benches. It was used by the Major government on an almost industrial scale. One Tory MP, Rupert Allason, who was absent in the confidence vote on the Social Chapter had the whip withdrawn. (It was restored the following year.) Eight Tory MPs who abstained on the EU (Finance) Bill had the whip withdrawn. Another, Sir Richard Body, resigned the whip in protest at the government's action. The existence of the nine whip-less MPs created problems for the government; it meant that technically it no longer had a parliamentary majority and after six months the whip was restored to the eight abstainers. It was another eight months before Body accepted the restoration of the whip. Despite the problems, the action – as with using votes of confidence – achieved its intended purpose. The government got its legislation.

REPUTATION

There are two points to emphasise from this narrative. The first is the extent to which John Major was at the heart of the government's position on constitutional issues. He articulated the case against radical constitutional change and was central to the government's handling of constitutional issues that it faced when he took office – on devolution, Northern Ireland and Europe. He was also responsible for generating a programme of open and accessible government, at the heart of which was the Citizen's Charter.

The second necessarily flows from the first, and that is the extent to which Major was held responsible for the outcomes of the government's approach to constitutional issues. His legacy is very different from how his performance was seen at the end of his tenure in Downing Street. The premiership of Tony Blair seemed to confirm the extent to which Major had been seeking to resist an incoming constitutional tide. His policies were berated as not having achieved their purpose. According to Barry Jones, 'by any objective measure, Major's devolution policy was a total failure'.[22] In addition to implementing a scheme of devolution, the Blair government enacted the Human Rights Act, a Freedom of Information Act, and set up an independent commission to review the voting system for parliamentary elections. Constitutional reform was a feature not only of the Blair government, but of succeeding administrations under David Cameron.

On Northern Ireland, the policies pursued by Major and Brooke/Mayhew enjoyed cross-party support, but failed to end the conflict in the province. Major recognised that he had 'to reckon on the long haul'.[23] He ended his premiership, as he acknowledged, with the job uncompleted. On Europe, he achieved passage of the Bill giving legal effect in UK law to the Maastricht Treaty, but it proved a bruising fight, badly divided the parliamentary Conservative Party, and created the impression of a party tearing itself apart.

Major's handling of issues affecting the monarchy were seen as maladroit, not least delaying a decision on commissioning a successor to HMS *Britannia* (the decision was rescinded by the Blair government), and his handling of the Nolan report on standards in public life seen as being too willing to put party before country. 'The decision lost him the respect of liberal opinion, as well as losing him the moral capital which he had made so many sacrifices to build up over the previous years.'[24]

His Citizen's Charter was seen by some as worthy, but was remembered especially for the cones hotline, where people could ring to complain about traffic cones being left out unnecessarily. It was also seen as being confused in its objectives. As Peter Hennessy has observed, the Charter was the most famous of Major's public service initiatives. 'It was also the most derided.'[25]

In the wake of his departure from Downing Street, his stance on constitutional issues was seen as out of tune with the times and his own initiative as limited and complex, failing to address the needs of citizens.

LEGACY

However, Major's legacy can be revisited. There are five dimensions. The first is contextual. Major inherited significant problems. He assumed the premiership when the consensus on the British constitution had dissipated and attitudes on constitutional issues divided both his own party and public opinion. 'Major had the difficult task of managing strong and complex trends of parliamentary and public opinion, which moved decisively in a Eurosceptic direction in the 1990s.'[26]

Critics were demanding radical constitutional change. The pressures were not solely external to the Conservative Party, or indeed the government. As we have recorded, his party was badly divided on the issue of European integration. There were also some Tory MPs who favoured devolution and some who were committed to a more hard-line Unionist approach on Northern Ireland. His predecessor proved a lurking presence, with a body of backbenchers more committed to her views than to Major's. These backbenchers were not isolated individuals, but organised in different groupings within the parliamentary party, including the 92 Group and the No Turning Back Group. Margaret Thatcher's stance on the UK constitution was, as we have said, instinctive rather than reflective and, out of office, became one of supporting paradigmatic change, a stance at odds with Major's approach. 'No Conservative leader this century has had to contend with a predecessor so overtly questioning their leadership.'[27]

The second is the extent to which, in the face of these conflicting pressures, Major pursued his stance with a certain rugged determination. Though sensitive to criticism, he proved willing to take on advocates of constitutional reform and face up to rebels within his own parliamentary party – and indeed within his own Cabinet – and not let party resistance dictate his actions. The immediate focus of the media was the internal party battles rather than the fact that he succeeded in enacting the measures to which he was committed. Even those closest to him did not always share his belief in what his policies might achieve. The Citizen's Charter, they recognised, was not exactly setting the nation alight, especially given the other problems they were facing, but Major 'believes in it, passionately, believes it will change the quality of life of ordinary people'.[28]

This willingness to stick to his position, despite a precarious – and at times non-existent – parliamentary majority, and attacks by his predecessor and her allies, stands now in contrast with the stance taken by his successor as Conservative Prime Minister, David Cameron. Cameron had negotiated a coalition in 2010 in order to produce a parliamentary majority, but had to walk a tightrope between the stance of his coalition partners and his own backbenchers. He conceded a referendum on introducing a new electoral system as part of the deal to create a coalition. After initially resisting demands of Eurosceptic backbenchers, he eventually succumbed and promised a referendum on the UK's membership of the European Union.[29] He sought to renegotiate Britain's terms of membership, in so doing adopting a more self-confident approach than that adopted by Major, but one that failed to deliver what he expected of it. Whereas Major by his actions had managed to keep the UK in the EC, at the risk of splitting his own party, Cameron let party considerations dictate an approach that was to result in a referendum vote in 2016 to leave the EU.

The third is what has happened in terms of what Major sought to deliver. He arguably proved more effective than his predecessor in tackling constitutional problems, problems that his predecessor had, if anything, exacerbated. Robin Harris observed that 'John Major was in some respects a better politician than his predecessor'.[30] He was able to persuade and cajole in a way that was alien to Margaret Thatcher, yet at the same time followed her in knowing what goals he sought to achieve.

On European integration, Major had fought a crippling battle, but he achieved what he had set out to achieve. As Tim Bale has observed, it is hard to see how Thatcher, 'unless she had somehow become once again the person she was when she consented to the SEA in 1985', could have achieved the same deal.[31] Also significant was the fact that 'despite a chorus of demands from usually Tory-supporting newspapers and from Lady Thatcher, the government easily defeated calls for a referendum on the treaty'.[32]

On Northern Ireland, he had set in train a process that was to lead to the Good Friday Agreement the year after he left office.

> 'Major's concentration on Northern Ireland had one unintended legacy for Blair. By making it such a very high personal priority, in contrast to his predecessors as Prime Minister since 1969 when "the troubles" had re-erupted, it meant that no British Prime Minister for the foreseeable future could afford not to make it one of their principal priorities too.'[33]

Furthermore, his handling of the crisis in the monarchy may be seen, with hindsight, to have been more adept than it was apparent at the time, enabling it to come through, indeed survive, a critical period. His Citizen's Charter has also been subject to re-evaluation. The House of Commons Public Services Committee noted in 1997 that the initiative had made 'a valuable contribution to improving public services.'[34] As the House of Commons Public Administration Committee argued in 2008:

> Despite the criticisms, it is still the case that the Charter programme was one of the clearest articulations of the need to focus on the experience of public service users, and for services to be responsive to the people using them. It also popularised the ideas that performance should be measured and measurements made public, and that information about services should be readily available in plain language.[35]

Fourth, experience has tended to bear out his warnings as to what would happen. He failed to resist the oncoming tide of constitutional changes, but his warnings as to their effect have some resonance. This has proved to be especially the case in respect of devolution. As he made clear, it was for the people to decide whether to remain in the Union, but he warned of 'the unknown, uncharted waters of tempestuous change'. He raised not only the West Lothian question, but also what is now recognised as the English question. He also identified the problems of asymmetrical devolution.

> At the moment, the government spends more in Scotland and Wales than it raises in tax. Would that continue? And if so, who would fund it? Would we still have Secretaries of State for Scotland and Wales in the Cabinet? If yes, what if one party has a majority in Scotland or Wales, and another in Westminster? Which one would choose? Why give the Scottish Parliament the power to raise taxes and make Scots pay more tax than any other part of Britain? Why should Scotland have a tax-raising Parliament, but Wales only an assembly?[36]

He also raised a constitutional question over a referendum. 'Who would vote in this referendum? The Scots of course. But who else? Because the result would affect the whole of the United Kingdom.'

The points here are as much as anything important points of process as of principle – he had already made the principled case for the Union – but they anticipate some of the issues that were to create tensions once the path of devolution was embarked upon by the Blair administration. Secretary of State for Wales, Ron Davies, famously described devolution as a process and not an event. Major was in many respects anticipating the issues that were to cause, and continue to cause, tensions within the Union and a continuing process of seeking some balance within the system. Whereas Major thought about the constitution as such, his successors have thought about constitutional changes as discrete reforms. There has been a failure to think holistically about the constitution of the United Kingdom and the relationship between different changes to the constitutional fabric of the nation, a feature as much of coalition and Conservative governments as of the Labour government of Tony Blair.[37]

Finally, he is the last Conservative leader to think about the constitution *as a constitution*. His successors addressed constitutional issues, but not on any consistent and reflective basis. William Hague gave a major speech on the constitution early in 1998, but the constitution as such was not a theme of his leadership. Iain Duncan Smith and Michael Howard were essentially silent on the issue. David Cameron as Prime Minister had to deal with a range of constitutional dilemmas, but his stance was essentially responsive and pragmatic. He conceded compromises in order to achieve a coalition government and fought (successfully) to preserve the Union in an independence referendum and (unsuccessfully) to maintain the UK's membership of the European Union. He was instinctively a unionist, but he lacked a clear directing belief-system, motivated instead by a sense of public service.[38] He failed to articulate a view of the constitution he thought appropriate to the United Kingdom. There was thus no clear guiding ideological framework.

Major was not just the last Conservative leader to think seriously about the constitution, he was one of the very few Prime Ministers of recent times to do so. Gordon Brown is the only other premier in recent history to think about the nation's constitutional arrangements as such, pursuing the Governance of Britain programme.[39] It was more structured than Major's approach, but less coached in an overarching view of the nature of the British constitution. Tony Blair presided over major constitutional change, but had no great commitment to it, nor any clear embrace of a coherent approach to constitutional change.[40]

There is also a constitutional postscript to Major's premiership. He was the last Prime Minister to utilise the power to make a vote one of confidence and threaten an election in the event of defeat. The Fixed-Term Parliaments Act 2011 removed the capacity of the Prime Minister to ask the monarch to dissolve Parliament and call a general election.[41] The Prime Minister no longer has what may be seen as the nuclear option for maximising party support in the division lobbies. It is unlikely that Major would have conceded the case for such a measure.

ENDNOTES

1 J. B. Jones, 'Devout Defender of the Union: John Major and Devolution', in P. Dorey (ed.) *The Major Premiership: Politics and Policies under John Major* (Basingstoke: Palgrave Macmillan, 1996), p. 145
2 P. Norton, *The Constitution in Flux* (Oxford: Martin Robertson, 1982), pp. 379–87
3 The Conservative Manifesto 1997, *You Can Only be Sure with the Conservatives* (London: The Conservative Party, 1997), p. 49
4 J. Major, *Our Nation's Future* (London: Conservative Political Centre, 1997), p. 47
5 Ibid. p. 50
6 The Conservative Manifesto 1997, p. 49
7 Major, *Our Nation's Future*, p. 52
8 J. Major, *Trust the People* (London: Conservative Political Centre, 1992), p. 43
9 Major, *Our Nation's Future*, p. 55
10 J. Major, *The Autobiography* (London: HarperCollins. 1999), p. 264
11 Major, *Our Nation's Future*, p. 55
12 Norton, *The Constitution in Flux*, pp. 261–94
13 M. Stuart, *John Smith* (London: Politico's, 2005), p. 293

14 P. Norton, 'In Defence of the Constitution: A Riposte to the Radicals', in P. Norton (ed.) *New Directions in British Politics* (Aldershot: Edward Elgar, 1991), pp. 14–9
15 J. Patten, *Things to Come* (London: Sinclair-Stevenson, 1995), p. 55
16 Major, *Our Nation's Future*, p. 55
17 I. Lang, *Blue Remembered Years* (London: Politico's, 2002), p. 176
18 Major, *Trust the People*, p. 42
19 Major, *The Autobiography*, p. 436
20 D. Hurd, *Memoirs* (London: Little, Brown, 2003), p. 421
21 N. Lamont, *In Office* (London: Little, Brown, 1999), p. 134
22 Jones, 'Devout Defender of the Union: John Major and Devolution', p. 126
23 Major, *The Autobiography*, p. 489
24 A. Seldon, *Major: A Political Life* (London: Weidenfeld & Nicolson, 1997), p. 611
25 P. Hennessy, *The Prime Minister* (London: Allen Lane/The Penguin Press, 2000), p. 448
26 A. Seldon and M. Davies, 'John Major', in C. Clarke, T. S. James, T. Bale and P. Diamond (eds) *British Conservative Leaders* (London: Biteback, 2015), p. 343
27 Ibid. p. 337
28 G. Brandreth, *Breaking the Code* (London: Weidenfeld & Nicolson, 1999), p. 120
29 P. Norton, 'The Coalition and the Conservatives', in A. Seldon and M. Finn (eds) *The Coalition Effect 2010–1015* (Cambridge: Cambridge University Press, 2015), pp. 482–3
30 R. Harris, *The Conservatives: A History* (London: Bantam Press, 2011), p. 496
31 T. Bale, *The Conservatives since 1945: The Drivers of Party Change* (Oxford: Oxford University Press, 2012), p. 279
32 P. Riddell, 'Major and Parliament', in D. Kavanagh and A. Seldon (eds) *The Major Effect* (London: Macmillan, 1994), p. 53
33 A. Seldon, *Blair* (London: The Free Press, 2004), p. 349
34 House of Commons Public Services Committee, *The Citizen's Charter*, Third Report, Session 1996–7, HC 78-I, para. 92
35 House of Commons Public Administration Committee, *From Citizen's Charter to Public Service Guarantees: Entitlements to Public Services*, Twelfth Report, Session 2007–8, HC 411, para. 14
36 Major, *Our Nation's Future*, p. 54
37 See for example the comments of the House of Lords Constitution Committee, *The Union and devolution*, 10th Report, Session 2015–16, HL Paper 149
38 Norton, 'The Coalition and the Conservatives', pp. 474–6
39 See especially Ministry of Justice, *The Governance of Britain*, CM 7170, 2007
40 P. Norton, 'Tony Blair and the Office of Prime Minister', in M. Beech and S. Lee (eds), *Ten Years of New Labour* (Basingstoke, Palgrave Macmillan, 2008), pp. 89–102; P. Norton, 'From Elective Dictatorship to Isolated Presidentialism', *Political Quarterly*, forthcoming 2017
41 P. Norton, 'The Fixed-term Parliaments Act and Votes of Confidence', *Parliamentary Affairs*, Vol. 69 (1), 2016, pp. 3–18

6

'72 HOURS TO SAVE THE UNION': JOHN MAJOR AND DEVOLUTION

Catherine McGlynn and Shaun McDaid

INTRODUCTION

IN THE RUN-UP TO the 2014 referendum on Scottish independence John Major entered the debate on Scotland's future, using his public profile to bolster the credibility of promises made by Prime Minister David Cameron that a no vote would be rewarded with greater powers for Scotland. Despite this commitment to the devolution of more responsibilities, including fiscal ones, Major used an interview on Radio 4's *Today* programme to reaffirm his long-standing position on devolution for Scotland and his concerns about the referendum:

> I opposed devolution not because I thought the Scots couldn't govern themselves, of course they could. They've been a very talented nation and they have run a large part of the British Empire and been remarkably influential in building up the United Kingdom. My opposition to devolution was that it

> would be a stepping stone to separation. When I look at events that are taking place at the present moment I can see precisely why I thought that.[1]

This chapter assesses the substance of Major's opposition to devolution and how it relates to his understanding of conservatism. We will begin by comparing and contrasting Major's approach to devolution within Great Britain to that of his predecessor, Margaret Thatcher (Northern Ireland is covered in depth elsewhere in this volume). We will then assess the roots of Major's failure to create a constituency big enough to reject devolution when the Welsh and Scottish electorates were given the opportunity by Labour to vote on the issue in the referendums of 1997. His opposition to devolution was denounced by critics such as the former Deputy Prime Minister Lord Prescott as irrational, claiming Major risked a visit from the 'men with the white coats'.[2] Nevertheless, we argue that Major's concerns about the potential separatist sentiments which devolution, in Scotland if not in Wales, could foster were undoubtedly prescient even if, paradoxically, the way in which the concerns were framed seemed to further isolate the Conservative Party from the Scottish and Welsh electorates to which it tried to appeal.

Finally, we will look at Major's understanding of Britishness and Englishness and we will argue that although his anglicised view of the UK's history was an impediment to his own cause, it gave him a notable amount of insight into the rise of English nationalism. As with so much else in Major's premiership, all his manoeuvres and arguments must be seen in the context of difficulties within the Conservative Party caused by the issue of Europe and European Integration.

THATCHER AND MAJOR

The election of the Conservatives in 1979 put a block on aspirations within Wales and Scotland for either devolution of power or full independence. The referendums held earlier that year had seen Wales reject a proposed assembly decisively, while Scotland's 'yes' vote was nullified because it didn't meet the threshold of representing 40 per cent of the electorate's wishes.[3] Thatcher was not triumphalist about these defeats and she made vague promises when she took the reins of power that devolution was not dead, despite being a 'vehement Unionist'.[4] However, it became clear that devolution was covered in her mind by her overall objective of rolling back the state and most definitely not by introducing another layer of government. Major followed this Thatcherite interpretation of devolution of power, laying great stress on the increased accountability that he believed the Conservatives had created for citizens as consumers of services and that he was augmenting through his Citizen's Charter.

Major also followed Thatcher in the belief that the Conservative economic programme was ultimately of benefit to all citizens of the United Kingdom. He did acknowledge the trauma of what he saw as short-term consequences such as job losses, but claimed this was a price worth paying. With regards to Scotland, for example, he argued, 'Margaret Thatcher's economic medicine served Scotland well, and I carried it forward in the 1990s ... It was a sea change from the 1970s when Scotland's future seemed one of continual decline, palliated only by a drip-feed of subsidy.' That the Scottish patient seemed not to accept the diagnosis given, Major attributed to the increased self-confidence endowed by economic renewal.[5]

Finally, he shared with Thatcher a firm belief that Wales was of limited cause for concern when it came to any threats to the integrity of the state. Scotland needed management and mollifying, with emotional appeals to the British heritage created by figures such as Adam Smith, but also practical concerns about working with the Scottish Office and getting the right Secretary of State for Scotland on board as far as Scottish interests were concerned. In Wales, there was no sense that the Secretary of State even needed to be Welsh and the post was a way of absorbing more awkward elements of the party into the realm of Cabinet confidentiality, although Thatcher (perhaps unintentionally) managed this to the advantage of Wales more than Major did, as we shall see.

However, there were also key differences between the two leaders. Firstly, and most obviously, Major was simply not as unpopular and divisive a figure as Margaret Thatcher and particularly with the Scottish electorate, his arrival was seen as potentially positive.[6] Thatcher's imposition of the hated poll tax on Scotland a year early, as an experiment, had been particularly infuriating. And although Major's abandonment of the tax followed English reactions, he now had a chance to be listened to that she had forfeited. And despite the fact that he championed a unitary state, he did so with a more conservative understanding than could be allowed by Thatcher's innate radicalism. His presentation of the Conservative Party's Unionism as an essential part of its obligations to act as custodian of the organic, uncodified constitution could be presented as genuinely selfless, given the lack of Scottish and Welsh seats accruing to the party. And while this commitment to the unitary state could be fairly said to look like (and indeed be) intransigence, his focus on the constitutional delicacy of the United Kingdom and the vandalism that could be wrought by devolution had a coherence that his handling of the nationalist consciousness behind the drive towards changes in government for Scotland and Wales lacked. Major certainly believed that his commitment to the Union had been a feature in preventing annihilation in Scotland in 1992 (the party, in fact, gained another MP) and so, understandably believed that there was a still a Unionist case to be made throughout his time in office.

WALES

Wales received much less attention than Scotland when it came to the possibility of devolved government in the UK. Indeed, the region was described acerbically as the 'Cinderella of the constitutional reform debate'.[7] Major was confident that the outright 'no' of 1979 still represented a settled response, and while Plaid Cymru had picked up another seat at the 1992 election, they remained penned into their Welsh-speaking geographical base – something that actually made their votes count in terms of seats in the way that higher but more diffuse support for the Conservatives couldn't replicate. Welsh governance did receive some attention from Major's administrations, however. The Welsh Grand Committee was reformed, giving Welsh MPs, as the Tories put it, the chance to 'call ministers to account and debate legislation which affects those countries – something that would be impossible with separate Assemblies'.[8] Similarly, the Welsh Language Act of 1993 was a way of granting Wales a measure of cultural autonomy and thus assuaging demands around the issue that its nationalist party was most closely associated with, and this was enough action in this sphere as far as the Major government was concerned.

While Scotland needed to be managed and monitored, Major was more sanguine about Wales. In Wales, as in Scotland, disaffection with Conservative rule and policy was seen increasingly through a nationalist lens.[9] The ongoing lack of mandate in Wales for a Conservative government led to an alienation that was intensified by what was seen as an exceptional democratic deficit because of rule by quango.[10] This, Bradbury has argued, can be seen as evidence that the Conservative government demonstrated a 'blatant reluctance' to accept the legitimacy of locally elected representatives within Wales.[11] This, coupled with Welsh resentment that levels of public spending in Wales were at times most vociferously debated by right-wing, English MPs, ensured that it was Labour, the proponent of devolution, which stood to gain most from Major's principled opposition to what he regarded as risky constitutional meddling.

Major's refusal to listen to these concerns while he was so publicly 'taking stock' of Scotland's position (as discussed below) was problematic, but probably his worst move was in his choice of John Redwood for Welsh Secretary who Major later observed, did 'not take to the Welsh people, or they to him'.[12] Following Thatcher's view of the Welsh Secretary as a way of managing a faction could have been an example of clever leadership. However, Thatcher's choice of 'wets' like Peter Walker for the post meant that Wales had had a One Nation shield against the full onslaught of her economic policies. Putting Redwood in the post gave him a chance to deliver Thatcherism red in tooth and claw to somewhere that had rejected such policies in four elections, and he did so, hiving off even more functions from locally elected representatives to quangos as he went.[13] By the time he resigned to challenge John Major in a leadership contest in 1995, Redwood had arguably acted as the greatest recruitment officer to the nationalist cause. As Vernon Bogdanor observed after the 1997 referendum, the vote in favour of devolution was by the narrowest of margins. But in drawing support from both Welsh-speaking and industrial Wales, it reflected 'a real consciousness of Welshness' that he was right to predict would be strengthened by the resulting assembly.[14]

Following Major's departure, the Welsh Conservatives placed an increasing emphasis on British identity. The introduction to the 1999 Assembly election manifesto, penned by the colourful Rod Richards (who resigned his post as a junior minister in Major's government following a scandal concerning his personal life),[15] emphasised the party's commitment that devolution would 'not become an instrument that undermines our British identity and leads to the break-up of the United Kingdom'. The manifesto also displayed an increasing sense of Euroscepticism, cautioning against devolution facilitating 'a process that facilitates the creation of political union with Europe'.[16] While it could be argued this was largely due to the personal political preferences of Richards, who has since defected to the United Kingdom Independence Party (UKIP), Europe was an important aspect of Major's own attempts to recast and reshape British identity, in the context of political changes both within and beyond the UK.

SCOTLAND

The issue of Scottish nationalist aspirations was something that Major had greater awareness of and respect for. His foreword to the Scottish Office's White Paper on procedural reform offered the assurance of his understanding that 'no nation could be held irrevocably in a union against its will'[17] and so courting Scottish favour was important. This did not involve joining the Scottish Constitutional Convention set up in 1989 to agree a vision of Scottish self-government among politicians and civil society groups.[18] Instead, after convincing himself that the 1992 election result had affirmed his hope there was space to make a case for alternatives to devolution, Major worked on a number of strategies. Firstly, the White Paper was drawn up as a tangible example of a promised taking stock of Scotland's needs and position within the UK. Secondly, he sought to find ways to convince a Scottish audience of the worth of the Thatcher revolution. Thirdly, he sought to harry the Labour Party over devolution and expose the paucity of planning and commitment to Scotland's cause he felt he discerned, particularly once Tony Blair had taken over from the more straightforwardly enthusiastic John Smith.

Strategy one, the investigation of how to deliver a greater sense of Scottish participation and partnership, did not make the impact Major had hoped for. The White Paper didn't really offer much beyond minor procedural changes to parliamentary workings and the role of the Scottish Office, and ideas such as holding the Scottish grand committee in a range of different venues was hardly going to measure up to plans for day-to-day responsibility over Scotland's affairs. And that it was being offered in conjunction with a strategy of selling Thatcherism as the painful medical treatment that was now going to deliver its benefits. The flood of sentiment that Thatcher, both as a person and as the personification of a policy programme, had unleashed, had convinced huge swathes of the Scottish electorate that the Tories were an innately anti-Scottish party,[19] and telling them that this was all for their benefit was both unconvincing and condescending. The figure who Major settled on as the conduit for this message was Michael Forsyth, his second Secretary of State for Scotland, whom he believed to have a 'sharp-toothed feel for the saleable parts of his Thatcherite inheritance, particularly those saleable in Scotland'.[20] But while Forsyth had an eye for symbolic acts, such as returning the Stone of Destiny, without which legend held that Scottish kings could not be legitimately crowned, the simple matter was that by the 1990s there was not much about Thatcherism that could be sold to Scotland. It could be pointed out that other parts of the UK had fared as badly, if not worse, or that many constituencies in the north of England had also rejected the Conservatives four times in a row, 'but that is not the point. The distinguishing feature here is national consciousness.'[21] And that had become allied to the idea of the Conservatives as a hostile force.

The third strategy of exposing the holes in Labour's plans for devolution carried the most promise. Discussions around any future Scottish Parliament had done nothing to resolve constitutional issues around Scottish MPs having a say in English affairs without English representatives being able to reciprocate (popularly known as the West Lothian question). And Labour's initial unthinking support for the idea of a parliament with tax-raising powers was summed up by the Conservatives as a 'tartan tax' on the Scottish population. Focusing on tax-raising powers also allowed the Conservatives to challenge Labour's key aim, that of shedding the tax-and-spend image that had contributed so much to its failure to beat the Conservatives in 1992. During the election campaign of 1997, Major's confidence in his unionist position (exemplified by a whistle-stop tour of the four constituent parts of the United Kingdom under the banner of '72 hours to save the Union') contrasted with the muddle Blair got himself into with an interview in *The Scotsman* that saw him liken the proposed parliament to a parish council and carried the rather smug assertion that 'sovereignty rests with me as an English MP and that's the way it will stay'.[22] However, as Major ruefully noted in his autobiography, poking holes in Labour's proposals forced them to sharpen up and hit on the plan of a referendum for both devolution and tax-raising powers which distanced them effectively from having to justify a policy that wasn't of the heart. So this strategy, too, did not achieve its intended aim.

The electoral wipe-out in Scotland in 1997 was blamed by Major on the hostility of other parties and the media who had joined the 'devolution bandwagon'[23] as well as wider problems for the Conservatives such as the loss of economic credibility after Black Wednesday. This is in many ways a fair assessment, but to acknowledge the wider picture of misfortune only works if the 1992 result in Scotland is also accepted as in large part due to the failures of Labour rather than the brilliance of a pro-union message. It is also clear that it was Major himself who closed off any potential space that he had to reformulate a vision of Scotland's place in the UK that was Conservative without being Thatcherite, and thus he was always on the back foot.

Major's Unionism undoubtedly kept him alive to the separatist undercurrents sparked by Labour's plans for devolved assemblies in both Cardiff and Edinburgh. What, he asked in 1994, should happen 'at some stage in the future if the Scottish National Party were to have a majority in the Scottish parliament and asked to leave the United Kingdom?'[24] And in the party's 1997 general election manifesto, it was argued that 'the development of new assemblies in Scotland and Wales would create strains which could well pull apart the Union'. The desire not to create a new, competing, layer of government in the proposed devolved regions, 'hungry for power', perhaps weighed equally on the mind of Major and many of his party contemporaries.[25]

But the views Major held were sincere, and the evidence from Wales suggests there was no objection to increasing bureaucracy in principle, so long as it did not carry with it a party-political edge, and thus threaten the Conservative Party's electoral position. Furthermore, it did little to counter the perception abroad, particularly in Scotland, that the Tory Party was Anglocentric and out of touch. The desire to leave the constitution unaltered ultimately blinded Major to the need for policies which took greater account of the variegations within both Conservatism and Unionism across the United Kingdom.

The Scottish Conservative Party subsequently attempted to address the failures of Major's (and indeed Thatcher's) approach to Scottish politics in the 1999 Scottish parliamentary elections. Scottish Tory leader, David McLetchie, introducing their manifesto referred explicitly to the 1997 election result as the people of Scotland letting the party know it was 'out of touch', but that the result marked a 'turning point' for the party. What the electorate told them during the course of over 500 'listening meetings' was that the party 'didn't listen; that our decisions and policies had London stamped all over them, with little relevance, or sympathy, for the needs of the Scottish people'.[26]

What Major arguably did recognise more than most, however, was the extent to which questions about the future of Scottish governance, and Scotland's future role within the United Kingdom, were inextricably linked to wider issues within identity politics. Although himself accused of displaying the 'unacceptable face of English nationalism' by Sir Menzies Campbell, if anything, Major recognised the potential difficulties which posing the 'English question', much less leaving it unanswered, could hold for the UK's future – both at home and abroad.[27]

EUROPE, BRITAIN AND ENGLAND

The final element of discussion here for Major's attempt to recast Unionism is Britishness, in the context of both Europe and of Englishness. Major has been accused of inconsistency for insisting on the principle of subsidiarity during the Maastricht negotiations while dismissing the validity of any sub-state devolution of power.[28] He has also been taken to task for presenting an ideal of Britishness to be defended from the blight of European integration that was distinctly English at heart as 'even though Britain is mentioned, the thinking is unmistakably the pervasive notion of England as an ancient, continuous nation'.[29] Evidence for this can be found in his much-quoted speech to the Conservative Group for Europe in 1993.[30]

On the issue of subsidiarity, it is clear that Major had thought about the connection between sub- and supra-national levels of government and this was not necessarily an inconsistent position. He saw how Plaid Cymru and the SNP were keen to make use of the idea of a Europe of the Regions a means of circumventing the UK as a self-contained member state of the coming EU. He was also willing to try and find pragmatic ways of accommodating this, for example by agreeing to more Welsh and Scottish representatives on the Maastricht Treaty's Committee of the Regions that originally envisaged local and regional authorities having a greater say at the heart of European governance. More problematic in fact was the condescending attitude that once again Scotland was being saved from its propensity to damage its own health, this time by exclusion from the Social Chapter, one of his key opt-outs. He claimed that foreign investors were coming to Scotland because, 'they are attracted here by the enterprise culture built by the Tories, the corporate tax structures, designed by the Tories, and our lack of the Social Chapter insisted on by the Tories.'[31]

Major's conception of Britishness was peppered with contradictory assumptions and often Anglocentric in focus. In a parliamentary debate on constitutional reform (or lack thereof) he made the claim both that the UK was a 'proud nation-state' and that it was comprised of 'four nations', namely England, Scotland, Wales and Northern Ireland.[32] In this, though, he was not alone, and the way in which Europe threw the UK into relief as a cohesive nation-state, the archetypal player on the world stage in conservative thinking, reflects the way Britishness was, in Linda Colley's words, forged in large part through its world role, most notably as an imperial force that was in conflict with the French.[33] Pleas to connections between the component parts through loyalty to overarching ties such as the monarchy and the army may seem archaic. But political attempts, particularly in the Gordon Brown era, to reformulate Britishness failed spectacularly to supersede this narrative.

Most interesting about Major's hostility towards devolution is his conscious acknowledgement of Englishness. The diminished or even dismantled UK he saw resulting from devolution would, he argued, pit Scotland 'against an England in thrall to nationalism'.[34] Even if Scotland was to stay within the UK, what he saw as an overly advantageous funding structure for Scots would be exposed and 'stir up latent English nationalist resentment, leading to a backlash.'[35] Though the idea of a tolerant England paying Scotland's bills is open to challenge in a number of ways, Major's predictions about the increasing salience of Englishness, especially in relation to anti-Scottish sentiment (and arguably vice-versa), have not turned out to be empty.[36]

CONCLUSION

The Scottish and Welsh questions, and devolution in particular, proved, in their own ways, just as difficult for John Major to navigate as his predecessor, Margaret Thatcher. This was unexpected to some extent, since Major did not attract the levels of personal animus from the Scottish and Welsh electorates that Thatcher did. Nevertheless, in failing to execute more skilful political management of Conservative policy in both regions, Major found himself attracting the ire of voters in both regions. In the case of Wales, this manifested as an inability to perceive that the ideological preferences of his choice of Welsh ministers were out-of-step with the preferences of the Welsh electorate, who had rejected the economics of the New Right in successive elections, and did little to engender the common sense of Britishness across the UK which Major himself was so keen to promote. This tendency to see British identity in more cohesive terms than was the reality was evident in Major's approach to Scotland, also. Here, Major's ministers took a more conciliatory approach than the likes of John Redwood did in Wales, although Major's inability to see that the appeal of Thatcherite policies in Scotland was limited, to say the least, led him to misjudge the Scottish mood regarding devolution. It is equally likely that he misjudged the appeal of the Unionist message during the general election of 1992, which with the gain of a single seat was hardly a Lazarus-like revival and instead represented only a temporary reprieve from total defeat.

It is arguable that the case of England is where Major's insights on devolution proved most prescient. Since 1997, the English question has indeed risen to the fore of the political agenda. Although unfairly accused of English nationalism himself (it would be more accurate to say his vision of Unionism was at times Anglocentric), he was certainly conscious that devolution could, if not carefully managed, lead to competition and resentment between the constituent parts of the UK, particularly England and Scotland, especially when it came to the allocation of public money.

It is unarguable that the political character of the UK is even less homogenous since the onset of devolution than it had been previously, although it is on the issue of Europe – which so plagued John Major during his premiership – that these divisions have been most obviously manifest. The Scottish and Welsh electorates differ significantly on the question of Europe; the former voting to remain in the EU, and the latter opting to leave, in line with their English counterparts.

The issue of Europe has divided the Conservative Party as much as it has the nations of the United Kingdom. Context aside, perhaps the main difference is in the subtle shifts in the political nomenclature: the hard Eurosceptic 'bastards' of the Major era have been replaced by 'new bastards', who seek the closest possible post-Brexit ties with the EU.[37] Indeed, what form the UK's future relationship with the EU takes could have a significant impact on Scottish (although probably not Welsh) separatist sentiments in the future. Thus the challenge faced by Major in trying to define a British Unionism which can accommodate the diversity of opinion within an increasingly divided national polity remains as elusive today as it was during his premiership.

ENDNOTES

1 Interview with John Major on *Today* BBC Radio 4, 18 June 2014

2 *The Independent*, 31 December 1994. Prescott claimed that Major's emotive reaction was due to his succumbing to pressure from Tory grandees such as the 1922 Committee, which plagued his tenure: otherwise known as the 'men with the grey suits'. See also, *The Independent*, 18 June 1995

3 R. Hazell, *The English Question* (Manchester: Manchester University Press, 2000)
4 C. Pilkington, *Devolution in Britain Today* (Manchester: Manchester University Press, 2002) p. 56
5 J. Major, *The Autobiography* (London: Harper Collins, 1999), p. 416
6 D. Denver, J. Mitchell, C. Pattie and H. Bochel, *Scotland Decides: The Devolution Issue and the Scottish Referendum* (London: Frank Cass, 2000)
7 *The Guardian*, 17 February 1997
8 Conservative Party, *1997 Conservative Party General Election Manifesto: You can only be sure with the Conservatives* (London: Conservative and Unionist Party, 1997)
9 J. Tomaney, 'End of the Empire State? New Labour and Devolution in the United Kingdom' *International Journal of Urban and Regional Research* 24:3 (2000), pp. 675–68
10 Pilkington, *Devolution*
11 J. Bradbury, 'The Devolution Debate in Wales during the Major Governments: The politics of a developing union state? *Regional & Federal Studies*, 8:1 (1998), pp. 120–39
12 Major, *The Autobiography*, p. 621
13 For a fuller discussion of the impact of Thatcher and Major's choices of Secretary of State for Wales see J. B. Jones, 'Devout Defender of the Union: John Major and Devolution' in P. Dorey (ed.) *The Major Premiership 1990–1997: Politics and Policies under John Major* (Basingstoke: Palgrave, 1999), pp. 126–45
14 V. Bogdanor, *Devolution in the United Kingdom* (Oxford: Oxford University Press, 1999), p. 200
15 *The Independent*, 2 June 1996
16 Welsh Conservative Party, *Fair Play for All: Your Voice in the Assembly*. (Cardiff: Welsh Conservative Party, 1999)
17 Scottish Office, 'Scotland in the Union: a Partnership for Good' (Edinburgh: HMSO, 1993), pp. 5–6
18 The convention had also been boycotted by the Scottish National Party (SNP) who baulked at the idea of joining a grouping that had attracted Labour and Liberal Democrat representation and was therefore destined to stop well short of independence. They later backed a yes vote in the referendum for a devolved Scottish Parliament on the basis that it represented a genuine stepping stone towards their ultimate goal.
19 For a detailed quantitative analysis of the impact of perceptions of the Conservatives as the anti-Scottish party see A. Brown, D. McCrone, L. Paterson and P. Surridge, *The Scottish Electorate: The 1997 General Election and Beyond* (London and Basingstoke: MacMillan, 1999)
20 Major, *The Autobiography*, p. 426. Malcolm Rifkind and Ian Lang also served in this post during Major's time in office.
21 A. Brown, 'Asymmetrical devolution: the Scottish case' *Political Quarterly*, 69:3 (1998), p. 216
22 Quoted in D. Butler and D. Kavanagh, *The British General Election of 1997* (London & Basingstoke: MacMillan, 1997), p. 109

23 Major, *The Autobiography*, p. 415

24 *The Independent*, 31 December 1994

25 Conservative Party, *1997 Conservative Party General Election Manifesto*

26 Scottish Conservative Party, *Scotland First* (Edinburgh: Scottish Conservative and Unionist Party, 1999)

27 See *Irish Times*, 9 January 1995

28 See T. Heppell, *The Conservative Party Leadership of John Major 1990 to 1997* (Lewiston New York: Edwin Mellen Press, 2006); Jones, *Devout Defender of the Union*

29 J. Mitchell, *Devolution in the United Kingdom* (Manchester: Manchester University Press, 2011), p. 195

30 J. Major, Speech to the Conservative Group on Europe, 22 April 1993

31 J. Major, Speech to the Scottish Conservative and Unionist Association Conference, 12 May 1995

32 Debate on Constitutional Reform (Hansard official record), 20 February 1997

33 L. Colley, *Britons: Forging the Nation 1707–1837* (New Hampshire: Yale University Press, 1992)

34 Major, *The Autobiography*, p. 415

35 Ibid. p. 419

36 For a helpful overview of these developing attitudes, see the Institute for Public Policy Research report of 2012, *The Dog that Finally Barked: England as an Emerging Political Community*, available from http://www.ippr.org/publications/the-dog-that-finally-barked-england-as-an-emerging-political-community.

37 *The Guardian*, 13 December 2016. On Euroscepticism more generally, see P. Taggart and A. Szczerbiak, 'Contemporary Euroscepticism in the Party Systems of the European Union Candidate States of Central and Eastern Europe', *European Journal of Political Research*, 43/1 (2004), pp. 1–27

7

LOCAL GOVERNMENT

Tony Travers

LOCAL GOVERNMENT FINANCE WAS a significant contributor to Margaret Thatcher's downfall and thus to the nature of her succession. Her ill-starred 'community charge' proved massively unpopular and, in the last resort, helped to undermine her efforts to remain Prime Minister when challenged for the Conservative leadership in November 1990. After more than a decade of struggle with town halls, Mrs Thatcher was finally brought low by her efforts to reform local taxation. Councils had their collective revenge.[1]

John Major was the immediate beneficiary of this terrible policy failure. In their magisterial book *The Blunders of Our Governments*, Anthony King and Ivor Crewe see the poll tax as an epic example of how British governments frequently become mired in inescapable policy disaster: 'we might be tempted to call it the blunder to end all blunders'.[2] Thatcher paid a swift price for the failure of her commitment to the reform of council funding. National politicians in Britain remain traumatised by the potential political consequences of reforming local taxation.

BEGINNING IN LAMBETH

Before considering Major's local government inheritance from Thatcher, it is worth examining the former's route into politics. John Major was one of only three post-1945 Prime Ministers to have been councillors before they became MPs and, eventually, Prime Minister. Clement Attlee had been mayor of Stepney (in today's Tower Hamlets), while Theresa May was a member of Merton council from 1986 to 1994. All three ex-local government Prime Ministers had been members of London councils. Also, all three have had a reputation for being solid, pragmatic and for avoiding unnecessary ostentation.

Aged twenty-one, Major stood as a Conservative candidate in Lambeth in the first-ever elections to the contemporary London boroughs in 1964. Having failed to get elected, he stood again in 1968 and won a seat in the Conservative landslide victory in the capital that year. It is instructive to note that at the height of the revolutionary late-1960s, the Tories were more successful at winning local government elections in the capital than at any time since. Lambeth, both the new council and its predecessor of the same name, had been controlled by Labour since the 1930s. Labour councillors in Lambeth were generally traditionalists and often socially conservative. London was in decline at the time and still coping with housing challenges resulting from the destruction of World War Two and an inheritance of dilapidated old houses.

The Tory victory in 1968 brought a breath of fresh air and, more importantly, a move away from the social conservatism of traditional Labour control. Major became chairman of the housing committee and was married at St Matthew's Church in Brixton. Under Major's chairmanship, the council built significant additional council housing and adopted fairer (particularly to ethnic minorities who had suffered significant discrimination hitherto) housing allocation policies.

There was a big shift back to Labour in the 1971 borough elections, and Major lost his seat. On the same day, another soon-to-be-famous politician won a seat. Future leader of the Greater London Council (GLC) and Mayor of London Ken Livingstone observed of Major's defeat: 'poor old John Major didn't deserve to lose the night I won in Lambeth in 1971. That Tory council was the best for thirty years – highly imaginative and I agreed with almost everything it did.' Livingstone's remarks (admittedly made many years later) provide a sharp insight into many observers' views of Major ever since. His three years on Lambeth council had resulted from a random electoral upheaval, but once in office he had proved socially concerned, moderate and efficient.

MRS THATCHER AND THE WAR WITH LOCAL GOVERNMENT

Nineteen years later, another electoral upheaval projected John Major into Downing Street. The struggle over the poll tax did not on its own destroy Mrs Thatcher, but it can certainly lay claim to be the straw that broke the camel's back. In fact, the introduction of the community charge was the culmination of a war between central and local government which had raged ever since Thatcher herself had entered Downing Street in 1979.

Mrs Thatcher had long seen councils as bastions of inefficiency and, more broadly, wished to 'roll back the frontiers of the state'. As all governments discover, forcing local authorities to make cuts is far easier than taking on ministerial budgets in Whitehall. From the start, Thatcher and her Environment Secretary Michael Heseltine had cut council grants, introduced spending targets and, soon enough, capped individual councils' budgets. An avowed market liberaliser, Mrs Thatcher also believed in centralising power within government so as to reform the state by spending cuts, privatisation and internal competition. Local authorities of all parties, like most public and private institutions, were uncomfortable with such radical change. By the early 1980s, conflict between central and local government was part of daily politics in Britain.

Councils were forced to expose services to private competition. Council housing was sold off and not replaced. A punitive grant regime was introduced to force councils to cut their spending. Rates were capped. The GLC and six metropolitan county councils were unceremoniously abolished. At the zenith of the Thatcher government's radicalism towards local authorities it was proposed, following modest internal studies, to abolish domestic rates and replace them with a flat-rate poll tax.

From the Thatcher government's point of view, all of this anti-local government reform was justified not only by 'waste' in local government but also by the emergence of the 'loony left' in a number of urban authorities. Liverpool, Lambeth, Southwark, Islington, Sheffield, the GLC and a number of other Labour-run councils were led by radical 'New Left' councillors, some of whom were members of (or closely associated with) fringe leftist groups such as the Militant Tendency or the Socialist Workers Party. The political debate about such 'entryism' during the 1980s was very similar to that which has occurred concerning the activities of Momentum since Jeremy Corbyn became Labour leader in September 2015.

Labour councillors in places such as Liverpool and Lambeth were explicitly engaged in a struggle with 'Thatcher'. The New Left within local councils and Mrs Thatcher's government fed off each other, providing the fuel for ever-more lurid attacks on each other. In reality, most Labour councils continued to be run by moderates, but the perception of a war of all-against-all evolved. With this remarkable struggle as a background, the community charge emerged as an even more impressive weapon to aim at local government.

The poll tax proved to be a local tax reform which turned into a world-class policy disaster and, as observed above, profoundly damaged Mrs Thatcher. Senior ministers found themselves publicly selling a policy they knew was catastrophic. By loyally sticking to the decision to go ahead with the reform in the teeth of much expert advice and opposition from within the Conservative Party, the government dug itself into a hole which could only be escaped by a change of leadership. This simple lesson should probably be learned by all Prime Ministers who embark on major reforms when the overwhelming majority of moderate expertise is warning of catastrophe.

The November 1990 Conservative leadership race was fought with the future of the poll tax as a major element. Michael Heseltine, who triggered the contest, was committed to a 'fundamental review' of the tax if elected leader. Once Thatcher had failed to win the first round leadership ballot by a wide enough margin, Douglas Hurd and John Major entered the race. Both committed themselves to reviewing poll tax. One of Major's key backers observed, 'we can't let a chink of light come between us and Heseltine on the poll tax'.

This promise was sufficient to neutralise any risk that Michael Heseltine's long-held opposition to the poll tax would be enough to win the leadership for him. Major, once in No. 10, appointed Heseltine as Environment Secretary (as he had been at the start of Thatcher's government) to review the poll tax. In April 1993, the council tax replaced the poll tax as Britain's sole local tax, though not before John Major had been the key beneficiary of his predecessor's doomed efforts to reform local taxation.

THE RETURN OF PEACE

By the time of Major's arrival in Downing Street, Labour had come to realise that its municipal reputation was suffering because of a perception of extremism in town halls. The real problem was not simply that the tabloids had run hundreds of stories about 'loony' policies, but rather that in a number of Labour councils, services were failing badly. From 1990 onwards, Labour at the local level shifted back towards pragmatism and in many cases adopted a more pro-business stance.

Thus the stage was set for an outbreak of post-struggle reconstruction in the relationship between central and local government. John Major's style, together with his background in local politics, ensured that the tone of his government was significantly different from Mrs Thatcher's. Even if the content of many policies (apart from poll tax) did not to alter radically, the tone of debate improved.

Unlike every Prime Minister since Attlee, Major had been responsible for a major council spending programme and knew the realities of local provision. Lambeth council may have become a byword for extremism since he had left it in 1971, but Major remained committed to the area and the needs of its people. A strangely moving 1992 party political broadcast (directed by John Schlesinger) involved him being driven round Brixton and pointing out homes his family had lived in and places he used to visit. It could have been cheesy, but actually felt authentic.[3] It showed a Prime Minister who could speak in ordinary language about ordinary things.

It is a measure of how far central-local relations had deteriorated during the 1980s that the House of Lords set up a select committee to consider the issue. Chaired by Lord Hunt of Tanworth, the committee concluded the relationship was not in good condition. Speaking in a House of Lords debate about the committee's report in 1996 Hunt, who had been Cabinet Secretary in the mid-1970s, relied on mandarin understatement to make his point: 'we were left in no doubt that relations between central and local government, although perhaps better than a few years ago, were unsatisfactory. There is a high degree of unconstructive tension between them.'[4]

'A few years ago' was, of course, the late 1980s and 1990, when the central-local relationship reached its nadir. The Lords report was important for noting that a turning point had been reached. The ministers appointed by John Major, notably Michael Heseltine and David Curry, approached local government very differently from their predecessors. Heseltine had a track record from his previous period at the Department of the Environment. Although not enthusiastic about local tax autonomy (capping was retained) Heseltine believed in greater local autonomy over the management of resources. In particular, he believed in 'challenge funding' whereby councils applied for government grants for specified regeneration-related purposes.

One of the Major government's first local government policy changes was to cut poll tax bills by £140 per person in Norman Lamont's March 1991

Budget. This was an unabashed populist move, but one which suggested a firm commitment to kill off the poll tax. VAT, a far less perceptible tax, was put up from 15 to 17.5 per cent to replace the lost revenue. Average poll tax bills fell from £392 to £252.[5] The newish government had taken the sting out of Mrs Thatcher's poll tax. This needed to be done because it would be impossible to replace it before the inevitable 1992 general election. A within-government review of the tax had been initiated and just after the 1991 Budget; Heseltine announced it would be abolished and replaced by a new property-related levy. Council tax was introduced in England, Wales and Scotland on 1 April 1993: Mrs Thatcher's least helpful legacy was replaced by one which is still in use today. Heseltine also launched a separate review of the structure of local government in non-metropolitan parts of the country.

The decision to consider moving towards single-tier councils was less than popular with Conservatives in rural areas. Labour had traditionally been the party of 'unitary' local government, while the Tories had their power base in non-metropolitan counties and districts. Michael Heseltine, for his part, had long been an advocate of directly elected mayors. He had pushed for such a policy in the late 1980s after he had resigned from Margaret Thatcher's government. To operate as mayor effectively, a single tier of local government (or groups of unitary authorities) appeared to be a pre-requisite.

STRUCTURAL REFORM

A commission was set up under the businessman Sir John Banham, who had previously been chief executive of the Audit Commission. The Local Government Commission for England was given the task of reviewing the structure of designated areas of the country. Avon, Cleveland, Hereford & Worcester and Humberside were all abolished and their constituent districts turned into all-purpose unitary authorities. Later reviews created unitary councils in big cities such as Bournemouth, Brighton & Hove, Bristol, Hull, Leicester, Derby, Milton Keynes, Nottingham, Portsmouth,

Stoke-on-Trent, Southampton, Stockton and Plymouth. Subsequently, under the Blair government, a number of additional district, county and part-county based unitaries were created.

Local government in Wales and Scotland was also reformed. The two-tier system which had been put in place in the early-1970s was replaced by a single tier of unitary councils. Although the Major government could not have known it at the time, in making this change, the stage was set for the Blair government's post-1997 devolution reforms. By removing one tier of local government, the creation of new governments for Scotland and Wales became far simpler to deliver than if there had been a parallel requirement to reorganise local authorities.

The rolling process of local government reorganisation was disruptive and led to a number of court challenges. But it was welcomed in cities which had formerly been county boroughs and which regained their independence. Major, by appointing Michael Heseltine to the role of Environment Secretary, triggered local government structural reforms which were to become the building blocks of future attempts at regional and, more successfully, city regional policies. Heseltine also had particular views about interventionist urban policy which he had the opportunity to deliver for a second time within a decade.

URBAN REGENERATION

The regeneration of declining urban Britain had been attempted by Labour in the late-1970s. The Thatcher government had appointed development corporations and, as far as possible, avoided using local councils in urban regeneration projects. But by the early 1990s, both central and local government had started to change. In July 1991 Heseltine introduced the City Challenge programme which encouraged councils in deprived urban areas to make competitive bids for Whitehall resources. Out of fifteen bids, eleven winners were announced, including a project to regenerate the Hulme area of Manchester.

More were selected subsequently. 'City Challenge encouraged an integrated approach, with a focus on property development, but cutting across a range of topic areas, including economic development, housing, training, environmental improvements, and social programmes such as crime, and equal opportunities.'[6] Partnerships involving the public, private and community sectors were incentivised. Projects were encouraged to leverage in private capital.

Heseltine, as he had in his first period as Environment Secretary, prioritised urban regeneration. But unlike in the early 1980s, local government was now given a role in the process. Many councils, including Labour ones, enthusiastically embraced their new role. London boroughs such as Southwark, Greenwich and Lambeth; and cities, including Liverpool and Manchester, began to embrace the property-led development programmes which have, ever since, been the hallmark of much urban government in England.[7] The mid-1990s saw the development of more formal and stronger links between councils in Greater Manchester. In the aftermath of the abolition of the metropolitan counties and the Greater London Council, new relationships evolved between districts and boroughs in major cities which were to play a major part in the emergence of city-regional governance from 2010 onwards.

Further urban and housing programmes followed. In 1993, the Single Regeneration Budget (SRB) was introduced, bringing together a large number of previous programmes. It continued with the approach of City Challenge, being bid based and attempting to deliver wider benefits to neighbourhoods by bringing together public and private resources.[8]

HOUSING

Housing Action Trusts (HATs) were another feature of the Major government's approach to local government. Council estates constructed since the 1960s had, in many cases, fallen into serious disrepair. Thatcher's Housing Act (1988) allowed the government to appoint HATs to take over council housing within designated areas. HATs were set up in Hull, Waltham

Forest, Tower Hamlets, Birmingham, Liverpool and Brent. The latter five were created during the Major years and took responsibility for targeted programmes to deliver the repair and improvement of housing, improved management and greater diversity of tenure.

During the 1990s, 'housing policy [emphasised] the importance of breaking up the most unpopular estates through selective demolition, transfers to new landlords and mixing tenures.'[9] Generally, such policies would work well, but there was a risk that problems could simply be displaced. The housing policies pursued by the Major government, often initiated by Michael Heseltine, have become the model for those which succeeded them. Lessons about the construction and mixed tenure of social housing learned between the early 1970s and the end of the 1980s came to maturity between 1990 and 1997.

The 1990–97 government continued to offer discounts to council tenants who wished to exercise a 'right to buy' their homes. The policy had been popular since its introduction in 1980 and virtually all Conservatives agreed with it. In 1993, a 'Rent to Mortgage' scheme was unveiled which allowed tenants who were unable to afford the full, discounted, price of their property to pay for a proportion of the property initially, creating 'shared ownership' with the local authority until the full price would eventually be paid.

The government also introduced a Rough Sleepers Initiative to reduce the number of people sleeping on the streets of London. Originally intended to run from 1990 to 1993, the programme was extended to the end of the Major government and beyond. It was extended to other cities with similar problems. Sir George Young, the housing minister responsible for delivery of the policy was, like John Major, a liberal Conservative with a desire to reduce social problems.

EDUCATION

Major sustained Mrs Thatcher's reforms to education. The Education Reform Act 1988 had set out a series of changes which, together, were designed to reduce local authority control over education. The need for reform had been foreshadowed by Labour Prime Minister James Callaghan in a speech at Ruskin College in 1976, where he had outlined the need for reform in education, particularly in relation to the school curriculum. Successive Conservative and Labour governments have, ever since, struggled to produce governance and accountability arrangements which would improve the performance of schools.

The post-1990 government built on the 1988 Act by developing policies which were designed to increase parental choice within a 'quasi market' where schools competed for pupils. Competition, it was argued, would raise academic standards. Local government was seen as an impediment to parental market forces and, thus, to improvement. 'Another recurrent theme [was] the need to raise the standards of education for the mass of ordinary children by overturning the current "producer dominated" system of education. Taking schools out of LEA control was seen as one means of removing education from the influence of "the smug complacency of educationalists".'[10]

Grant Maintained (GM) schools, like City Technology Colleges which had also been introduced by the 1988 legislation, functioned outside local government control. Their governing bodies were, in effect, mini-quangos. GM schools received resources directly from the Department for Education, and, after 1994, from a new 'Funding Agency for Schools' (FAS).[11] Ministers and other supporters of the policy saw it as a chance to 'take education out of the hands of planners and return it to parents where it belongs and a means by which educational standards would be improved and school provision diversified.'[12]

Between 1990 and 1997, provisions enabling local management of schools (which had also been a feature of the great Education Reform Act of 1988) led to a significant shift of control within all remaining 'maintained' local government schools. School governors and head teachers were given their own budgets and, thus, greater autonomy from town halls.

In 1992, a Further and Higher Education Act transferred control of further education colleges from local government in England and Wales to new appointed bodies, the Further Education Funding Council for England and an equivalent body for Wales. Advanced further education, mostly provided by polytechnics, had been nationalised in a similar way in 1988. Thus, by the mid-1990s, virtually all post-school education in England and Wales was the responsibility of central government. The creation of the FAS created a vehicle for the gradual transfer of many local authority schools to a similar form of central oversight.

Major enacted a number of radical transfers of educational responsibility from local to central government. His government picked up the baton from Margaret Thatcher's government and pushed on with the diminution of local authority responsibility for education. Tony Blair's government was to do much the same after 1997. Although GM schools were brought back within local control, academies were created which were significantly free of local government. By 2007, schools' funding was fully ring-fenced and, effectively, outside local control altogether.

CARE IN THE COMMUNITY

Another key reform during the period from 1990 to 1997 was the further implementation of 'Care in the Community' policies. Official inquiries and reports during the 1980s, notably the 1988 Griffiths report, had highlighted the need to transfer as much social care as possible out of institutions such as hospitals and care institutions and into people's own homes.[13] The National Health Service and Community Care Act (1990) gave local authorities a duty to assess the care needs of their residents and to ensure provision was available. Councils were put in the position where they purchased care services from NHS institutions or their own and from non-profit or private providers. The option of providing social care in individuals' or families' own homes was encouraged.

The reform was intended to generate a 'quasi-market' in care provision while reducing the need for institutional service delivery. It built on the

New Public Management reforms which had been initiated by the Thatcher government and which were intended to make public provision more efficient and less dominated by producer interests. As with structural changes to local government and education reforms, the development of community care during the Major years paved the way for much that was to come under subsequent governments.

PERFORMANCE INDICATORS AND THE CITIZEN'S CHARTER

Another significant public management innovation was the decision to introduce the Citizen's Charter and, of particular relevance for local government, performance indicators (PIs). Both policies were designed to improve the accessibility, transparency and quality of public services. The Charter was intended to provide members of the public with rights to service standards, while PIs were expected to allow comparisons between the performance of different councils and of other public service providers.

According to the House of Commons Public Administration Select Committee's analysis of the policy, 'the most prominent aspect of the Citizen's Charter initiative was the creation of the individual service charters. The basic idea of the charters was that they would form a kind of contract between service users and service providers. The charters would inform citizens of their entitlements to public services, and make clear to providers the level and standard of service they in turn were committed to meet. By clarifying these commitments, service providers were encouraged to improve both standards and responsiveness to service users. By 1997, there were forty-two national charters covering the main public services and over 10,000 local charters.'[14]

The government's original White Paper on the Citizen's Charter contained a commitment to make local authorities publish performance indicators. The White Paper also promised that the Audit Commission would publish league tables of councils' individual performance. Proposals were enacted in the Local Government Act (1992).

Regulations stipulated that local authorities would have to publish data on a wide range of performance attributes, including 'process' measures such as the time it took to answer telephones and letters, the way in which complaints were dealt with and the number of complaints made to the Local Government Ombudsman. In relation to housing, councils had to collect and release data about activities such as the numbers of new housing lettings, empty properties, response times for repairs, rent levels, homelessness and performance in the rent collection. There were analogous measures for education, social care and other provision. The police and fire services were required to publish 999 response times, and other indicators about (for the police) crime rates and detection and (for fire brigades) rescues.[15]

The Audit Commission, which had been created in the early 1980s, acted as the collector and publisher of this mass of new indicators. The government believed that councils would change their behaviour if they appeared to be doing badly in league tables, while the public and local press would agitate for improvement. The actual impact on performance proved hard to measure, though (as discussed above in relation to council structures, education and community care) Labour, after 1997, built on the foundations of Major's performance indicators with its own 'Best Value' regime, though the latter was less concerned with 'lowest cost' and rather more about service quality.

LONDON

By the time of Major's arrival in Downing Street, it was three and a half years since the abolition of the Greater London Council (GLC) and six metropolitan counties in the other great cities of England. Following the GLC's abolition, the Inner London Education Authority (ILEA), which provided education in the twelve inner-London boroughs and the City of

London, had been reconstituted as a separate, directly elected, institution. But in 1988, Conservative MPs, led by Norman Tebbitt and Michael Heseltine, voted through an amendment to the Education Reform Bill which had the effect of abolishing the ILEA. Thus in 1990, Major's first year as Prime Minister, the authority followed the GLC to oblivion and its responsibilities were passed to the boroughs and the City.

But the vacuum created by the abolition of the GLC generated new pressures for mechanisms to replace a number of the features of city-wide government which were lost in 1986. Coincidentally London's population, which had declined from 8.6 million in 1939 to 6.6 million in 1986, started to increase once more. Pressure built up not only to create some form of London governance but also to re-invest in the capital's crumbling transport infrastructure.

A number of changes were made. Steve Norris, who was to go on to be Conservative candidate for Mayor of London in 2000 and 2004, was appointed Minister for Transport in London in 1992. This new post gave voice to the capital's need for significant reinvestment in its rail, Underground and bus networks and also for new services to accommodate rising demand. The Jubilee line extension was being constructed at this time. A Cabinet Sub-Committee for London was also set up in 1992, with responsibility to coordinate the activities of central government in the city. The Secretary of State for Agriculture, Fisheries and Food, John Gummer, styled himself as 'Minister for London' and was seen (even by political opponents) as effective in promoting initiatives within London.[16] In parallel with these changes to the machinery of government, in 1992 a number of leading London companies created London First, a new lobby for the capital's business interests.

Then, in 1994, a more radical change was made. 'Government Regional Offices' were appointed for all nine English administrative regions. London witnessed the creation of the Government Office for London (GOL), headed by a senior civil servant. GOL and its director, Robin Young, became a kind of 'prefect of the Thames', operating a new form of London-wide government.

These innovations in London were evidence of the Major government's changing attitude to the Thatcher legacy. The oddity of having no London-wide government was addressed, though without directly returning to an elected city authority. John Major and his ministers were signalling it was moving on from the political struggle of the 1980s, creating a bridge (though they did not know this at the time) to the early Blair years.

CONCLUSION: PRAGMATISM AND CONSOLIDATION

Local government under Major started the process of constitutional recovery from the bitter ideological wars of the 1980s. In the UK, a large unitary state without a written constitution, the interaction of central and local government is a key element in the flexible working of the checks and balances required by any effective democracy.

There is no evidence that John Major and his senior colleagues had a thought-out plan to repair central-local relations, or that they believed in any broad constitutional theory. The position of local government in Britain had been in decline since at least 1945, with a succession of service transfers from localities to the centre and an erosion of councils' fiscal freedom. Countless books have catalogued this trend.[17] Major's government set about the pragmatic task of rebuilding a rational relationship with councils rather than attempting to move towards a defined role for local authorities within the UK constitution. In fairness, Tony Blair's government showed little evidence that they were reconstructing the constitution within a particular theoretical framework when, later in the 1990s, it created devolved governments for Scotland and Wales, while restoring London's citywide government.

This chapter has argued at several points that Major generally delivered pragmatic and less confrontational local government policies than his predecessor. These policies did, however, build on those inherited from Mrs Thatcher. The scrapping of the poll tax was the major, cathartic, break with the past. But policies relating to the structure of local government, education, urban regeneration, housing and London built on those of Mrs Thatcher's eleven years. The inference from all this must be that John Major ran a government which consolidated policy towards local councils rather than initiating a new settlement. Indeed, the decision to transfer part of the burden of local taxation to the Exchequer (cutting the poll tax by increasing VAT) represented a further shift to fiscal centralisation.

Central-local relations improved between 1990 and 1997, though against the backdrop of 1979 to 1990, this was more of a corrective than a bold new path. British local government had limited powers by international standards, but a corner had been turned away from the struggles of the 1980s. Subsequent governments have attempted to devolve power to local government, though twenty years later the scale of change is very limited. John Major's government stopped the pain, but did not cure the illness.

ENDNOTES

1 For a full account of this story see: D. Butler, A. Adonis and T. Travers, *Failure in British Government The Politics of the Poll Tax* (Oxford: Oxford University Press, 1994)

2 A. King and I. Crewe, *The Blunders of Our Governments* (London: Oneworld Publications, 2013), Chapter 4

3 'Conservative Party election broadcast', 18 March, 1992 http://www.screenonline.org.uk/tv/id/1389782/index.html

4 Hansard, HL Deb, 18 November 1996, vol. 575, cols. 1–58

5 Butler, Adonis and Travers, *Failure in British Government The Politics of the Poll Tax*, p.175

6 B. Cullingworth, V. Nadin, T. Hart, S. Davoudi, J. Pendlebury, G. Vigar, D. Webb and T. Townshend, *Town and County Planning in the UK*, 15th Edn (Abingdon, Routledge, 2015), pp. 450–1

7 See S. Fainstein, quoted in T. Travers, *London's Boroughs at 50* (London: Biteback, 2015), pp. 122–3

8 A. Harding and B. Nevin, with K. Gibb, N. Headlam, P. Hepburn, P. Leather and L. McAllister, *Cities and Public Policy: A Review Paper*, Future of Cities Working Paper (Foresight, Government Office for Science, 2015)

9 Estate Regeneration Briefing for Expert Panel, Joseph Rowntree Foundation Briefing (York: Joseph Rowntree Foundation, 2016), p. 7

10 J. Fitz, S. Power and D. Halpin, 'Opting for Grant-maintained Status: A Study of Policy-making in Education' *Policy Studies* 14.1 (Spring 1993), pp. 4–20, p. 4

11 Records of the Funding Agency for Schools (London: The National Archives, 2017) http://discovery.nationalarchives.gov.uk/details/r/C191

12 Ibid, p. 4

13 R. Griffiths, *Community Care: Agenda for Action* (London: HMSO, 1988)

14 *From Citizen's Charter to Public Service Guarantees: Entitlement to Public Services*, Public Administration Committee, Twelfth Report, Session 2007–08, HC411, London: TSO, paragraph 8

15 E. Wood, *Local Authority Performance Indicators*, House of Commons Research Paper 95/39, House of Commons Library, 1995

16 T. Travers and G. Jones, *The New Government of London* (York: Joseph Rowntree Foundation, 1997), pp. 22–5

17 M. Loughlin, M. D. Gelfand and K. Young (eds.) *Half a Century of Municipal Decline* (London: Allen & Unwin, 1985)

8

NORTHERN IRELAND

Cathy Gormley-Heenan

UNDERSTANDING POLITICAL LEADERSHIP IN the context of any conflict or peace process is complicated. It cannot be reduced to a story of heroes and villains, of foxes and lions or other 'great men' of history. Nor can it be reduced to an overriding normative assumption that to lead is to do the 'right' thing. And yet the more complex and often nuanced realities of political leadership in a conflict and peace process still seem to get lost in the overall narrative thanks to such reductionist approaches. For example, much of the analysis of political leadership during the Northern Ireland conflict and peace process focused on the personalities involved and their perceived leadership style. At various points Gerry Adams was applauded as a statesman, or as a man of warmth and vision;[1] John Hume was given the accolade of 'Saint John' and seen by supporters as 'a man suffused with goodness, shining Ghandi-like in the gloom of local politics'.[2] David Trimble was likened to a prophet;[3] Ian Paisley, David Ervine, and Gary McMichael were all described as charismatic, too often to reference each individually. Other comments were rather more pejorative. Adams was described as a terrorist;[4] Hume was still called 'Saint John' but the tone had become more wry; Trimble was denounced as 'a hard-line sectarian bigot';[5] and Paisley was still charismatic but the inference was towards the darker side of charisma. This chapter reflects then on John Major's leadership in relation to Northern Ireland during his time as Prime Minister, but does so in terms of his particular role, capacity and overall effectiveness rather than as consideration of his leadership in more personal terms. In this latter 'personal' aspect he was often considered to be a weak and ineffectual leader insofar as his achievements were almost invisible while his failures were all too obvious.[6] Deconstructing the concept of political leadership into the constituent parts of its role, capacity and effect has been useful in previous research to demonstrate that political leadership in Northern Ireland suffered, at times, from confused roles, undermined capacity and negated effects.[7] Applying a similar framework of analysis for Major's leadership allows us to reappraise the record of John Major in Northern Ireland, twenty years after his departure from office, and reconsider the current political context against this.

SETTING THE CONTEXT

Major was the fifth Prime Minister to inherit the problem of Northern Ireland in the post-1969 period. Heath, Wilson, Callaghan and Thatcher all held office during the conflict before the Irish question passed over to John Major for his consideration. Heath was best known for introducing direct rule for Northern Ireland in 1972 during a particularly volatile period in the conflict. He tried to introduce power sharing in 1973 through the Sunningdale Agreement, though this lasted for only five months and he was criticised heavily by both nationalists and unionists for his interventions. Wilson produced a 'doomsday scenario plan', which would have meant a British withdrawal from Northern Ireland, though this was a plan that did not come into the public domain until 2008 when the files at Kew were declassified.[8] Callaghan, who was preoccupied by economic and social difficulties, did not encourage any new political initiatives in Northern Ireland.

Thatcher's name was always indelibly linked to both her uncompromising stance on the 1981 hunger strike and to the signing of the Anglo-Irish Agreement in 1985, which gave the Irish government a consultative role in the affairs of Northern Ireland. And only weeks before John Major's election as Prime Minister in 1990, Peter Brooke, the Secretary of State for Northern Ireland at the time, had made an important speech stating that Britain had no 'selfish strategic or economic interest' in Northern Ireland and would accept the unification of Ireland by consent. It was against this new backdrop in Northern Ireland's troubled history that John Major was elected Prime Minister in November 1990.

DECLARATIONS, DEADLOCKS AND DOCUMENTS, 1990–97

In the days following his election, Major drew up a short list of priorities for his tenure in office. Of the four key things he wanted to achieve overall, the Irish question was second (the other priorities were inflation, public services and unemployment).[9] He said at the time: 'I always believed Northern Ireland should have been given a higher profile and that it was not acceptable to have any part of the UK engulfed in that sort of bloodshed and treated almost as though it was a matter of course.'[10] Given these remarks in the early days, expectations of his leadership approach to Northern Ireland were high, even within republicanism. In fact, soon after his election the IRA held a three-day Christmas ceasefire – the first time that this had happened in fifteen years – with some suggesting that this was the IRA's greeting to the new PM.

Major was not starting with a blank sheet of paper when it came to the Irish question. He had inherited in those early days the preparations for a three-stranded, multi-party talks process from the Thatcher administration (known as the Brooke/Mayhew Talks). Strand one consisted of internal talks between the Northern Irish parties alone. Strand two focused on talks between the Northern Irish parties and the Irish government, and strand three was made up of talks between the British and Irish governments. The actual agreement signed in 1998 – the Good Friday Agreement – was based on the same three strands used in the talks and was divided up into internal relations, north-south relations, and east-west relations. The talks, which began in 1991, were routinely attended by the British and Irish governments and all of the Northern Ireland political parties with the exception of Sinn Féin. Although these talks collapsed in 1992, they did lead directly to the 1993 Downing Street Declaration.

The 1993 Downing Street Declaration, signed by John Major as British Prime Minister and Albert Reynolds as Irish Taoiseach, was regarded by commentators at the time as the most important intervention which any British government had made since the conflict began and that John Major's involvement in the development and delivery of the declaration was central to its publication. Learning from the lessons of the 1985 Anglo-Irish Agreement, which had been so poorly received by Unionism in Northern Ireland, Major focused on securing an agreement that would gain the consent of mainstream Unionism. The eventual declaration achieved three main things. Firstly, it recommitted the British government to its position of having 'no selfish, strategic, or economic interest in Northern Ireland'. Secondly, it enshrined the principle of consent as the necessary foundation of any future agreements made between the various protagonists, with a clear statement that the British government would 'uphold the democratic wish of a greater number of people in Northern Ireland' and that the people of the island of Ireland had a right to 'exercise the right of self-determination on the basis of consent freely and concurrently given, north and south, to bring about a united Ireland if that is their wish'. And, thirdly, it made explicit the view of the British and Irish governments that those parties with links to paramilitaries would now be able to take their place in any subsequent talks processes, provided that their parties renounced violence beforehand. External reaction to the declaration was wholly positive, but in Northern Ireland the response was more sceptical. The large degree of ambiguity in the text concerned both unionists and nationalists, with Major himself acknowledging afterwards that 'it would not have won an award for plain and unambiguous language'.[11] Unionists were concerned about the continued Irish influence in Northern Irish affairs, and nationalists thought that the declaration had not gone far enough in its stated ambitions.

Although at the time the Downing Street Declaration was marked by many as another new beginning resolving the Northern Ireland problem, Major himself, reflecting back on that period, was rather more reserved. 'Historians like to identify turning points. Northern Ireland's history did not appear to turn on 15 December 1993; and when it did begin to turn, it was not solely as a result of the Downing Street Declaration. The declaration itself had its origins in several sources and in many hands, and was most certainly influenced by the Hume–Adams talks which began during Thatcher's period of office.[12]

Historians may also point to the 1994 IRA ceasefire as another turning point. With the initial news headlines stating that 'It's Over', it was not inconceivable to think, at that time, that John Major might go down in history as the British Prime Minister who had brought peace to Northern Ireland. In retrospect, the ceasefire was only another step in the dry stone wall of its history, another stone critical to creating the stability needed for the overall structure to stay intact. Major wanted assurances that the ceasefire indicated a permanent rejection of violence before he would allow the parties associated to paramilitaries access to any talks process. When these assurances were not as forthcoming as hoped, he brought in the Americans, through the establishment of an international commission, to examine the issue of decommissioning and spent much of 1995 in negotiations around the *Framework for the Future* document, which formalised the demands for the IRA to give up its weapons and begin the process of decommissioning in advance of Sinn Féin's participation in any future political negotiations on the constitutional status and future of Northern Ireland. By 1996, amidst Republican concerns that the peace process would not survive, due to the slow pace of the 'talks about talks' and the various preconditions now set down for engagement, the IRA ceasefire collapsed with the detonation of a large bomb in London's Canary Wharf district and the accompanying IRA statement declaring that 'instead of embracing the peace process, the British government acted in bad faith, with Mr Major and the Unionist leaders squandering this unprecedented opportunity to resolve the conflict'. The peace process was not derailed by this ceasefire lapse in 1996. Discussions continued and Major announced elections to a new Forum for multi-party talks, which would include Sinn Féin, provided they committed to the principles of non-violence.

In 1997, when John Major was defeated by Tony Blair in the general election, peace was as elusive as ever. And John Major did not go down in history as the British Prime Minister who had brought peace to Northern Ireland. Yet only a year later, the 1998 Good Friday Agreement was signed between the British and Irish governments and was endorsed in referendums in the north and south of Ireland some weeks later. Arriving for the closing days of the multi-party talks process at Castle Buildings in Stormont, Blair commented that 'a day like today is not a day for soundbites, really. But I feel the hand of history upon our shoulders. I really do'. Looking back, the Good Friday Agreement was momentous and another historical turning point but it too was not the end, and Blair can no more be credited with having brought peace to Northern Ireland than his predecessors, though Major credits him with promising a continuity of approach and standing by all of the agreements that Major had made, from principles of the Downing Street Declaration through to the Framework Documents.

This raises the question of whether there is scope to reappraise the record of John Major as Prime Minister, and his contribution to the Northern Ireland peace process.

THE ROLE OF MAJOR'S LEADERSHIP

Moving beyond the chronological overview of events and activities during the Major premiership, it is important to reflect on what role Major's personal leadership actually played in addressing the Irish question. It is argued that Major took an active and engaged approach to the Northern Ireland problem, an approach 'which contrasted with previous attempts at keeping Northern Ireland affairs out of mainstream British politics'.[13] That is true. As Major himself acknowledged: 'working for a Northern Ireland settlement was the most difficult, frustrating and from 1993, time-consuming problem of government during my premiership. It was also the most rewarding. I have never regretted my decision to get involved in such a direct way.'[14] What is more interesting is whether that degree of direct engagement was undertaken with a particular preferred outcome in mind. Was his role that of broker? Certainly, in the 1993 Downing Street Declaration, it was made clear that the British government's role was to 'encourage, facilitate and enable' the peace process without expressing any preference for the eventual outcome. At this time, Unionists criticised him for failing to make the case for Northern Ireland's place in the Union with the same degree of conviction that he did for Scotland and Wales. But on the other hand, it was clear that if the eventual outcome was for Northern Ireland to remain as part of the UK rather than secede from the UK into a united Ireland, then the type of government envisaged for Northern Ireland within the UK appeared to be non-negotiable, with Major's speeches and statements ruling out both integration and joint authority but supporting the development of a power-sharing arrangement.

When one considers the idea of the Union which Major put at the heart of his broader constitutional position in respect of the UK, with a strong defence of parliamentary sovereignty and opposition to devolution, there is an obvious contrast in terms of his approach to Northern Ireland and the more flexible approach taken towards the possible constitutional outcomes as a result of any settlement.

In response to criticisms of his differing approach he said:

> What we have suggested for Northern Ireland is radically different from the plan that the Labour Party has for Scotland and Wales. There is no suggestion of an assembly with tax-raising powers. There are no pluralist politics in

> Northern Ireland, as there are in Scotland and Wales. There is no representation by parties likely to form a United Kingdom government. What we are seeking in Northern Ireland is a widely accepted accommodation based on consent. That would provide the surest possible foundation for maintaining Northern Ireland's place firmly within the United Kingdom. That is our wish.[15]

There was always a link between his attitude towards Northern Ireland and the rest of the UK and that manifested itself in the principle of consent. And so, throughout his time in office, Major's role was in searching for a formula which would a) secure the Union according to consent while also b) devising possible arrangements for Nationalists/Republicans to consent to working institutions within the UK and c) securing the agreement or consent of Dublin in 'jointery'. Three sets of relationships and three types of consent.

THE CAPACITY OF MAJOR'S LEADERSHIP

John Major's capacity for securing such consent on the Irish question was said to have diminished somewhat following the 1992 general election. While this election was an electoral victory for the Conservatives under his leadership, it returned a government with a much-reduced parliamentary majority of just twenty-one. In those first days of this government's term of office, a reduced parliamentary majority did not diminish Major's desire to make progress on the Irish question. Even with the breakdown of the multi-party talks process in 1992, and an IRA bombing campaign in England, the communication channels with the IRA were kept open. These secret talks were always denied in the House of Commons, to the extent that Major famously commented on the floor of the chamber that talking to the IRA 'would turn my stomach over. We would not do it.' A story by *The Observer* newspaper shortly afterwards demonstrating that talks had actually taken place through a series of back channels, began to affect Major's credibility. The fact that there had already been secret talks with the IRA and the British government in the 1970s did not diminish the impact of *The Observer*'s revelations on Major's leadership at that time. That said, the revelations did not deter Major in his willingness to shift away the talks from constitutional parties only, to finding ways and means to give cover to the fact that he knew that future negotiations would have to include representatives from parties and spokespersons aligned to those responsible for the majority of the violence and deaths – republican and loyalist paramilitaries.

His capacity to remain as a broker on the Northern Ireland issues was questioned most when his parliamentary majority in the House of Commons diminished further as the term wore on. As early as 1993 Major's majority was so slim in Westminster, owing to a series of by-elections and a rise in the number of Tory rebels, that he relied heavily on the support of the Ulster Unionist Party, with its nine MPs under the leadership of James Molyneaux, to carry through some of the government's crucial votes. Because of this, Major was accused of pandering to Unionism. While Major always denied that any 'deal' had been cut with the Ulster Unionists to secure their votes at the critical moments, and while both Major and Molyneaux said 'nothing was asked for, nothing was given', whatever understanding or agreement had been put in place for the final votes on the Maastricht Bill was regarded as 'a fickle one'.[16] The question is whether such an understanding with the Ulster Unionists impacted significantly on the outcome and effect of Major's leadership.

Of course, these were not the only difficulties that he had to contend with which affected his capacity as a political leader. James Molyneaux had wanted a long period of Sinn Féin 'decontamination' before he believed talks could be sold to the Unionist constituency; and Sinn Féin refused to 'advise' the IRA to disarm in that period after the first IRA ceasefire in 1994 and before its subsequent breakdown in 1996. Such stalling tactics and political difficulties, significantly and repeatedly, slowed the negotiation timetable down (though did not manage to bring it to any grinding halt).

As time moved on towards the inevitable general election, the notion that Major was incapable of now 'delivering' anything grew stronger and nationalists particularly thought that they might fare better under a new Labour government should that potential scenario come to pass. His capacity to deliver ended with the landslide election of the Labour Party in May 1997.

RETHINKING JOHN MAJOR AND NORTHERN IRELAND

During his tenure and in the days afterwards, John Major faced repeated criticisms for his role in Northern Ireland. He was accused of failing to build on the momentum of the 1994 IRA ceasefire, which lead to its collapse some time later; for failing to meet with Sinn Féin once the ceasefire was in place directly, despite their repeated requests for him to do so; conversely, for then failing to be tougher on Republicans after the collapse of the IRA ceasefire in 1996 and in allowing their participation in the multi-party talks process that had been established during that period. Christopher Norton concluded some two years after Major's departure as Prime Minister that: 'John Major's handling of the peace process was not without its fault but whether he can be accused of mishandling the process to the point of collapse is questionable … And if a breakthrough does emerge, based on the principles of consent and a balanced settlement acceptable to both governments and the majority of Unionist and Nationalists, then history may record the Major premiership in a more generous light.'[17]

Such generosity can be detected in places today. There is more agreement that John Major was primarily guided by a belief soon after taking office that that the Republican movement was genuinely committed to breaking with paramilitarism, and that it was important to involve them in the political process. In the spirit of this belief, he took risks that were not recognised until some considerable time later.

Firstly, he knew that officials from his government were engaged in secret talks with Republicans for some time and he was content for this contact to be pursued in the interests of peace. Despite his initial denials that this was, in fact, the case he eventually acknowledged the contact, weathered the subsequent political and media storm, and assuaged Unionist concerns by agreeing to a long-standing request from Unionist MPs for a Northern Ireland Affairs Select Committee at Westminster. Denial, admittance, and the perception of assuagement were all high-risk strategies which could have cost him his premiership.

Secondly, he continually faced down more Unionist-oriented members of his own political party in his pursuit for progress in Northern Ireland. The relationship between Unionism and the Conservative Party was one steeped in a long history of an elective affinity between the two in terms of its historical, ideological and institutional contexts, and many senior political players within the party disagreed with Major's actions and overtures because of their strong sense of affinity for their Unionist colleagues and because, by extension, they did not necessarily believe that overtures made by the Irish government, by nationalism and by republicanism in the North, were genuine but rather that they were designed to expose the British government for its naivety in extracting concession after concession from them. Facing-down party colleagues when he needed to make as many alliances as possible, given his small parliamentary majority and the propensity of party colleagues to rebel against him, cannot have been particularly easy. As Sir John Holmes, who managed the transition from the Conservatives to the Labour Party in 1997, said: 'Major was the one who was … incredibly dedicated to try and find a solution even though there was absolutely nothing in it for him politically; quite the reverse.'

Thirdly, when comparing the key documents, agreements and principles which were developed during the Major era, but which did not bear fruit until the 1998 Good Friday Agreement, the effect of his time in office on the eventual agreement cannot be ignored. The two key documents of that period: the 1993 Downing Street Declaration and the 1995 Framework Documents, illustrate this.

For example, the 1993 Downing Street Declaration was committed to a talks process with the objective of achieving a new form of government for Northern Ireland. That new form of government was put in place through the three strands of the 1998 Good Friday Agreement. Also of note was that the 1993 Downing Street Declaration was committed to the principle of consent by both the British and Irish governments. Article 1 (ii) of the 1998 Good Friday Agreement says that the participants 'recognise that it is for the people of the island of Ireland alone, by agreement between the two parts respectively and without external impediment, to exercise their right of self-determination on the basis of consent, freely and concurrently given, north and south, to bring about a united Ireland, if that is their wish, accepting that this right must be achieved and exercised with and subject to the agreement and consent of a majority of the people of Northern Ireland.'

In addition, in the 1993 Downing Street Declaration, the governments agreed that they may have to revoke its constitutional claims in respect of Northern Ireland as laid out in Articles 2 & 3 of the Irish Constitution and in the Government of Ireland Act 1920. Both the British and Irish governments amended and/or repealed their constitutional and their legislative positions, taking effect when the 1998 Northern Ireland Act became law in November 1998.

Latterly, the 1995 British government document, 'A Framework for Accountable Government in Northern Ireland' (which was part of the broader Framework documents) put forward more proposals for power-sharing devolution, with a ninety-member NI Assembly elected by a form of proportional representation, holding both legislative and executive powers, complimented by a system of assembly committees, a system of detailed checks and balances intended to sustain confidence in the institutions, as well as a series of possible arrangements for the architecture around north-south relations and east-west relations. The 1998 Good Friday Agreement made provision for the establishment of a Northern Ireland Assembly made up of 108 MLAs (Members of the Legislative Assembly) with cross-community consensus or 'parallel consent' required for any key decisions taken by the assembly; the establishment of a Northern Ireland Executive with a mandatory coalition of both the majority and minority communities; and the use of the D'Hondt system of voting to allocate the ministerial seats proportionate to the size of the parties as well as the total number of seats allocated to each party within the Northern Ireland Assembly. The 108 Assembly seats have been further reduced to a ninety-member body for the 2017 Northern Ireland Assembly election, taking the number back down to that originally suggested by the Framework documents.

Of course, the 1998 Good Friday Agreement itself has had to be amended through a series of subsequent Agreements including the 2006 St Andrews Agreement, the 2010 Hillsborough Agreement and the 2015 Stormont House Agreement, but the 1998 Good Friday Agreement is still heralded as *the* agreement which changed Irish history. It is clearer now, however, that much of the architecture of the historic 1998 Agreement on which so much of the political progress in Northern Ireland has been based came from the Major era.

Fourthly, John Major successfully built a different type of relationship with the Irish government and officials than any of his predecessors in office. The strong relationship between Tony Blair, the Irish Taoiseach Bertie Ahern, and their respective officials was based on the significant steps already taken to build a relationship with their counterparts at that time. This had been helped by the fact that both John Major and his counterpart, Taoiseach Albert Reynolds, had both met previously as finance ministers at EU meetings in Brussels, and had developed a relationship before beginning to discuss the Irish question. The out-workings of this building up of relations for British–Irish relations have been profound. In 2017, notwithstanding the concerns over Brexit and its implications, the strength of the relations between the two states has never been stronger. In the first official state visit by a British monarch in almost 100 years, the Queen visited Ireland in 2011 and subsequently hosted President Michael D. Higgins for the first-ever state visit to the UK by an Irish President in 2014.

Of course, some might argue that the time was ripe for political progress on the Irish question; that all sides were jaded and were looking for a way out and that Major himself was not a key variable. But in reflecting on Major's particular style of leadership, Tim Bale, author of *The Conservatives Since 1945*, asks whether this same progress in the peace process would have been made under Thatcher had she remained in power after 1990 given that she had already signed the Anglo-Irish Agreement back in 1985 and engaged with Dublin officials to deliver on this. He convincingly argues that 'it is difficult to imagine [her] going anything like as far as Major both in terms of the compromises required to get the process going (direct, if secret negotiations with the IRA) and the compromises which subsequently resulted.'[18]

CONCLUSION

The political leadership of British Prime Ministers involved in the Northern Ireland conflict and peace process is as complicated as that of the local leadership. It too cannot be reduced to a story of heroes and villains, of foxes and lions or of the 'great men of history'. And yet Major was in some ways portrayed as 'John the Baptist' to Blair the 'Irish Messiah', with the analogy that Major (at least) helped 'prepare the way' for Blair. As the line from John's gospel goes: 'He was not that Light, but was *sent* to bear witness of that Light.' This was an especially potent analogy in 1998, when Blair was still basking in the radiance of the 'New' just as Major was identified with the wilderness or the sleaze of the 'Old'. There was indeed that sense at the time that Blair's light would guide the way of the hand of history. Major's reputation might, rather ironically, now stand higher. Major was not 'John the Baptist' to Blair the 'Irish Messiah' but rather he sustained a set of commitments which might otherwise have dissipated under a different leadership, especially when the IRA resumed bombing after the collapse of their ceasefire in 1996. And of course, the reality is that the Good Friday Agreement was nothing 'new'. It was almost like a register of all of the previous agreements and initiatives with bits of the Sunningdale Agreement, rolling devolution and the Anglo-Irish

Agreement and the British dimension thrown in, and despite the Good Friday Agreement, Blair inherited all of the problems that Major had to deal with too. As the subsequent collapses of the Northern Ireland Assembly, in 2002 and again in 2017, have shown, the Good Friday Agreement was not a defining moment but another brick in the dry stonewall of Anglo-Irish history.

Reflecting afterwards on the experiences of high office Major said:

> I have never believed there would be a single defining moment at which the Irish question would simply be "settled". The problem has too long and bitter a history. Attitudes and fears are deeply ingrained. Sectarianism will take a very long time to erode ... we can be certain there are further difficulties ahead... This is an incremental process ... whatever setback there may be, I do not believe that the clock can now be turned back fully.[19]

In this regard, he was right. Northern Ireland began 2017 with yet another political crisis and the necessary intervention of the British Secretary of State, in calling a snap Assembly election. But the electorate has been used to political crises in Northern Irish politics. None have been single defining moments.

Except perhaps one. The UK's decision to leave the EU in the 2016 referendum. Anticipating this outcome, and putting old party political differences to one side, both Major and former Prime Minister Tony Blair came to Northern Ireland together to urge the Northern Irish electorate to vote 'remain' in the days before the referendum vote. In the coverage of their visit, both were referred to as 'instrumental' in the Northern Ireland peace process, assuring John Major's place alongside Tony Blair in the history books. Both have articulated their vested interest in the continued progress of the peace process. Both argued strongly that any exit from the EU could put at risk that peace. John Major said: 'I believe it would be a dreadful mistake to do anything that has any risk of destabilising the complicated and multi-layered constitutional settlement that underpins stability in Northern Ireland. But that is what a British exit from the EU would do: it would throw all of the pieces of the constitutional jigsaw into the air again, and no one could say where they might land.' The subsequent UK vote for Brexit has once again put the border question back into the heart of Irish politics as Northern Ireland becomes the only jurisdiction in the UK with a land border to an EU member state. It is difficult to imagine how there will not be further difficulties ahead.

ENDNOTES

1 D. Aitkenhead, 'Time and Gerry' *The Guardian*, 4 August 1997
2 J. Collins, 'Lessons in the Ignoble Art of Politics' *Irish News*, 21 August 2003
3 M. Gove, 'Preface', in D. Trimble, *To Raise Up a New Northern Ireland: Articles and Speeches, 1998–2000* (Belfast: The Belfast Press, 2001)
4 J. Stevenson, 'Northern Ireland: Treating Terrorists as Statesmen' *Foreign Policy*, 105 (1996), pp. 125–40
5 See R. Dudley-Edwards, 'Trimble and I', *Sunday Independent*, 12 March 2000
6 M. Foley, *Tony Blair and a Conflict of Leadership: Collision Course* (Manchester, Manchester University Press, 2002), p. 153
7 C. Gormley-Heenan, *Political Leadership and the Northern Ireland Peace Process* (Basingstoke: Palgrave, 2006)
8 '"Impotent" Prime Minister Considered Doomsday Scenario of Quitting Ulster', *The Guardian*, 1 January 2005 https://www.theguardian.com/uk/2005/jan/01/past.nationalarchives6
9 C. Norton, 'Renewed Hope for Peace? John Major and Northern Ireland' in P. Dorey, (ed.) *The Major Premiership: Politics and Policies under John Major, 1990–1997* (Basingstoke: Palgrave, 1999), pp. 108–25. See p.109
10 A. Seldon, *Major: A Political Life* (London: Phoenix. 1997), p. 134
11 J. Major, *The Autobiography* (London: Harper Collins, 1999), p. 455
12 Ibid. p. 454
13 P. Lynch, *The Politics of Nationhood* (Basingstoke: Palgrave, 1999), p. 120
14 Major, *The Autobiography*, pp. 491–2
15 John Major's Commons Statement on the British Constitution, 20 February 1997, htttp://www.johnmajor.co.uk/page828.html
16 Lynch, *The Politics of Nationhood*, p. 123
17 Norton, 'Renewed Hope for Peace?', p. 125
18 T. Bale, *The Conservatives since 1945: The Drivers of Party Change* (Oxford: Oxford University Press, 2012), p. 280
19 Major, *The Autobiography* p. 493

PART THREE

POLICIES

9

ECONOMIC POLICY

Wyn Grant

As the Major premiership has come to be viewed in a more favourable light, little of the focus has been on economic policy. Major has been praised for establishing the fundamentals of the Northern Ireland peace accord and for fighting a successful war in the Gulf that did not have a protracted aftermath. Britain's resurgence as an Olympic nation has been traced back to the funds provided by the National Lottery that he set up in 1994. The one economic achievement that gets mentioned is a negative one, keeping Britain out of the euro through an agreement successfully negotiated at Maastricht.

In fact the UK economy was performing much more successfully when Major left office in 1997 than when he entered it in 1990. However, the Conservatives received no electoral credit for this improved performance. Their reputation for economic competence was fatally damaged by the forced exit from the Exchange Rate Mechanism (ERM) of the European Union (EU) in 1992. The economic policy of the Major government falls into two phases, that when Britain was a member of the ERM and the period after

1992 when policy had a different basis. However, in both periods, the control of inflation was a central economic policy objective.

MAJOR'S OBJECTIVES

That John Major prioritised inflation is not, of itself, surprising. For the Thatcher government, control of inflation had displaced full employment as the central economic policy objective. The inflation mean was lower in the 1980s than the 1970s, although to some extent this was helped by external circumstances. The 'Lawson boom' of the late 1980s saw inflation surge again, peaking at 10.9 per cent in September 1990. During the period of Ken Clarke's Chancellorship from 1993 to 1997 it remained within the target range of 1 to 4 per cent.

For Major the defeat of inflation was something more than a matter of pursuing an established policy objective or practical politics. It was a personal rather than a theoretical concern. He saw inflation as a tax on the poor and a benefit for the rich, with the losers being those who had least. Thus, when he became Chancellor of the Exchequer, 'the principal objective was the destruction of inflation, an insidious demon, always waiting in the wings, that I had every reason to loathe. Inflation is disastrous and morally corrosive, and it destroys lives.'[1]

The mechanism that was used to drive down inflation was the ERM, which Britain had entered shortly before John Major became Prime Minister but when he was Chancellor. It is important to note that there was a broad policy consensus in favour of membership. It was supported by most politicians, by financial services and industry, by the Bank of England and the OECD, the trade unions and the vast majority of economic commentators and analysts. With the benefit of hindsight, a number of criticisms were made of the way in which entry had taken place.

There was criticism of the decision to enter at a central rate of DM 2.95 to the pound, which was subsequently thought to be too high. However, Mrs

Thatcher thought that a high rate reflected a strong currency and would even have favoured a higher rate, as did some in the Bank of England. It was the current rate and was in line with the average of the previous few years. Other member states would have been reluctant to allow Britain to obtain a competitive devaluation at the point of entry. Above all, it imposed the strong anti-inflationary discipline that was thought to be required.

Unfortunately, entry was accompanied by an ill-judged cut in interest rates which Mrs Thatcher insisted on to make entry palatable in the run-up to the Conservative Party conference. The groups most affected by high interest rates, such as mortgage payers and small business owners, formed the heartland of Conservative support. It could be argued that participation in the ERM required a commitment to follow German interest rates, whatever the implications for the UK economy or domestic politics. Between the beginning of 1991 and June 1992, following the consequences of reunification which led to higher inflation, the German discount rate rose by 2.75 per cent, something which the Treasury had not anticipated. Base rates edged down from 14 per cent in the autumn of 1990 to 10 per cent just before the ERM crisis, a cautious reduction in seven stages. Membership of the ERM did make interest rate cuts easier, at least initially, as it reinforced the government's anti-inflationary credibility.

Major's attitude towards interest rates was much more pragmatic than his moralistic stance on inflation. He saw them as a policy instrument to be deployed as circumstances required, albeit that lower rates were to be preferred to higher ones and were seen as a measure of economic policy success. This did not mean that he was insensitive to political considerations, far from it. When he was Chancellor in 1989, there was pressure for an increase in interest rates. He thought that the economic case was finally balanced, but there was no political argument for an increase. There would have been dissatisfaction in Parliament and Mrs Thatcher thought it would be portrayed as an economic price to be paid for her falling out with Nigel Lawson. Major's approach to economic policy was always informed by a sense of what was politically possible and desirable. When Ken Clarke raised interest rates by fifty basis points in September, Major implored him to drop the idea, which he thought would be highly politically unpopular.

In the summer of 1992 a number of economic and political factors came together to put pressure on the UK's membership of the ERM. There was considerable uncertainty about the outcome of a referendum in France, scheduled for late September, which threatened to derail the Maastricht Treaty. European leaders were calling for reductions in what were seen to be high German interest rates, but these were felt to be necessary by the Bundesbank in the wake of reunification with the east. German interest rates were increased on 16 July and it was indicated that they might be increased further. The UK domestic economy was weak with high unemployment, net output per worker well below German levels and a developing budgetary crisis.

Global economic factors were not helping. The dollar was weak because the Federal Reserve decided to lower interest rates to boost economic growth in the United States. Money found its way from the US to London where it was invested in deutschmarks, driving up the value of the German currency. Preoccupied with their own domestic inflationary problems, the Germans were not disposed to be helpful to other countries in the ERM.

It was becoming increasingly apparent in the summer of 1992 that the rate of the pound against the deutschmark was becoming unsustainable. However, Major and the government were determined to stick to the central plank of their economic policy. Why did Britain not try for a realignment of the pound within the ERM? Admittedly, there had not been such a realignment since 1987 and countries were expected to adhere to the rate band at which they entered. Other member states were resistant, but that does not mean that it was impossible and Britain does not seem to have pushed very hard on the issue. One concern seems to have been that it would have meant higher domestic interest rates. Treasury officials also felt that it would not have solved the main problem, which they saw as the impact of German monetary policy on British interest rates.

It was hoped that some kind of solution could be found at the Ecofin meeting of finance ministers and Central Bank governors scheduled to meet in Bath at the beginning of September with the Chancellor, Norman Lamont, in the chair. As it turned out, neither a realignment nor a reduction in German interest rates was achieved. Many saw Lamont 'as the principal culprit for his uncompromising chairmanship and *idée fixe* about pressurising Germany rather than exploring multilateral realignment options'.[2] Major did not, however, blame his Chancellor: 'however clumsily the meeting had been handled, it was clear that the Germans were not prepared to give way on interest rates without a realignment, and the French were not interested in that. Norman may have irritated his colleagues, but I do not believe that he threw away any opportunity.'[3]

Germany did make a very small cut in interest rates, which at least was seen as an indication of a willingness to ease them, but any benefits it might have brought were offset by incautious remarks by the president of the Bundesbank, Dr Schelsinger, which indicated that there might be further devaluations beyond that taken by Italy. This precipitated the chaotic events of so-called 'Black Wednesday', although some came to see it as 'Golden Wednesday' because of the way in which devaluation boosted the economy. Rises in interest rates, from 10 to 12 per cent and then to 15 per cent, failed to calm the markets or ease the pressure on the pound. Rather belated attempts were made to contact the German Chancellor, the French Prime Minister and other key European figures.

All this was to no avail and the decision was taken to suspend British membership of the ERM and a de facto devaluation of the pound followed (by February 1993 it was at DM2.30). A shell-shocked Norman Lamont made a terse statement about what had happened in the Treasury courtyard. Because it was considered that no minister could give interviews, the party chairman, Norman Fowler, was summoned and had to cope with a topic with which he was not familiar, had only been lightly briefed, and was clearly out of his depth.

Presentational issues aside, this was a devastating blow for the Major government, which had lost the central plank of its economic policy. It never recovered its reputation for economic competence. Major considered resignation and was never sure whether he made the right choice in deciding to stay. The immediate task for the government was to find a new basis for its economic policy.

A NEW ECONOMIC POLICY

Norman Lamont survived the immediate aftermath of the ERM exit, remaining as Chancellor for another eight months until he was replaced by Ken Clarke. Lamont did not see why he should take all the blame for what happened and he was a useful political lightning conductor for Major. However, his usefulness declined as he became the subject of a media campaign. Never a commanding figure, he became increasingly weaker politically, not something that was sustainable in such a crucial post. His popularity with backbenchers and voters was low. Events which had nothing to do with economic policy, or were even fabricated, undermined his credibility and hence that of the government.

While Lamont was still in office, the government had to act quickly to find a new anchor for economic policy. It was decided to adopt an inflation target with an initial range of 1–4 per cent, with the objective of reducing it to 2.5 per cent by the end of the parliament, as the basis for policy. For some this was the start of an effective battle against inflation, although globalisation effects that produced cheaper imports undoubtedly helped. The inflation mean in the 1990s was reduced to 3.9 per cent.

The inflation targets were accompanied by a unified Budget which examined spending and revenue together, and monthly monetary reports from the Treasury. The Bank of England would prepare a quarterly inflation report and assess the government's progress in meeting its target. The Treasury would set out in detail the basic policy decisions after meetings between the Chancellor and the Governor of the Bank of England. In 1994 Ken Clarke announced that the minutes of the meetings between the Chancellor and the Governor would be published after a short delay. Even this small step in the direction of bank independence was almost too much for Major. At first, not much notice was taken of the minutes until they recorded a disagreement on interest rates between the Chancellor and the Governor.

Some saw this as the start of the process of depoliticisation of economic policy, which was taken further by the first Blair government with the creation of a quasi-independent Bank of England. However, it was a relatively weak form of depoliticisation and Major was explicit about the limits of how far he was prepared to go in that direction. Norman Lamont wanted to grant independence to the Bank of England. Major 'disliked this proposal on democratic grounds, believing that the person responsible for monetary policy should be answerable for it in the House of Commons. I also feared that the culture of an independent bank would ensure that interest rates went up rapidly but fell only slowly.'[4]

The economic slowdown had reduced tax revenues and increased spending on items such as unemployment benefits. In the spring of 1991 the public sector borrowing requirement was estimated to be £8 billion; the estimate on which the 1991–92 round was based put it at £19 billion; by the time of the 1992 Budget the figure had risen to £32 billion; by early 1993 it was projected to rise to £50 billion or 8 per cent of national income. Clarke was determined to reverse what he saw as the fiscal irresponsibility of the period running up to the 1992 election, to tighten fiscal policy and to achieve a balanced budget over the economic cycle.

It was evident that the system of public expenditure control was breaking down. The extent to which this was happening in the late 1980s was masked by rapid economic growth that enabled the headline total of public expenditure to GDP to fall. The system, if it can be called such, was based on bilateral discussions between the chief secretary to the Treasury and spending ministers of which Major had direct experience in his two years in that post. The final resort, if agreement could not be reached, was the 'Star Chamber', a committee of non-spending ministers. The process was very messy and unsystematic and highly politicised with spending ministers making leaks to the press to bolster their case.

Major wanted a top-down system, in which a global total was agreed by the Cabinet and then shared out between departments. Lamont came up with a mechanism in the form of the EDX committee. This was chaired by the Chancellor and serviced by Treasury officials. It offered regular scrutiny of departments rather than operating as a court of appeal. The discussion focused on conformity to the control total rather than the merits of departmental bids. It is generally thought to have worked quite well, although possibly less so towards the end of the government's term in office. However, an improved mechanism could not by itself overcome the underlying problems and the government was forced to take some unpopular decisions on taxation which may have caused it lasting political damage.

Although controlling inflation was a central economic policy objective for Major, he also wanted to reduce the burden of taxation, but in practice this proved difficult. His first task was to reduce the burden of the unpopular poll tax which had brought about Thatcher's downfall. This came at a cost of £4.5 billion and required an increase in value added tax from 15 per cent to 17.5 per cent. The replacement of the poll tax by a new form of property tax, the council tax, was a long drawn-out affair, given that some right-wing Conservatives were still attached to it, as well as Mrs Thatcher herself. By playing it long, while opening him to accusations of dithering from the opposition, Major was able to overcome the objections, although it did make local authorities even more reliant on central government revenue.

OECD figures show that total tax revenues in the UK as a percentage of GDP were 32.9 per cent in 1990 when Major took office, a figure slightly above the OECD average. By 1997, they were 32.3 per cent, slightly below the OECD average. This might suggest progress of a kind, although such figures are subject to fluctuations in GDP. From a purely political point of view, Major was not able to reduce the basic rate of income tax as quickly as many Conservatives would have liked. It was reduced to 24p in the 1995 Budget and by a further 1p in the 1996 Budget. The right had wanted large income tax cuts in 1995 and 1996, but Clarke took the view that any tax increases had to be sustainable in the longer term.

A number of 'stealth' taxes were introduced, such as those on insurance premiums and air travel, which produced a target for political opponents. Labour constantly referred to '22 tax increases since 1992'. Having campaigned on the taxation issue in the 1992 general election, voters now started to think that the Conservatives were no more likely to reduce taxes than Labour. A new 20 per cent income tax band for the first £2,000 of taxable income, to benefit four million of lower pay, was introduced in the 1992 Budget, but the income tax burden was increased by lower allowances in the 1993 Budget. Indeed, Clarke raised the tax burden by more than any single Budget since 1945.

What Clarke did seek to do was to move towards the abolition of tax relief on mortgage interest. This had been seen as consistent with the Conservative commitment to home ownership and had been particularly favoured by Mrs Thatcher. Clarke believed that it fuelled housing booms and mired purchasers in excessive debt. It was not finally eliminated until Gordon Brown became Chancellor.

The political room for manoeuvre of the government on taxation was limited. The Treasury was interested in applying a lower rate of VAT to zero-rated items. Major saw that extending VAT to such items as food, passenger transport, children's clothes, books and newspapers would be politically unattractive. However, it was agreed that in Lamont's 1993 Budget that domestic fuel should be subject to an 8 per cent rate of VAT. This was presented as being compatible with the environmental commitments made at the Rio Earth Summit in 1992. In 1994 this was increased to 17.5 per cent, leading to a backbench rebellion and a defeat in the House of Commons. The government's inability to secure support for a key element in its Budget damaged its credibility.

PRIVATISATION

One view of John Major is that he represented a return to a more One Nation centrist view of Conservatism. An alternative view is that he simply represented an emollient form of presenting Thatcherite policies. When it came to privatisation, Major seemed to be resolved to complete the task that Mrs Thatcher had begun. The difficulty was that all the low-hanging fruit had been taken and what was left presented complex challenges. Indeed, Thatcher had decided that the three remaining significant candidates for privatisation (coal, the railways and the Post Office) were best left well alone.

Coal was in some respects the most straightforward of the three. Its main customer, the electricity industry, had already been privatised and was diversifying its sources of supply. Security of supply was no longer the issue that it was. The powerful National Union of Mineworkers had been defeated by Mrs Thatcher and was unable to offer any effective political resistance to a pre-privatisation closure plan. The breakaway union, the Democratic Union of Mineworkers, which had been crucial to the Thatcher government's victory in 1984–85, did feel betrayed as its members thought that they had been given assurances about the future of their pits. Many miners took the relatively generous voluntary redundancy terms on offer. The government survived a backbench revolt on the issue. The deep-mine pits were divided into five packages that were offered to their open-cast neighbours. Major doesn't even mention the privatisation in his lengthy memoirs.

The Post Office posed a much more difficult challenge. Major was anxious about the politics and the Chief Whip feared a backbench revolt. Ken Clarke, on the other hand, saw it as a way of raising some money. The Post Office had a highly positive image in the minds of the public. There were concerns that rural post offices might be at threat. Opposition came from the far left and the far right of the parliamentary party. Traditionalists on the right saw it as undermining a national institution, rather like privatising one's regiment as one MP put it, while those on the left saw it as an essential service that should remain in public control. Faced with problems on other fronts, Major was unwilling to risk political capital on something that he was unconvinced about anyway. Rather than face a defeat in the Commons he backed down, but in doing so made himself look weak.

The railways offered the most complicated privatisation task and, in the long run, proved to be the least successful. The privatisation of the railways is discussed in detail in a later chapter in this volume. Demands for their renationalisation today enjoy widespread public support. In part, this is because expansion in demand for rail services since privatisation has not been matched by an expansion of capacity, which is not easy to achieve with a system with a Victorian inheritance, in which some routes which would be useful today were closed during the Beeching cuts in the 1960s. The expansion in demand is not so much a result of privatisation, as structural changes in the economy, including an increase in commuting in the south-east. Commuters and others often have to put up with delayed and overcrowded trains, exacerbated in some cases by industrial-relations' problems.

It is difficult to work out what Major's objectives were in his three major privatisation attempts, particularly given that he says very little about them in his autobiography, suggesting that he did not regard them as one of the achievements of his time in office. He was asked to justify the policy of rail privatisation in 2008 and could only come up with one positive argument, that privatisation was the only way in which adequate investment funds could be attracted because government would never provide them. His defenders would say that he was simply approaching them on a pragmatic case-by-case basis. He was ready to retreat when the Post Office privatisation attracted political opposition, but in the case of the railways he was not ready to challenge the Treasury's view of how privatisation should be carried out. His attention was really elsewhere, not least because of the challenges of party management that he faced.

THE REAL ECONOMY

The Major government has been criticised for its failure to tackle the underlying structural problems of the real economy. Although productivity had improved under the Thatcher government, in part because of a 'batting average' effect in which under-performing enterprises were squeezed out, a number of fundamental problems remained. In particular, the UK remained deficient in skill formation in its labour force, particularly below degree level.

The Major government did show more concern for the fate of the manufacturing industry than the Thatcher government and in particular restored an effective working relationship with the CBI. Concern about poor relations with business led the government to start a series of breakfast meetings between Cabinet ministers and executives from small- and medium-sized companies. However, the government abolished one of the last remnants of tripartite cooperation between government, business and the unions: the National Economic Development Council. It may have been seen as a hangover from a corporatist past, but its sectoral work did provide a forum in which employers and unions could work together to tackle problems of innovation and competitiveness.

The task of improving relative economic performance was largely subcontracted to Michael Heseltine at the Department of Trade and Industry (DTI) through his 'competitiveness agenda'. This terminology avoided any reference to the industrial strategies of the past which were seen as having too interventionist a tone, although Heseltine was frank about his interventionist intentions. Heseltine set up a Competitiveness Division in the DTI staffed from the public and private sector. Although productivity was seen as the test and indicator of success, Heseltine saw his task as changing attitudes as much as anything so that complacency was replaced by a realistic appraisal of national strengths and weaknesses.

The question remains about the effect that his competitiveness White Papers had on the real economy. There were political concerns about whether Heseltine was using competitiveness to raise his own political profile and seize control of the domestic agenda. However, in many respects, the competitiveness White Papers were a damp squib. The first of them in 1994 was greatly heralded, but 'the policy announcements offered little new, continuing to stress the importance of training, contained no hint of a return to 1970s-style industrial policies and implicitly confirmed the continuing decline in DTI spending. There were no concessions to critics such as the House of Commons Trade and Industry Committee, which had called for greater research and development spending by governments.'[5]

Heseltine did attempt to do something about the chaotic structure of trade associations in Britain which he rightly saw as a weakness in terms of policy formation and implementation. He set up an initiative for trade association improvement in 1993–94, which was based on a 'model association document' with development funds provided by the DTI. This was subsequently managed through a Trade Association Forum, hosted within the CBI. Although there were some successes, the initiative as a whole came up against the interests of particular industrial sectors and association staff. Heseltine also wanted to reinvigorate the chambers of commerce movement, but obligatory membership on continental European lines was never going to be acceptable, and local coverage by the chambers remained patchy, with some very effective organisations but also many indifferent or under-funded ones.

In contrast, attention to competition policy slipped back under the Major government, perhaps reflecting the renewed influence of the CBI on policy. Competition policy shifted in a more pro-business direction with more emphasis on the costs of compliance for firms. Major mergers were not referred to the Monopolies and Mergers Commission, against the advice of the Director General of Fair Trading, and the Office of Fair Trading started to complain that the government had gone soft on competition policy. Anticipated changes to the Restrictive Practices Act and a new law on abuse of market power failed to materialise. It was left to New Labour to bring about needed legislative changes to give greater force to competition policy.

Perhaps some of the major changes occurred in labour-market policy. The trade unions had already been marginalised under the Thatcher government and this policy stance was not reversed. There was also a conscious effort to promote a more 'flexible' labour market, which in practice often meant driving down wages and reducing or removing worker protection. For example, the Wages Councils, which had laid down minimum wage rates for 2.5 million low-paid workers in non-unionised sectors of the economy, were abolished. These had not always been very effective bodies, but there was concern that the removal of any form of legal protection for low-paid workers would leave them more open to exploitation by employers and a driving down of their wages.

The government's general approach to labour market policy was set out in its February 1992 White Paper *People, Jobs and Opportunities*. This emphasised the importance of the individual employee and anticipated a further decline in collective bargaining, especially the replacement of national by local-level agreements. The government made clear its preference for what it saw as a lightly regulated, decentralised and flexible approach to employment and labour-market issues, which it contrasted with what it perceived to be a centralised, regulated and uniform model being pursued by other EU member states. There was a notion that the UK could be a 'tiger' economy like Pacific Rim countries such as South Korea and Taiwan.

Of course, the move to a more flexible labour market was not just a consequence of government policy. It also reflected structural changes in the economy, such as the shift from manufacturing to services, and was in part a reflection of pressures created by globalisation. Nevertheless, the government enthusiastically embraced these changes and took a number of steps to facilitate them, a policy stance continued by New Labour.

The old tripartite system of industrial training run by the former Manpower Services Commission was finally replaced in 1991 by eighty-two employer-dominated Training and Enterprise Councils (TECs) in England and Wales. They were given the responsibility of meeting the training needs of local labour markets and were generously financed through the use of taxpayers' money (£2.3 billion in 1993/94), although the lines of accountability were far from clear. Inevitably, they risked a patchy approach in terms of the quality of the training that was provided. They did not survive under New Labour, but then no government has really found a satisfactory institutional framework for tackling the need for better skill formation.

CONCLUSIONS: WAS THERE A MAJOR EFFECT?

The economy continued to recover, but the Conservative reputation for economic competence did not. By 1995 John Major and Michael Heseltine had used every opportunity to repeat a mantra of the highest rate of growth, the lowest unemployment and the lowest inflation in the European Union. Unemployment, having stood at 2.9 million early in 1993, had dropped below 2 million by the end of 1996. Inflation stayed under three per cent, except in 1995. The misery index, combining inflation and unemployment, thus fell away from previously high figures. The rate of growth moved up to 4 per cent by late 1994.

However, it was largely a voteless recovery. In large part, this was because of considerations that had nothing to do with economic policy: the impression of a divided party given by continued disputes over the EU; the scandals involving Conservative MPs referred to as 'sleaze'; and incompetence in handling events such as the outbreak of BSE (commonly known as mad cow disease). In contrast, New Labour was able to present an image of a competent, modernising and moderate party that would address voters' concerns about the deterioration of public services. 'By 1996 the British Election Study panel found a modest recovery among 1992 Conservative voters in the government's perceived economic competence. But this was offset by their dissatisfaction with its record on health and education, while voters discerned few differences between the Labour and Conservative parties on economic issues.'[6]

Too many voters had experienced large tax increases and cuts in their own standard of living. The exit poll from the 1997 general election found that '35 per cent agreed that the economy had grown stronger over the previous five years but 31 per cent thought the opposite and, strikingly, only 25 per cent thought that their own standard of living had improved over the period while 38 per cent actually thought it had worsened.'[7] Economic optimism did grow in the twelve months to polling day, but not to the benefit of the Conservatives.

Did the Major premiership have any significant impact on economic policy or was it just an interval between Thatcher and New Labour with little distinctive content of its own? Was it simply a case of completing the remaining items on the Thatcherite agenda, as in the case of privatisation? As Major himself said: 'in economic policy, in further privatisation ... I was no counter-revolutionary. In these policies, I led the Thatcherite march onwards with conviction – for I believed in it.[8] Leaving aside the consequences of the forced exit from the ERM, Major faced three constraints in developing a distinctive economic policy.

The first of these was the constraint he faced as a Prime Minister who had not (initially) won a general election, but had been selected by his party. It might be observed that this has not discouraged Mrs May from striking out in a number of new policy directions after taking over from David Cameron. However, John Major faced a particularly challenging policy-making environment even before the ERM crisis. As an unexpected Prime Minister, he did not have time in opposition to sort out his objectives and priorities. 'Rarely had a Prime Minister arrived at Number Ten with so little ground prepared.'[9]

Second, having made the perhaps unfortunate choice of Norman Lamont as Chancellor, once Lamont was gone, Major was beholden to his successor. As Major noted, 'losing one Chancellor was a desperate affair, and losing two would be above the normal ration'.[10] Major had an effective working relationship with Clarke, with whom he was and remained personally friendly, and the Chancellor did not enjoy the wide range of authority that Gordon Brown did under Tony Blair. Nevertheless, Major's attention was often elsewhere, either trying to cope with the challenges of party management or pursuing his own pet projects such as the Citizen's Charter. Many of the policy initiatives in the area of economic policy thus came from Clarke and the Treasury.

Clarke recalls: 'I paid proper attention to (Major's) opinions on economic policy. He, in his turn, never attempted to overrule me.'[11]

Third, the government was constrained by its small majority after 1992, which was further eroded through by-election defeats. It did not take many government MPs to frustrate a policy initiative, as was noted in the case of Post Office privatisation.

In many ways the economic policy significance of the Major government was that it started new policies or projects that were then taken further and with greater enthusiasm by New Labour. Steps were made towards greater independence for the Bank of England, albeit with Major's reluctant consent. Major was an enthusiast for the Private Finance Initiative as a means of offering a new form of partnership between the private and public sectors. No contracts were signed under the Major government, but New Labour took up the baton, although with mixed results in terms of value for money. The flexible labour market policy emphasised with the Major government also found favour with New Labour.

Some might argue that all government policies end in failure and therefore that governments should follow Salisbury's statecraft of having no policies. It might be possible for a Prime Minister to get away with that in the late nineteenth and early twentieth century. However, modern governments are expected to do more than react to events. In the sphere of economic policy, they are expected to assess the obstacles to greater prosperity and to try and do something about removing them.

Even allowing for the misfortune of the ERM episode, economic policy under Major lacked an overall organising theme as was the case for his predecessor and successor. Just like Churchill's pudding, policy requires a theme. What one often had, particularly after the exit from the ERM, was largely a pragmatic reaction to events. In terms of the main economic indicators, this worked quite well, albeit helped by forces that had nothing to do with the government or its policies. However, the underlying structural deficiencies of the economy were largely ignored or at best targeted by incomplete or flawed policy initiatives.

ENDNOTES

1 J. Major, *The Autobiography* (London: Harper Collins), p. 136
2 A. Seldon, *Major: a Political Life* (London: Weidenfeld & Nicolson, 1997), p. 311
3 Major, *The Autobiography*, p. 325
4 Ibid. p. 675
5 N. F. R. Crafts, 'Industry' in D. Kavanagh and A. Seldon (eds.) *The Major Effect* (London: Macmillan, 1994), pp. 206–22
6 D. Butler and D. Kavanagh, *The British General Election of 1997* (London: Macmillan, 1997), p. 34
7 Ibid. p. 228
8 Major, *The Autobiography*, p. 215
9 Seldon, *Major: a Political Life*, p. 131
10 Major, *The Autobiography*, p. 681
11 K. Clarke, *Kind of Blue: a Political Memoir* (London: Pan Macmillan, 2016), p. 322

10

INDUSTRIAL RELATIONS

Andrew Taylor

INTRODUCTION

TRADE UNION AND INDUSTRIAL relations reform had been central concerns of the Thatcher governments because they were regarded as fundamental to the government's ambition to transform the UK; realising this objective inevitably involved confrontation with the unions. After passing five major pieces of legislation, and following a sharp decline in union membership and the incidence of industrial conflict, there was an assumption that union and industrial relations reform were problems solved. One of the main reasons for John Major's emergence as party leader and Prime Minister was that he was perceived as less aggressive and confrontational than Mrs Thatcher, and there was an expectation by some that this changed tone would apply to industrial relations.

The Major government was not ideologically different from its Conservative predecessors.[1] Smith and Morton, for example, portray the Major years as 'another step in the evolution of the Conservative government's project to diminish union power and one which marks a new confidence and a willingness to jettison past inhibitions'.[2] The memoirs of John Major and his ministers devote little space to industrial relations or union reform, which testifies to their reduced significance; however, the Major government was responsible for one major piece of legislation, the Trade Union Reform and Employment Rights Act (TURERA, 1993). This showed the government remained wedded to the Thatcher government's strategy of legal change, promoting free markets and deregulation, and responding to events that revealed lacunae in legislation.[3] The government's approach and emphasis on individual rights (*'Every business, every worker, freedom from the dictatorship of union militants'*) fitted neatly with the Citizen's Charter, which John Major regarded as the centrepiece of Conservatism in the 1990s.[4] It is therefore wrong to regard the Major government as a non-event in policy terms.

This chapter argues the Major government was the first to oversee the industrial relations system that developed out of the changes begun in the 1980s and manage the consequences of the shift from an industrial to a post-industrial economy. Three features of post-industrialism command our attention. First, the collapse of manufacturing industry and the decline of its associated unions saw the rise of the service industry economy with a low level of unionisation. Union membership as a proportion of employees declined from 38.6 per cent in 1989 to 30.2 in 1997, with membership in the public sector being significantly higher than in the private sector. So, second, the decline of private sector trade unionism and collective bargaining was not matched in the public sector where unions remained relatively more powerful. The percentage of private sector employees covered by collective agreements in 1997 was 22.0 and 74.9 per cent in the public sector. Third, some unions remained strategically important, developing responses that utilised the legislation as well as exploiting growing job insecurity, inequality, recession, de-regulation, and privatisation.

Did the legal and other changes of the 1980s constitute a degree of change sufficient to solve the union and industrial relations problems? Whatever the answer, the political case for legislation remained strong. Conservatives had enjoyed the reputation of being the party best able to deal with the unions and industrial relations, and the Labour Party suffered from the opposite evaluation. This reputation created an incentive for legislation for party-political advantage intended to embarrass Tony Blair and New Labour.[5] However, it proved difficult to brand New Labour as the trade union party. Other reasons justifying further legislation were internal Conservative politics and the Major government's acute consciousness of the threat posed by the EU's social agenda to party unity and the changes of the 1980s.[6] The next section considers the Major government's inheritance.

JOHN MAJOR'S INHERITANCE

In 1979 industrial relations were dominated by collectivism and the voluntarist tradition, which held that in general the law should interfere as little as possible in employee-employer relations conducted *via* collective bargaining. The negotiation and distribution of reward through collective bargaining was essentially a private activity albeit one supported by the state. But this collectivist-voluntarist tradition was progressively weakened during the 1980s, and by 1990 this tradition was undermined fatally. The earlier conception of industrial relations was delegitimised and subject to extensive attack; the critical period was 1984–90 and the pattern established continued in the 1990s.[7] By 1998, many workplaces continued to recognise unions but not collective bargaining, and the result was a 'hollow shell' compared to what had existed before. This decline in joint workplace regulation was accompanied by a sharp fall in union membership (Table 1, p. 175) with indications that employees had lost their appetite for union membership. In workplaces of more than twenty-five employees, collective bargaining remained fairly intact, but there were sharp declines in private sector manufacturing and services.[8]

One difference between the Major government and its predecessors was a change in tone. Talk of 'the enemy within' faded with the decline in union membership, industrial action, and changes in industrial relations, which meant this charge carried little conviction with the public. Given John Major's political persona and strategy, such language would have seemed incongruous. However, the change in tone was of secondary importance compared to the government's fixity of purpose and commitment to his predecessor's strategy. The 1992 Conservative manifesto declared that the previous Conservative governments' legislation had transformed industrial relations, returning power from militants to ordinary union members.

This individualisation was part of a wider programme of deregulation (removing obstacles to the market's operation and managerial prerogatives) intended to promote job creation, and the manifesto promised further measures to promote these objectives.[9] In his autobiography John Major described his government's economic inheritance as 'unpromising' (in 1991 1,150 companies went into liquidation and unemployment was 2.3 million, or 8.3 per cent). But notwithstanding this, Major insisted the UK had been transformed. Union and industrial relations reform had been central to this transformation because it 'had removed the stranglehold of militancy over our affairs. Supply-side economic changes had boosted the flexibility and well-being of the economy. Privatisation had broken down the monolith of public ownership, and once-derelict public services were now hugely competitive private companies. Private enterprise had won the battle against socialism.'[10] Trade union and industrial relations legislation was a signifier of contemporary Conservatism and a key measure of its success, and so inevitably would feature in the Major government's policy repertoire. The overall strategy rested on the premise that the unions were voluntary associations that had outgrown their legitimate role and become serious obstacles to economic growth as well as disruptive political actors, so their power had to be reduced.

A notable feature of the 1990s was the decline in industrial action and the salience of industrial relations and trade union power as a political issue. The number of working days lost due to disputes peaked in 1979, followed by a sharp and continuing decline (Table 1, p. 175). The Major government, therefore, enjoyed historically low levels of industrial conflict. This decline was accompanied by a decline in union membership, which had also peaked in 1979. In the 1990s membership declined continuously, a decline that was the result of domestic economic changes such as the closure of large, heavily unionised plants and workplaces in the public and private sectors and the effects of globalisation (the data shows that the already high openness of the UK economy increased during the 1990s).[11] The 1980s legislation addressed three problems: first, the gap between the interests of union leaders and members; second, that unions enjoyed too much power in the polity and workplace; and third, that unions were controlled by extremists. Table 2a (p. 176) shows that around 40 per cent of union and non-union members agreed union leaders were out of touch with their members; Table 2b (p. 176) shows one-third agreed unions were too powerful but over time this declined to one in four; an average of 74 per cent of union members disagreed with this preposition compared to 55 per cent of all adults. Despite the decline in industrial action, around one in three agreed unions were controlled by militants and only a bare majority (57 per cent) of union members disagreed (Table 2c, p. 176), but the legitimacy of unions (Table 2d, p.177) as protection was accepted by both groups (an average of 78 and 89 per cent). Unions were still considered to be necessary, but this was balanced by public opinion's continued perception of unions being under militant control and their leaders being disengaged from the membership. However, the Conservatives lost strikes and the unions as an issue. In answer to the question '*Which political party do you personally think would handle the problem of strikes and industrial relations the best?*', Labour overtook the Conservatives after May 1992 (between 1992 and 1997 Labour's average was 40 per cent agreed, the Conservative average was 36 per cent) and industrial relations ceased to be the 'most urgent problem' facing the country.[12] The residual ambivalence of public opinion towards aspects of trade unionism, however, created an incentive and opportunity for the Major government to undertake further legislation.

John Major's inheritance had three broad components: the deregulation of the labour market, the promotion of individual over collective rights, and squeezing the unions out of policy-making. Their exclusion from policy-making was an essential contribution to creating a governance that stressed the primacy of government authority, while the unions' exclusion from employment relations would be a signal contribution to creating a low-tax, flexible, high-productivity economy in which the state's role was to facilitate domestic adaptation to an increasingly globalised political economy. Further legislation was promised in the 1992 Queen's Speech and John Major and his ministers expected this would be controversial.[13] Union exclusion thus remained the object of policy but the Major government sponsored no initiatives comparable to those of the 1980s. Nevertheless, government policy posed a serious threat to the remaining organisational strength and presence of trade unions, and its actions showed the government had 'perfected the art of spinning legal webs around them.'[14] The next section considers the policies of the Major government.

GOVERNMENT POLICY

The Major government's emphasis was, as I have argued, on exclusion: 'reducing the role of unions within the labour market, the employment relationship and as representatives of a separate "labour interest" in society'.[15] By the time Mrs Thatcher left office the political case for legislation seemed less strong and Michael Howard, the Employment Secretary, speculated in January 1990 that the reform agenda was now complete.[16] Michael Heseltine, the President of the Board of Trade, hinted at a broader agenda, seeking to use the changes of the 1980s, which had de-fanged the unions and brought them under the rule of law, as an important foundation for his competitiveness agenda and intervention strategy.[17]

In 1991 the Department of Employment issued a Green Paper, *Industrial Relations in the 1990s*, and in 1992 published the White Paper, *People, Jobs and Opportunity* that outlined the post-Thatcher approach. Neither departed from Thatcherism's precepts.[18] The continuity between the Thatcher and Major governments meant the rejection of any idea that nothing more needed to be done; the government was interested in extending, not consolidating, Thatcherism, and any relationship with the unions would be contained in this framework.[19] Howard argued that the Green Paper built upon existing changes, addressed weaknesses in the legislation, and increased the rights of the public and union members through an emphasis on ballots and changes to union governance. As a result of previous policies 'we have now', Howard declared, 'reached a decisive stage in the history of industrial relations in this country. As a result of the legislation that the government have introduced since the 1980s, our industrial relations have achieved a degree of stability and a maturity that seemed unattainable during the 1970s.'[20] The proposals combined regulation and restriction based on an individualist conception of citizenship that undercut collective action and sought to force unions to abandon collective action and recast themselves as 'service providers' to their members and, ideally, management. TURERA was the *point d'appui* of an established approach that reflected the Major government's determination to complete the transformation of industrial relations.[21]

Thatcherism's approach to industrial relations was restated in the Green Paper and the White Paper, and both embodied an individualist ethos in industrial relations, with further measures restricting and regulating union activity and governance. Building on the foundations laid in the 1980s, the Major government focused on continuing the unions' exclusion, and reducing and circumscribing their role in the employment relationship, in the labour market, and the policy process. Exclusion was encapsulated in the oft-stated intention of 'giving the unions back to their members' that meant creating a pattern of individualised participation, captured by the emphasis of ballots, that inevitably and necessarily de-emphasised the collective.[22]

The 1992 crisis over pit closures is not directly relevant to the Major government's industrial relations or trade union policies, but the closures provide an insight into Britain's changing industrial relations. Industrial relations in the deep-mined coal industry had been transformed on lines familiar throughout the rest of industry as a result of the NUM's defeat in 1984–85 and the founding of the Union of Democratic Mineworkers (UDM) as a competitor to the NUM. The decision to privatise the remnants of deep mining had been announced in the 1992 Conservative manifesto but the closures (an essential precursor to the privatisation of both the coal and the electricity supply industries), coming three weeks after the UK's humiliating ejection from the ERM, seemingly confirmed the government's reputation for incompetence and mismanagement. The majority of closures were concentrated in the Nottinghamshire and Central coalfields, where the majority of mineworkers were members of the UDM who had played a crucial role in the defeat of the NUM. Ingratitude was therefore added to the charge of incompetence. Notwithstanding the public and political outcry over a poorly prepared and presented policy, the primacy of privatisation and the de-regulation of the electricity supply industry triumphed and the affected mines were quickly closed.[23]

Rothwell thought 1992 was possibly a 'watershed year' for industrial relations but the continued recession and the fallout from the UK's ejection from the ERM included redundancies at, *inter alia*, Ford, Jaguar, Rolls-Royce and British Aerospace. Surveys of management found 80 per cent expected restructuring to continue and that this would stimulate extensive cultural change in the workplace that would be to the unions' detriment. Labour's defeat in the 1992 general election ended the immediate prospect of a Labour government instituting pro-union changes and this was reinforced further when Tony Blair became party leader, determined to recast the traditional party-union relationship. Another potential avenue for change was blocked by the ERM crisis. The ERM crisis stimulated and reinforced Conservative hostility to the EU's social role, which reinforced the Major government's determination to opt out of as much of this European social agenda as possible.[24] However, this proved difficult. For example, many of the measures in TURERA dealing with individual employment rights were the result of EU policies (Figure 1, p. 174).

TURERA further regulated union activity and governance. Gillian Shephard, Howard's successor as Employment Secretary, argued the Bill continued an established reform process and it had two strategic objectives: 'first to strengthen and extend the rights of the individual – both employees and individual trade union members; secondly, to increase the competitiveness of the economy and remove obstacles to the creation of new jobs'.[25] Legislation had, for instance, played a crucial role in the decline in industrial action, and so

> Now more than ever we need to make sure that the progress we have made … is maintained in the future. Without investment we shall not have the new jobs that we want to see. But without industrial peace there will be no investment. Nothing could be more damaging to the prospects of employment growth than a return to the strike-happy ways of the 1970s.[26]

Fewer than 50 per cent of the workforce was now covered by collective bargaining and only 30 per cent by national agreements and Shephard presented the case for continued reform as a series of questions:

> what is unreasonable about allowing trade union members freedom to choose which union they join? What is unreasonable about giving trade union members a right to a postal ballot before they are called out on strike? What is wrong with allowing union members to decide how they pay their subscriptions? And what is wrong with giving the citizens of this country the protection of the law if they are victims of an unlawful strike?[27]

Auerbach argues the legislation was presented as delivering modest, common-sense changes designed to promote the individual rights agenda but TURERA's effects went far wider than this.[28] Neither recession nor the post-ERM economic upturn fed through into increased disputes or union membership, which was interpreted as signalling the acceptance and institutionalisation of 'the new industrial relations'. TURERA, while not on the scale of the earlier legislation was, notwithstanding, a significant measure, extending the law even deeper into union governance and further promoting union exclusion. Miller and Steele concluded TURERA 'evidences a determination ... to continue the Thatcherite agenda' and the Act's overall effect was to continue to 'slay the union dragon' despite it having 'lost much of its fire and is increasingly constrained by legal requirements'.[29]

Two other developments testify to the unions' exclusion from the policy process. The first was the abolition of the National Economic Development Council (NEDC, or 'Neddy') founded in 1962, a tripartite – management, government and unions – quasi-corporatist planning-consultative body with sectoral offshoots (the 'little Neddies') intended to promote economic growth. The NEDC had been ignored in the 1980s and in 1995 the Major government delivered the *coup de grace.* The second event, the abolition of the Department of Employment (DE) as part of John Major's post-leadership election reshuffle in June 1995, was more significant. The DE's abolition marks the end of an institution and political style that dated from the establishment of the Ministry of Labour in 1916 (which traced its antecedents back to the Board of Trade's Labour Department in the 1890s) as labour's *entrée* to the bureaucracy as the demands of total war and governance required the unions' participation in making policy. After 1916 the Ministry of Labour became the major conduit for the labour interest into the state (and vice versa) and in its various incarnations it represented a type of quasi-corporatist politics that was the dominant form of governance in British politics for much of the twentieth century, but which the post-1979 Conservative governments were determined to eradicate.[30] The DE's functions were transferred (for example, its industrial relations function to the Department of Trade and Industry; unemployment and training services to Education and Training) to a variety of other government departments. In macro-political terms the abolition of the DE expressed the political exclusion of organised labour and the end of quasi-corporatist politics.

The response of the Trade Union Congress (TUC) to this hostile environment under its General Secretary, John Monks, was to try and develop the 'New Unionism', which was influenced by foreign models such as that employed by the AFL-CIO in the United States. This 'New Unionism' (a successor to then TUC General Secretary, Len Murray's 'New Realism' of 1983) focused on delivering benefits to union members as selective incentives to encourage union membership. Fundamentally this was a recruitment strategy that aspired to reflect the diversity of the emerging workforce (such as the growth in part-time women workers and the rise of the service economy) and rebuild the union movement from the bottom up. In terms of the relationship with management the New Unionism urged unions to cooperate with employers, sometimes described as 'fighting for partnership', promote workforce flexibility and improve productivity.

In July 1994 David Hunt, the Employment Secretary, addressed a TUC conference offering cooperation on achieving full employment. But this went nowhere as the dominant Conservative attitude was that full employment was best achieved by free markets and de-regulation. Monks' approach was criticised by some union leaders and activists as legitimising the government's accusation that unions did not truly represent their members' interests, and it proved difficult to implement by the TUC organisationally in the face of both union activist and employer opposition. New Unionism regretted the demise of cooperation between the government and the TUC and placed considerable emphasis on the positive role of the EU and the potential of its social agenda for augmenting the unions' influence, something which the government strongly opposed. John Monks argued that what had emerged was an unstable, rather than a flexible, labour market, that was unsustainable, but he conceded the changes were not reversible: 'we have largely decentralised the labour market since the break-up of most private-sector national negotiating bodies. It is no longer feasible for the nation's pay to be set in talks between the government, the TUC and the CBI in smoke-filled rooms over beer and sandwiches.'[31] Although not calling for a return to beer and sandwiches, Monks argued that the absence of any central contacts or coordination would result in adverse consequences for the country and he pointed to the success of European social models. Moreover, there remained the potential for significant industrial unrest.

In 1996 there occurred 'the Summer of Discontent II' (the 'Summer of Discontent I' occurred in 1989) and involved, among others, the postal service, the Liverpool docks, London Underground, the airline and car industries, and the public sector. These disputes were often defensive, concerned with protecting established working practices and the cooperative conduct of workplace industrial relations in the face of managerial aggressiveness. The mini-strike wave led to the government threatening legislation against strikes in essential services. In reaction to the postal dispute, the government ended the Post Office monopoly on deliveries. The public funding of union ballots and the rights of unions to be consulted over redundancies were ended, and the government also threatened to remove the employment rights of workers in small firms. Continued privatisation led to the further undermining of centralised collective bargaining. These led the ILO to condemn the British government for failing to observe its legal obligations.[32]

CONCLUSIONS

The data shows that in the 1990s industrial conflict was no longer a serious problem, although this did not rule out crises, over, for example, pit closures and the Summer of Discontent II, but the unions were no longer the presence either in the workplace or the polity they had once been. These changes were the combined result of legislation, radical change in the structure of industry, changing managerial attitudes, and the shift of power in the workplace, especially the private sector workplace. The Major government's legislation, TURERA, led *inter alia* to further restrictions on union immunities, the conditions of union membership, union governance, and abolished minimum wage regulation. The government abolished the last vestiges of corporatism (the NEDC and the Wage Councils) and continued public sector wage restraint; more state industries were returned to the private sector. Significant also was the institutionalisation of a globalised post-industrial economy. Rosamund concludes that, 'the attitude of the

Major government to trade unions displayed continuity with the previous Thatcher administrations as well as change'.[33] True, but the similarities and continuities were infinitely more significant than the dissimilarities and discontinuities. In marked contrast to his predecessor, however, John Major lost the unions and industrial relations reform as Conservative issues.[34] The Major government continued to identify Labour as the party of union power but the growth of New Labour and Tony Blair's commitment to a recasting of the party-union relationship, as well as the decline of the unions as a political issue, reduced markedly the effectiveness of this charge. However, the successive Conservative changes made the legislation irreversible, reinforcing Tony Blair's New Labour project.

Union power, as understood previously, was diminished and managerial prerogatives were restored, and the voluntarist-collectivist tradition in workplace and polity was eliminated. Legal intervention, de-industrialisation and globalisation had destroyed the voluntarist non-interventionary tradition in industrial relations, but many Conservatives remained convinced there was still work to do. The EU's Social Chapter was significant because the TUC and some unions saw the EU as offering an opportunity to defend and even extend union influence and this was something Conservatives, both Eurosceptic and Europhile, opposed. From the government's point of view, hostility to EU social policy was relatively politically cost-free because hostility to the EU meshed with the party's hostility to the trade unions and its commitment to transform industrial relations. Several of TURERA's provisions enacted EU social legislation but were couched in the language of extending individual, not collective, rights. Despite the transformation of the 'sick man of Europe', the 1997 manifesto promised the banning of strikes in essential services; legal immunity would be removed from individual actions having a 'disproportionate' (not defined) effect, and strikes would need a majority of all eligible voters and be repeated at regular intervals to be legal.[35] Some Conservatives also urged further action on union funding of the Labour Party, and in privatising the rail and coal industries the Major government could plausibly claim to be more radical than Mrs Thatcher's.

The Major government's significance lies less in its policy than in presiding over a post-industrial political economy and the emergence of many of the features and problems associated with contemporary Britain. The determination of all British governments to create a high-wage, low-tax, high-productivity, flexible labour market capable of exploiting the globalised international economy has not been realised. The continuing decline of manufacturing and dependence on services, low skills, poor productivity, casualisation, labour-force insecurity not flexibility, and gross income inequalities first emerge clearly during the 1990s under John Major.

Figure 1: Trade Union Reform and Employment Rights Act (1993) Main Provisions

The Public

- Individuals able to seek injunctions against unlawful action

Trade Unions

- Creation of Commissioner for Protection Against Unlawful Industrial Action
- Seven days' notice of ballots and of industrial action
- The members to be balloted to be clearly specified
- Replacement of TUC's Bridlington procedures on union recognition
- Written consent required from employees for check-off of union dues every three years
- Union financial records, including officials' salaries, to be public
- Independent checks on election ballots
- Independent scrutiny of strike ballots
- All industrial action ballots to be postal
- Postal ballots on union mergers
- Certification Officer to check union finances
- Higher penalties against unions failing to keep proper accounts
- 'Wilson/Palmer' Amendment (offered incentives to those moving to individual employment contracts)

Individuals

- Maternity leave increased to fourteen weeks with no length of service requirement
- Right to a written statement of duties within eight weeks for those working over eight hours a week
- Unlawful to dismiss health and safety representatives during the course of their duties and those walking off an unsafe site
- Individual right to challenge collective agreement in contravention of equal treatment terms
- Changes to Transfer of Undertakings Regulations
- Consultation on changes to redundancy terms

Miscellaneous

- Abolition of Wages Councils
- Changes to Employment Tribunals procedures

Source: http://www.ier.org.uk/resources/chronology-labour-law-1979-2008

Table 1: Trade Union Membership and Working Days Lost, 1990–98

Year	Trade Union Membership	Total Working Days Lost (000s)
1990	9810	1903
1991	9489	761
1992	8929	528
1993	8666	649
1994	8231	278
1995	8031	415
1996	7938	1307
1997	7801	235
1998	7852	282

Source: DBIS, *Trade Union Membership 2015. Statistical Bulletin* (London: DBIS, 2016). https://www.gov.uk/government/uploads/system/uploads/attachment_data/file/525938/Trade_Union_Membership_2015_-_Statistical_Bulletin.pdf

Table 2: Attitudes to Trade Unions

a) 'Trade union leaders are out of touch with their members'.

	All Adults			Trade Union Members		
	Agree	**Disagree**	**Net**	**Agree**	**Disagree**	**Net**
Aug 1993	45	22	+23	48	30	+18
Aug 1994	42	27	+15	38	41	-3
Aug 1995	41	26	+15	42	35	+7
Average	47	25	18	43	35	17

b) 'Trade unions have too much power in Britain today.'

	All Adults			Trade Union Members		
	Agree	**Disagree**	**Net**	**Agree**	**Disagree**	**Net**
Dec 1989-Jan 1990	35	54	-19	15	75	-60
Aug 1990	38	45	-7	22	66	-40
Feb 1992	27	64	-37	14	82	-68
Dec 1992	24	56	-32	16	71	-55
Aug 1993	26	55	-29	17	70	-53
Aug 1994	26	56	-30	7	79	-72
Aug 1995	24	57	-33	14	73	-59
Average	29	55	-26	15	74	-59

c) 'Most trade unions are controlled by extremists and militants.'

	All Adults			Trade Union Members		
	Agree	**Disagree**	**Net**	**Agree**	**Disagree**	**Net**
Aug 1990	50	30	+20	43	44	-1
Dec 1992	34	42	-8	26	26	-30
Aug 1993	35	40	-5	28	55	-27
Aug 1994	30	47	-17	19	68	-49
Aug 1995	31	45	-14	23	61	-38
Average	36	41	-5	28	57	-29

d) 'Trade unions are essential to protect workers' interests.'

	All Adults			Trade Union Members		
	Agree	**Disagree**	**Net**	**Agree**	**Disagree**	**Net**
Dec 1989-Jan 1990	69	21	+48	85	10	+75
Aug 1990	80	11	+69	90	7	+83
Feb 1992	81	14	+67	93	6	+87
Dec 1992	74	12	+62	86	9	+77
Aug 1993	80	10	+70	92	4	+88
Aug 1994	82	10	+72	93	6	+87
Aug 1995	79	10	+69	88	4	+84
Average	78	12	66	89	7	+82

Source: Ipsos MORI, *Attitudes to Trade Unions 1975–2014* London: Ipsos MORI 2014). https://www.ipsos-mori.com/researchpublications/researcharchive/94/Attitudes-to-Trade-Unions-19752014.aspx

ENDNOTES

1 T. Bale, *The Conservative Party from Thatcher to Cameron* (Cambridge: Polity Press, 2010) p. 34

2 P. Smith, and G. Morton, 'Union exclusion - the next steps,' *Industrial Relations Journal*, 25/1 (1994), p. 6. See also, P. Smith and G. Morton, 'Union Exclusion and the Decollectivisation of Industrial Relations in Contemporary Britain,' *British Journal of Industrial Relations*, 31/1 (1993), pp. 6–23

3 In addition to TURERA the government passed the Trade Union and Labour Relations (Consolidation) Act (1992) that drew together existing trade union and employment legislation in a single Act; the Employment Rights Act (1992) covered conditions of employment, family, domestic, and parental leave, dismissal and unfair dismissal, and redundancy payments; and the Employment Tribunals Act (1996) that revised the procedures of the employment tribunals system.

4 S. Hogg and J. Hill, *Too Close to Call. Power and Politics - John Major in No10* (London: Little, Brown, 1995), p. 136

5 A. Seldon, *Major. A Political Life* (London: Phoenix Books, 1998), p. 739

6 K. Miller and M. Steele, 'Employment Legislation: Thatcher and After,' *Industrial Relations Journal*, 24/3 (1993), p. 223

7 S. Machin, 'Union Decline in Britain', *British Journal of Industrial Relations*, 38/4 (2000), pp. 631–45

8 D. Blanchflower, A. Bryson, and J. Forth, 'Workplace Industrial Relations in Britain, 1989–2004', *Industrial Relations Journal*, 39/1 (2007), pp. 285–302

9 Conservative Central Office, *The Best Future for Britain* (London: Conservative Central Office, 1992) http://www.conservativemanifesto.com/1992/1992-conservative-manifesto.shtml.

10 J. Major, *The Autobiography* (London: Harper Collins, 1999) p.203

11 The data below uses the KOF Globalisation Index which gives the degree to which an economy is globalised. Economic globalisation involves long-distance flows of goods, capital and services, plus the information and perceptions that accompany market exchanges. For definitions and method see: http://globalization.kof.ethz.ch/media/filer_public/2016/03/03/method_2016.pdf

	1990	1991	1992	1993	1994	1995	1996	1997
Germany	57.63	58.66	57.66	57.78	58.53	58.96	60.49	64.49
France	59.13	62.05	63.1	64.45	60.37	62.29	63.59	66.56
United Kingdom	67.21	66.71	65.77	67.51	67.77	68.44	69.8	71.36
United States	57.55	57.52	56.59	57.11	57.91	59.5	60.54	62.04

Higher values = greater globalization (100 = complete globalization/0 = complete closure).
Source of data: http://globalization.kof.ethz.ch/

12 A. King, R. J. Wybrow, and A. Gallup, *British Political Opinion 1937–2000. The Gallup Polls* (London: Politico's Publishing, 2001), p. 89

13 Seldon, *Major. A Political Life*, p. 291

14 T. Morris, 'Annual Review Article 1994', *British Journal of Industrial Relations*, 33/1 (1995), p. 126

15 Smith, and Morton, 'Union exclusion – the next steps', p. 6

16 S. Auerbach, 'Mrs Thatcher's Labour Laws: Slouching towards Utopia', *The Political Quarterly*, 61/1 (1993), p. 44

17 M. Heseltine, *Life in the Jungle. My Autobiography* (London: Hodder & Stoughton, 2000), p. 415

18 Department of Employment, *Industrial Relations in the 1990s*, Cm1602 (London: Department of Employment, HMSO 1991) and, *People, Jobs and Opportunities*, Cm1810 (London: Department of Employment, HMSO 1992)

19 For a brief discussion of the Major government's handling of Mrs Thatcher's legacy see, P. Dorey, *The Conservative Party and the Trade Unions* (London: Routledge, 1995) p. 167; and his 'No Return to "Beer and Sandwiches": Industrial Relations and Employment Policies under John Major, 1990–1997', in P. Dorey (ed.) *The Major Premiership: Politics and Policies under John Major, 1990–1997* (Houndmills: Macmillan, 1999).

20 House of Commons Debates, 24 July 1991, vol. 195, col. 1165

21 J. Purcell, 'The End of Institutional Industrial Relations', *Political Quarterly*, 61/1 (1993), pp. 6–23. This volume is a special issue on industrial relations in the 1990s.

22 P. Fosh, H. Morris, R. Martin, P. Smith, and R. Undy, 'Politics, Pragmatism and Ideology: The "Wellsprings" of Conservative Union Legislation', *Industrial Law Journal*, 22/1 (1995), p. 19

23 For an account of the closure crisis see A. J. Taylor, *The NUM and British Politics. Volume 2, 1969–1995* (Aldershot: Ashgate Publishing, 2005), pp. 297–318. The author remembers an early-morning train journey to London in late-1992 that was joined by the NUM President, Arthur Scargill, who was greeted with an ovation from a carriage full of business people.

24 S. Rothwell, 'Annual Review Article 1992', *British Journal of Industrial Relations*, 31/1 (1993), p. 135

25 House of Commons Debates, 17 November 1992, vol. 214, col. 168

26 Ibid. col. 175

27 Ibid. col. 180

28 Auerbach, 'Mrs Thatcher's Labour Laws', p. 48

29 Miller and Steele, 'Employment Legislation', p. 233

30 On macro-political significance of the DE and its predecessors see, K. Middlemas, *Politics in Industrial Society: The Experience of the British System since 1911* (London: Andre Deutsch, 1979) and R. Lowe, *Adjusting to Democracy: The Influence of the Ministry of Labour on British Politics, 1916–1939* (Oxford: Clarendon Press, 1986). On Neddy see K. Middlemas, *Industry, Unions and Government: Twenty-One Years of NEDC* (London: Macmillan, 1983), whose title captures the political style Conservatives were determined to extirpate.

31 J. Monks, 'Government and Trade Unions', *British Journal of Industrial Relations*, 36/1 (1998), p. 134

32 E. Heery, 'Annual Review Article 1996', *British Journal of Industrial Relations*, 31/1 (1997), p. 90

33 B. Rosamund, 'Whatever Happened to the "Enemy Within"? Contemporary Conservatism and Trade Unionism', in S. Ludlam and M. S. Smith (eds), *Contemporary British Conservatism* (Houndmills: Macmillan, 1996), p. 200

34 Seldon, *Major. A Political Life*, p. 741

35 Conservative Central Office, *You Can Only Be Sure With The Conservatives* (London: Conservative Central Office, 1997) http://www.conservativemanifesto.com/1997/1997-conservative-manifesto.shtml

11

TRANSPORT POLICY

Christian Wolmar

Any analysis of Conservative transport policy must start and end with a discussion of rail privatisation for it was one of the most important legacies of the Major years and should, therefore, feature prominently in his memoirs. It was, after all, a high-profile process creating controversy throughout his term in office and required considerable effort and acumen to push through in the face of considerable opposition. This hostility stretched across the political spectrum, encompassing a good sprinkling of people on the government as well as opposition benches, particularly in the Lords. Yet, mysteriously, rail privatisation barely features in his autobiography. There are a few vague mentions of privatisation in the 816-page volume published in 2006 but there is no account of the convoluted process that led to the decision to privatise, nor, even more remarkably, any mention of the struggle to get the whole industry in private hands by the time of the 1997 election.

There has been, of course, much criticism of rail privatisation but the Tories have consistently deemed it a great success. The railways have boomed with passenger numbers doubling and an unprecedented level of investment. Privatisation, they argue, was the catalyst for this remarkable boom. Therefore, on the face of it, a politician like Major should be shouting from the rooftops about this achievement, especially as his seven years in office saw precious few such long-lasting and significant changes. There are many more critical views on the outcome of privatisation, such as my own book *On the Wrong Line: How Ideology and Incompetence Wrecked Britain's Railways* and Major's silence on the issue seems inexplicable.

THE CONSERVATIVES AND THE RAILWAYS

It is all the more surprising given that it was under Major's premiership that the issue changed from being a vague idea raised from time to time by think tanks and MPs on the right of the party, to becoming a key manifesto commitment with the government machine behind it in order to turn it into reality within the space of a five-year parliamentary term. Although under Margaret Thatcher some fifty major state-owned businesses had been sold off, privatisation of the railways had never really been in her sights. A ragbag of British Rail-owned business had been disposed of, such as the hotels, the Hovercraft services and Travellers' Fare, but selling the core railway service was never considered in depth while Mrs Thatcher, who famously shunned train travel and showed little interest in the railways, was in No. 10.

One of her favourite ministers, Nicholas Ridley, fresh from having sold off and deregulated the bus and coach networks in the mid-1980s, approached her and suggested rail privatisation, only to be given short shrift, as a former British Rail Board member recalled: 'she told him [Ridley] never to mention the words again and that was it. She said "rail privatisation will be the Waterloo of this government. Never mention the railways to me again".'[1] It may simply have been that 'she thought the railways were so bloody awful she wouldn't wish them on the private sector'.[2]

Interestingly, though, the Lady Who Was Not for Turning, vacillated over the issue, her instinctive dislike for the public sector clashing with her political antennae, which had detected that the railways were much closer to the hearts of the British people than the recently sold utilities. Ridley's successor but one, Paul Channon, managed to get the issue put back on the agenda by persuading Thatcher that he could announce at the 1988 party conference that the idea was being considered, although no details were forthcoming. Soon after the conference, he set out five potential options for the sell-off but he was soon replaced by Cecil Parkinson, another of Thatcher's favourites, who was told to put the idea on hold. Parkinson was, however, allowed to revive it at the 1990 party conference and told Parliament soon after that the government was 'determined to privatise British Rail'.[3]

John Major, who replaced Parkinson with Malcolm Rifkind when he became Prime Minister, appeared to have none of his predecessor's doubts about selling off the railways. However, the lack of clarity about precisely what ministers were trying to achieve through this privatisation, and the way the industry would be structured continued under Major. Parkinson had established a working group of ministers and civil servants from the Department of Transport, the Department for Trade and Industry and the Treasury to consider the five options, which ranged from a BR plc, sold off as one entity, to the break-up of the railways with, specifically, the operations being separated from the infrastructure – vertical separation as it is known.

Rifkind had doubts about vertical separation, which was favoured by the Treasury – in particular the head of the privatisation unit, Sir Steve Robson, who was the most influential supporter of the track authority model – because it would enable competition between different operators. The Treasury had initially pushed for an extreme version, which would have involved the auction of train paths – or slots – so that, for example, the 8am from London to Leeds might be run by one company while the 9am could be operated by a rival. The working group concluded that vertical operation would be the favoured option though it accepted that it was probably inappropriate for commuter routes in London and the South East where some kind of vertically integrated railway would remain. However, Rifkind soon sowed confusion by expressing concerns about the workability of this hybrid model and consequently the Conservative Party went into the April 1992 election with the vaguest outline of its intentions in its manifesto, which emphasised competition rather than, as happened, the total privatisation of all parts of the network: 'we believe the best way to produce profound and lasting improvement on the railways is to end BR's state monopoly. We want to restore the pride and local commitment that died with nationalisation. We want to give the private sector the opportunity to operate existing rail services and introduce new ones, for both passengers and freight.' Although the manifesto suggested that 'franchising provides the best way of achieving' better services, it also raised the possibility that 'some services might be sold off outright', meaning that they would remain integrated.

It was not, as John MacGregor, who became Transport Secretary after the election said, 'quite a blank sheet of paper as our election commitment, but very close to it. Just a few outlines about how it [rail privatisation] might work.'[4] MacGregor, given a free hand by Major, set about furiously trying to devise a workable model. Working chiefly with Sir Christopher Foster, a veteran adviser to ministers and a strong supporter of privatisation, the result was radical, a complete vertical separation, though the auction idea was abandoned.

PRIVATISATION

As can be seen from this short account of the background to the most radical privatisation of the railways anywhere in the world, it was a chaotic process with many fathers but none, seemingly, ready or able to claim paternity. As Professor Jon Shaw, who has studied the privatisation process, puts it: 'the decision to adopt the track authority model should not be regarded as the result of a detailed policy analysis'.[5] The Treasury had largely got what it wanted, a structure that would best enable rail competition, its Nirvana. Moreover, Major had lost out. He favoured a vertically integrated model, perhaps a return to the Big Four model that prevailed in the interwar period. He later wrote that he was 'persuaded that the safest transport industry in the country was also the most fragmented: namely, civil aviation'.[6] Major was apparently persuaded to drop his Big Four idea because he had been told that it fell foul of European rules. Tim Collins, a Conservative Party vice-chairman, later explained on BBC Radio 4's *Any Questions?* that 'separating track ownership from the responsibility of running the railway services ... was imposed by Europe rather than by the national government. What John Major wanted to do was to recreate the pre-World War Two situation, where you had four national companies who would have been responsible for the tracks and the signalling and the train services in those areas. He was not allowed to do that because of European negotiations.'[7]

This was bunkum and Major should have seen through it. Europe did indeed pass a directive, 91/440, just before Britain embarked on privatisation, which required railway infrastructure to be separated from train services as a way of encouraging competition and open-access operators. However, the separation needed only to be an accounting mechanism, so that the same access charges could be levied on all operators, but there was no need for the radical separation envisaged by MacGregor. Indeed, more than two decades later, France, Germany and several other countries still have railways where the state both owns the infrastructure and operates the majority of train services.

There was, in fact, still time to stop what proved to be the biggest mistake of privatisation. MacGregor met Sir Bob Reid (known as Bob Reid II since there were two successive chairmen of that name), the BR chairman, and his chief executive, John Welsby, soon after the election and they argued strongly for the retention of the integrated model. They argued, too, to keep the structure of having three passenger businesses – InterCity, Network SouthEast and Regional Railways – which was widely recognised as having established BR's most productive period. The same point was made unanimously at a second meeting with the twenty-seven most senior BR managers, but all these pleas fell on deaf ears. In fact, ministers never bothered to consult with rail managers after that point. As Chris Green, who had formerly run both InterCity and Network SouthEast, recalled, 'the unique feature of rail privatisation is that the nature of the new structure was not decided by the experts working within the industry but by people from outside such as consultants, politicians and civil servants.'[8]

The result of MacGregor's hurried efforts was the thinnest of thin White Papers, just 100 paragraphs spread generously over twenty-four pages. It set out for the first time the concept of franchising – asking different operators to bid to run a specific set of services – based on the idea of minimum service levels. The White Paper seemed to allow for different structures, with, perhaps, some parts of the network remaining as integrated though in practice this never happened. There was a lack of clarity about several basic aspects of the future of the railways as it raised the possibility of future closures and did not guarantee that network benefits, such as through ticketing when changing trains and railcards for young and old, would be retained. The White Paper envisaged that a separate company (or companies) would be created to take over ownership of the track – though it never mentioned the name Railtrack – and be regulated independently.

As a result of its contradictions and confused remit, the Rail Privatisation Bill came up against concerted opposition, which continued when the sales actually started. Major, oddly, was largely absent from this debate. He left the fight to his transport secretaries, MacGregor, Brian Mawhinney, who succeeded him briefly in July 1994, and Sir George Young, who saw through the sell-off from July 1995 until the 1997 election.

Major was fortunate in that the main opponent of privatisation on the government benches, Robert Adley, the chairman of the Commons Select Committee on Transport and a knowledgeable rail enthusiast who was the author of several books on steam engines, died suddenly in May 1993 as the Bill was going through Parliament. The main parliamentary revolt over the Bill was an amendment tabled in the Lords to allow British Rail to bid for franchises, as had been implied in the White Paper. Ministers were adamant about not allowing such bids because they feared it would undermine the whole process and, indeed, result in major parts of the network not being privatised. An amendment allowing BR to bid was put forward by Lord Peyton, a former Tory transport minister, and just as it was about to pass, the government pulled a fast one by accepting the idea but delegating the final decision to the Franchising Director, the civil servant responsible for the franchising process. In the event, Roger Salmon, the first holder of the post, later barred BR from bidding and that was the end of it.

Despite the thinness of its parliamentary majority, which had started at twenty-one but was reduced over time, the government managed to get the legislation through. It was a highly complex Bill involving 132 clauses and was full of enabling powers which gave the government considerable leeway over the eventual shape of the industry. Railtrack was still not mentioned by name, for example, because the ultimate structure was still fluid. Nick Harvey, the Liberal Democrat spokesman on transport, rightly pointed out, 'it might have been preferable to have had a Bill of one clause which simply said: "The Secretary of State can do what he likes, how he likes, when he likes and where he likes." It would have had more or less the same effect.'[9] Labour promised renationalisation, with even Tony Blair, the Labour leader, intimating that he would take the railways back into public ownership, something he had no intention of doing, and this had the effect of destabilising the sales process, reducing the amounts received for, in particular, the rolling stock.

A rearguard action by British Rail insiders, who regularly leaked documents setting out plans they did not like, and attacks by opposition politicians and transport campaigners resulted in many of the hard edges of the original proposals being removed. The number of franchises, originally envisaged to be thirty-five to forty as a way of stimulating competition, was reduced to a more manageable twenty-five. There were numerous other retreats. The acceptance of railcards was mandated for the new private companies, through ticketing was to be guaranteed, ticket offices were to remain open (after a threat to close most of them), the idea of selling off stations separately was quietly dropped and, crucially, closures were to be made very difficult (and there have been none, apart from a few stubs of lines, on the network since privatisation). Fares for commuters and off-peak long-distance travellers would be regulated rather than left to the free market. The minimum service requirements for the new companies would, by and large, reflect the existing timetable.

On the other hand, a key radical development that had not been in the original proposal was pushed through by the first chairman of Railtrack, Bob Horton, and would prove to be a major mistake. He wanted the company to be privatised in order to be able to raise funds separately from government, and ministers, keen to garner a bit of cash to reduce the impact of the privatisation on Treasury coffers, eagerly acquiesced. Railtrack was sold to the public and its shares, originally priced at £3.80, soared to over £17 until reality hit the fan. An accident caused by a broken rail at Hatfield (2000) followed by what was called a collective 'nervous breakdown' of the whole system, as Railtrack managers with insufficient engineering experience imposed speed restrictions around the network, led to the company being forced into administration and effectively renationalised in 2002. Railtrack had also signed up to a deal with Virgin using new in-cab technology that would have involved dispensing with outside signals and its failure to deliver on that deal also contributed to its collapse. Privatising Railtrack, which had been carried out on Major's watch, proved to be a step too far and investors lost most of their money.

Another obstacle to the privatisation process was encountered when the Franchising Director attempted to scrap overnight sleeper services to Fort William, dubbed cleverly by the *Daily Telegraph* as the Deerstalker Express, because of heavy losses. A court case ensued and was won by protestors on a technicality, but this put paid to any hope by the government that loss-making services could be quietly shut down. No more attempts were made to impose cuts in services.

What was all this about? The Treasury wanted competition and to be rid of any public sector organisation. But what were the politicians seeking to do? The oddest section of the White Paper was how it lauded British Rail, which 'has made significant improvements in recent years. Its efficiency compares well with that of other European railways. InterCity and freight operate without subsidy.' This prompted the question of whether such radical change was really necessary if BR was doing so well? It was widely accepted among rail managers that after various fraught reorganisations and the aftershocks of the Beeching cuts (1963), BR had entered something of a golden period with a workable structure, a far more commercial approach and a healthy investment programme. Nevertheless, the Conservative government pressed on, regardless of any evidence that evolution, rather than revolution, would have served rail passengers better.

The privatisation had to be conducted rapidly as the Tories were well behind in the opinion polls and they wanted to ensure that Labour could not reverse the process. British Rail was broken up into more than 100 different companies, all of which were sold to the private sector. The twenty-five train-operating companies were sold off by the Franchising Director just in time for the election, but there were enormous initial difficulties. There was a paucity of bidders and although management buy-outs were encouraged, they had problems getting sufficiently capitalised. Of the first three franchises allocated for London, Tilbury & Southend, Great Western and South West trains, two of the original deals collapsed and the third, South West Trains, found a bidder, Stagecoach, only after desperate requests from the Department of Transport. Initial subsidies to the private companies were far greater than the amounts paid to the same train-operating units when they were part of British Rail, though the contracts were designed to ensure that the level tailed off over time. The first few deals were conducted on generous terms but over time, as more bidders came forward, the subsidies on offer were reduced and that was to cause problems, as within a couple of years several of the successful bidders found themselves in difficulties. Most of the franchises ended up in the hands of bus companies, which had emerged a decade previously out of the coach and bus deregulation and privatisation.

Railtrack was the only part that was sold to the public. The rolling stock, consisting of 11,260 coaches and locomotives, was broken up into three and sold to private investors, who leased them out to the train operators. The sale, which earned £2.65 billion, was later heavily criticised by the National Audit Office, which calculated that taxpayers lost out by £760m because of the rushed nature of the sale. British Rail Engineering was split into maintenance and renewal, broken up into thirteen units and sold to engineering companies. There was an attempt to split the main rail freight concern into three companies but eventually they were all sold, after a worldwide tour by civil servants desperate to find a suitable bidder, to the same US-owned company, Wisconsin Central, while the container traffic went to Freightliner. Other bits and pieces such as Red Star Parcels and various service companies were all sold, but several soon ended up being closed down or merged. Many aspects of British Rail were lost, such as its ability to design trains, to undertake research and to provide a strategic overview of the future investment needs of the industry.

The most damning aspect of the whole process was that the new structure was based on the fantasy that on-rail competition could be widely introduced and, worse, that ministers, and probably Major himself, who must have been told, knew that it was impossible to introduce widespread competition into the industry if the franchising model were adopted. That is because there was a basic incompatibility between franchising and open-access competition of the type envisaged by the Treasury. Franchisees needed basic assurances about the services they would provide. If an open-access competitor were allowed to cherry-pick the most profitable trains, say at rush hour, without having to run those operating off-peak, then the franchisee would require far more subsidy (or pay much less premium). In other words, there would be a high price to pay for allowing the free market to operate. There were other constraints, too, such as the lack of train paths on busy parts of the network and the impossibility of competitors being able to provide faster trains given the difficulties, on a two-track railway, for them to overtake those in front. Therefore almost as soon as the Bill was passed, the Regulator introduced rules on 'Moderation of Competition' that, with a few very limited exceptions, prevented any open-access operators from running services.

According to Jon Shaw, 'MacGregor argues that he knew on-rail competition would not work but delayed announcing this for tactical reasons.'[10] This is an extraordinary admission. In other words, the government was knowingly pursuing a policy that it knew could not deliver its stated aims and, moreover, had given the railways a structure that right from the outset was not fit for purpose. Intellectually it was an utterly dishonest and cynical exercise which promised the public a policy that could not be delivered. Overall, open-access companies such as Hull Trains and Grand Central operate around thirty trains per day, a tiny proportion of the 24,000 daily franchised services, which demonstrates that the very convoluted way the railways were broken up to enable competition was completely unnecessary.

In his book, Major offers no explanation for why he was so intent on privatising the rail industry or why a fundamentally flawed scheme was pushed through. Privatisation of the railways was covered only in general terms with a few banal classic Tory tenets about the private sector being more efficient and innovative than state-run enterprises. However, in 2008, a TV producer I was working with on a programme on rail privatisation wrote to Major about his reasons for pursuing the policy and whether, given the lack of any discussion of the whole fraught process in his autobiography, he considered it a success. Intriguingly, Major broke his silence by responding with a three-page letter which is worth quoting in some detail.[11]

He started by denying that BR was privatised for 'ideological reasons', but suggested instead that 'the impetus for privatisation was my wish to improve public service'. He 'thought British Rail was inefficient; had been inadequately funded for fifty years; was hidebound by tradition; and poorly managed'. His purpose was 'to create a better railway'. Services were, he said, in a 'calamitous state' before privatisation.

Defending the fragmented model, he said: 'initially I was in favour of a vertically-integrated rail system but persuasive arguments encouraged me to move away from that concept.' He referred to aviation and then added: 'I do not believe the British Rail monolith was the best model for the industry. These days, every part of industry is disaggregated with more specialisation, sub-contracting and flexibility than ever before.'

He then blames the failings of privatisation on the hostility of the Labour government that succeeded his premiership: 'Railtrack had ambitious plans to build new links between the lines to the North and South of London, and, of course, modernise the West Coast Main Line. However, when the Conservative government lost the 1997 election, the new privatised industry had to operate in the very hostile environment that ultimately brought about the collapse of Railtrack'. That is an extraordinary statement since, as mentioned above, Railtrack collapsed because of the fiasco after the Hatfield train crash of 2000 and its inability to deliver on the West Coast project. In a very odd series of events, Railtrack allowed itself to go into administration after failing to take up an offer from the regulator, Tom Winsor, to review its funding arrangements, effectively sealing its demise.

He justifies 'even in retrospect' the creation of the vertically separated railway on the basis that 'having one single Authority able to be held to account was the best way to ensure safety on the railways'.

Given this was written more than ten years after the process, it is surprisingly defensive and may explain his reticence on the issue. To claim that British Rail was in a parlous state does not accord with the views of impartial and academic writers such as Terry Gourvish, who wrote the definitive history of British Rail. He agrees with the view that the period from the mid-1980s to privatisation was something of a 'Golden Age' of British Rail when 'British Rail did not confine itself to managing decline' and that 'there was an authority and purpose in an integrated railway led by a strong manager.'[12] This was the result of the reorganisation of British Rail under the banner of 'Organising for Quality' under Sir Bob Reid I, which was widely regarded as a success.

The supporters of privatisation point to the fact that passenger numbers on the railways have more than doubled since privatisation and there have been high levels of investment. It has, however, been a bumpy ride, with a series of four major accidents in the early days that had their roots in the way the industry was broken up, the collapse of Railtrack and a series of ongoing difficulties with the franchising process as several went bust or threw in the towel and had to be rescued. Oddly, despite BR being barred from bidding, most franchises are now in the hands of foreign state-owned companies who have been actively encouraged to bid.

The cost base of the industry has soared, too, because of the large number of interfaces, a risk-averse culture necessitated by private-sector involvement and an ever reducing number of companies willing to bid for contracts in the industry. One of the stated reasons for privatisation was to reduce subsidy but in fact this has proved impossible and since the sell-off the level of state support has averaged well above the levels paid to British Rail. The upheavals to the industry were undoubtedly damaging and some of that legacy remains today, as witnessed by the enormous cost overruns on the Great Western electrification programme. The loss of engineering skills and the absence of an overall integrated management structure for the industry has damaged the ability of the industry to control costs and to respond to new situations. As Gourvish concludes: 'was it really worth all the trouble and risks to dismantle what the two Bob Reids erected?' Major's solution of four big regional integrated companies may well have been a far cheaper and simpler option but he did not have the will to push it through because he listened to the Treasury.

ROADS POLICY AND THE CHANNEL TUNNEL

While rail privatisation dominated the transport agenda during Major's term in No. 10, his tenure saw a shift in roads policy. Most surprisingly, perhaps, John MacGregor, who was Transport Secretary for the first two years after the 1992 election, began to consider seriously the issue of road pricing. He even travelled to Scandinavia to look at the experience of Norway where tolls had been imposed in two cities and said that the government would be examining the options. These efforts eventually came to naught. Despite a Green Paper which put forward the idea of tolling motorways and an examination of the technology of road pricing, MacGregor's brave attempt was soon squashed by the *realpolitik*, in particular the fear of the powerful motoring lobby.

Nevertheless, the Major government did move away from the big roads programme envisaged by Mrs Thatcher, and scrapped several schemes, recognising that it was impossible to build themselves out of congestion. After bitter battles over the M11 link road in east London and the Newbury by-pass, both of which were eventually built, the roads programme was reined in, partly to save money but also in recognition of the unpopularity of many schemes. In particular, it was recognised that the concept of urban motorways or expansion of conventional roads in towns and cities, was no longer feasible because of opposition and cost. The shift away from road-building was accompanied by a recognition that cycling was a form of transport that deserved government support. This marked a key shift away from previous Tory policies, which had been informed by the notion that cyclists were a hazard for car drivers and questions were raised about whether cycling should be discouraged. *A Blueprint for Cycling Policy* published in 1994 by the Department of Transport was the first time that the government recognised the needs of cyclists and the policies required to increase numbers, and marked the start of the more positive cycling policies gradually introduced since then.

The biggest transport event during the Major years was the opening of the Channel Tunnel in 1994, but there was considerable embarrassment that its only rail connection with London was by a slow, meandering line that took an hour to cover sixty miles. A plan to build a Channel Tunnel Rail Link had stalled but was eventually kick-started by the intervention of the Deputy Prime Minister, Michael Heseltine, who scrapped the original alignment that involved a tunnel under south London and replaced it with a line that crossed the Thames and ran through east London to St Pancras. It was a fortuitous decision as, when opened in 2007, it became a key component of

London's successful Olympic bid as it included a station at Stratford, the main site of the Games.

A FINAL WORD...

A final word on the railways. I met Major at a social event in 2014 in County Hall which was, bizarrely, to celebrate twenty years since the passing of the Railways Act. It gave me, at last, the opportunity to ask him why there was nothing about rail privatisation in his 2006 autobiography. He responded that there had not been sufficient time – even though it was published nine years after he left No. 10, and that the book had been getting too long which therefore meant he was unable to include it. I must say that I was not entirely convinced.

ENDNOTES

1 C. Wolmar, *On the Wrong Line: How Ideology and Incompetence Wrecked Britain's Railways* (London: Aurum, 2005), p. 50
2 *The Independent*, 29 August 1993
3 Hansard, 1990, col. 606
4 Quoted in J. Shaw, 'Designing a Method of Rail Privatisation' in R. Freeman and J. Shaw (eds.) *All Change: British Rail Privatisation* (London: McGraw Hill, 2000), p. 21
5 Shaw, 'Designing a Method of Rail Privatisation,' p. 22
6 Letter written by John Major, 15 May 2008. The full text of the letter is available in the online version of my book, *On the Wrong Line*
7 Broadcast on 13 April 2001
8 Wolmar, *On the Wrong Line*, p. 58
9 Hansard 218, cols. 156–255, 2 February 1993.
10 Shaw, 'Designing a Method of Rail Privatisation,' p. 23
11 Letter written by John Major, 15 May 2008
12 T. Gourvish, *British Rail 1974–1997: From Integration to Privatisation* (Oxford: Oxford University Press 2002), p. 444

12

SOCIAL POLICY

Ben Williams

BACKGROUND – THE THATCHER LEGACY

ON TAKING OFFICE AS British Prime Minister at the end of 1990, John Major governed in the aftermath of a powerful personality who had dominated and re-defined British politics and society during the 1980s. Margaret Thatcher's political approach had polarised opinion (including within her own Conservative Party), and in economic, cultural and social terms the UK had experienced radical transformation over the course of the decade. This was perhaps not unexpected given the fundamental Thatcherite analysis that she operated from; namely that the centre of British political gravity had moved too far to the left during the post-war era. Thatcher and her acolytes had forcefully argued that the centralised state did too much in both economic and social terms, resulting in a society where individualism was suffocated. The 1980s therefore witnessed some seismic shifts within the nature and structure of British society, with the role of the state being reduced and revamped in its scope, and which in turn entailed widespread social implications that required appropriate political responses in the ensuing years. With the pace of such dynamic change creating significant social upheaval, Major's premiership required a social policy agenda that would have to be appropriately framed in order to address these considerable social challenges.

Although John Major had been a member of the Thatcher Cabinet since mid-1987, his ascent to 10 Downing Street offered the prospect of a revised and refreshed approach to policy-making within a number of policy spheres, and this appeared to be a primary motive for his party (with a plummeting poll rating), for ousting his predecessor. The new Prime Minister particularly and publicly expressed an enhanced degree of social awareness that was lacking in Margaret Thatcher, and in doing so he seemed more attuned to the significance of this specific policy dimension. Indeed, for all of her apparent political dominance, Thatcher had finally succumbed to a fatal Cabinet rebellion that stemmed from unpopular policies such as the poll tax, a particularly toxic issue with negative social implications that she had appeared immune to. Thatcher's brutal removal ultimately reflected the deep-rooted tensions that existed at the upper echelons of the Conservative Party, particularly relating to an 'awareness' of and 'empathy' regarding various social issues and the evolution of appropriate social policy in response. Within this context, the new premier was keen to avoid a similarly confrontational scenario both when dealing with senior colleagues, as well as devising less contentious and more consensual and inclusive policies in practical terms.

This chapter will ultimately seek to assess and analyse just how much the transition from Thatcher to Major altered the Conservative Party's social policy agenda, to what extent and with what success the Major administration tackled the often troublesome Thatcherite social legacy with its own distinct policies, and to what degree there was continuity or change within social policy in the process. It will ultimately seek to offer concluding judgements as to how effective the Major regime was within this policy sphere, both in the long and short term.

A NEW APPROACH TO SOCIAL POLICY?

How extensive Major's 'new approach' to social policy was in terms of both style and substance has been open to question given his close involvement with the previous regime, but some specific political objectives did progressively materialise. With a more unifying persona than his predecessor, Major developed his own style of premiership, featuring an inherent social emphasis and focus from the outset. Coupled with a more soothing rhetorical narrative, this contrasted with the often harsh and confrontational Thatcherite language, and indicated the potential for a more inclusive political approach that accepted how a healthy social infrastructure could enhance the workings of the modern capitalist state, with socio-economic benefits for all. Major's early consensual proclamation that he wanted to preside over a smoother social order within 'a country that was at ease with itself, a country that was confident and a country that was able and willing to build a better quality of life for all its citizens'[1] suggested a new approach to policy with potentially controversial implications, specifically if it meant diluting an often tough, economy-centric legacy which many loyalist Thatcherites sought to vigorously protect.

This more socially orientated outlook was further consolidated by Major's repeated calls for a 'classless society', which was an explicit rejection of left-wing, class-based politics, yet which also appeared to acknowledge that various social divisions and fissures had continued to fester throughout the 1980s. These had been particularly evident in some urban and traditional working-class communities, and became more visible via a series of urban riots in the country's large cities in the first years of the decade; there were also long-running industrial disputes such as the 1984–85 miners' strike, as well as the poll tax riots of 1989–90. Indeed, despite a revival of the concept 'social mobility' during the 1980s, it was a decade when class-based divisions stubbornly remained and sporadically exploded to the surface of everyday life. A more consensual and 'classless' approach as advocated by the new Prime Minister after 1990 would therefore aim to appease rather than inflame such lingering social tensions.

Social policy was therefore an important tool at Major's disposal, and although he was a new Prime Minister, the party label had not changed and essentially the same group of politicians remained in power. Conscious that the Conservatives had been in national office for eleven and a half years when his premiership commenced, and with a general election less than two years away, Major sought to renew public interest in the party's 'brand' and appeal with innovative and popular policies. In addition to this specific challenge, he also had to address a perception that was increasingly prevalent in the more deprived parts of the country that the Conservatives were the party of the wealthy with an 'uncaring' attitude towards those from the lower income or social groups. This image was fuelled by the growing divide in income between rich and poor, rising unemployment in many northern urban inner cities, a notable growth in child poverty in particular, and an escalation of inequality as the 1980s had progressed.[2]

Consequently by the mid-1990s under John Major's stewardship, an estimated one in four people lived in poverty in the UK, compared to just one in ten in 1979, which was very much a negative element of Thatcher's legacy. By 1993, a further alarming statistic emerged that saw the growing gap between the highest and lowest salaries in the UK reach the widest levels since records began,[3] although it then stabilised and did not escalate further. As a reflection of such emerging socio-economic trends, the Conservative Party had suffered some notable electoral losses in the UK's northern industrial cities and Scotland in particular at the 1987 general election.

As someone with humble origins who had experienced a challenging upbringing in inner-city Brixton, Major was not the typical Conservative Prime Minister, and he remarked that 'my own life history was different from that of most of my predecessors at Number 10'.[4] He was subsequently keen to dispel the notion that the Conservative Party symbolised a 'social elite', and he exploited his 'ordinary' image to potent effect during the 1992 general election campaign,[5] with floating voters warming to his reassuring 'classless' tones. Major therefore seemed to epitomise aspiring social mobility, having overcome social hardship and closed the social divide through hard work, determination and without a reliance on an overbearing state. Regardless of his links to the Thatcher regime and its messy demise, he subsequently received the largest number of votes for a winning party at any post-war election (over 14 million), being returned to power in April 1992 with a healthy 7.6 per cent lead in the popular vote (although with a reduced parliamentary majority of twenty-one).

Major's 1992 electoral victory was seen as a reflection of the electorate's preference for the security and reassurance that he offered, as opposed to the uncertainties, experimentation and relative change proposed by Labour. His electoral victory was also fuelled by emerging signs of economic growth and its associated potential for renewed social stability, despite the continued existence of historically high unemployment levels (the legacy of a damaging economic recession) and underlying social discord lingering from the previous decade. In the aftermath of the Conservative Party's fourth successive election victory, Major was therefore given the opportunity of abandoning the somewhat indecisive aura of having inherited power, and could now govern with a more confident policy agenda of his own. However, the challenge of devising popular and practical policies with an enhanced social edge to bolster the validated Conservative political agenda was a tough one. From 1992 onwards the party was entering its thirteenth year in power, and Major's electoral triumph was subsequently hindered by the small parliamentary majority which would create problems in terms of implementing a distinct, emboldened and coherent social policy narrative.

THE LEGACY OF ONE NATION CONSERVATISM

John Major's early rhetoric had indicated a degree of retreat from the Thatcherite policy agenda, and instead signified the revival of a more compassionate and socially themed One Nation approach. This was a theme that Thatcher had rejected, her disdain stemming from a hostility to its perceived influence over the policy failures, high public spending and bloated social policies of the post-war 'years of consensus'. Consequently, during the 1980s various paternalistic figures were derided as 'wets' and progressively despatched from Thatcher's Cabinet line-up. Yet Major resurrected aspects of this Conservative political legacy, which had been cast into obscurity since the mid-1970s. Such internal party realignments offered an implied criticism of his high-profile predecessor, which in turn generated a significant degree of intra-party friction that would be a source of persistent instability to plague Major's premiership from its inception.

The One Nation narrative was traditionally attached to the notion of greater social unity, inclusion and cohesion, alongside more explicit empathy and compassion. These were key components of the type of Conservatism that Major sought to revive after 1990, which raised the suspicions of Thatcher loyalists who gradually doubted his commitment to their patron's cause. Despite Major being originally viewed as 'one of us' by the Thatcherites, and being their preferred choice for leader when their heroine was ousted, his apparent revisions of her social policy narrative contributed to his questionable loyalty to the Thatcher brand as the 1990s progressed. Thatcher's allies were sceptical of a return to a One Nation influenced agenda (and those that advocated it), while apparently oblivious to the evident social strains that had contributed to her downfall. Their suspicions were exacerbated by Major's otherwise constructive attempts to bring together all wings of the party, particularly with the symbolic appointment of Thatcher's principal assassin and key One Nation advocate, Michael Heseltine, to a prominent Cabinet position, and eventually the role of deputy Prime Minister.

REVIVED 'CIVIC CONSERVATISM'

There has been much subsequent academic and political debate as to what extent Major followed up his initial verbal sentiments with clear and focused policy objectives regarding social policy agenda. He had intimated his desire for increased levels of social unity and enhanced class harmony by reviving elements of Disraelian One Nation politics, yet much attention was subsequently focused on the specific and practical degree to which he sought to detach and disentangle his administration from what had gone before. Aligned with his more unifying political style, Major was consequently accused by critics of harbouring an unrealistically nostalgic attachment to a social vision of Britain that had long ago dissolved – possibly reflecting a conservative reluctance to embrace further significant social transformation – with Major instead emphasising a required period of social reconstruction and consolidation. Such sentiments were particularly evident in a speech he made in 1993 when he somewhat romantically and vaguely talked of a Britain featuring 'long shadows on county grounds, warm beer, invincible green suburbs, dog lovers and pools fillers'.[6]

Yet it can be argued that a revived and specific variant of Conservative social policy cautiously emerged during the Major premiership, linked to the ideas of David Willetts, a cerebral former political adviser to Thatcher who was elected as a Conservative MP in 1992.[7] Willetts provided an intellectual bulwark in the evolution of a more civic conservatism, and his role in attempts to refresh the party's social policy agenda was significant given his one-time Thatcherite pedigree. This reflected a growing awareness within elements of the Conservative hierarchy that the social consequences of policy-making may have been disregarded from the thematic blueprint of the New Right during the 1980s. Willetts therefore provided enhanced credibility to this emerging social agenda, which articulated an alternative model of a renewed 'civil society' that refocused on an individual's social and communal role, rather than their individualised economic primacy as elevated by Thatcherism.

This new perspective emphasised a healthier civil society, the importance of the mutual social relationship between citizens, and the nature of citizens' relationships with a number of interconnected yet separate political institutions (as opposed to the monolithic, centralised state). Such social policy goals subsequently aspired to transcend the 'years of consensus' with its often excessive state regulation and control, while also transcending the more explicit neo-liberal ethos of free-market economics that had prevailed during the 1980s. This revived attention from the political right on an appropriate combination of individual civil action, communitarian localism and the subsequent creation of a more diverse range of public service providers could be viewed as a legitimate response to the 'Third Way' an ideologically-light and fairly flexible philosophy that had been derived by the academic Anthony Giddens in 1994, and embraced by the Labour leadership of Tony Blair. This New Labour perspective simultaneously embraced concepts such as communitarianism, stake-holding and social justice from the leftist political tradition, alongside free-market 'efficiency' and economic liberalism of the political right. This was therefore the intellectual furnace under which social policy making simmered and evolved during the Major premiership.

SOCIAL POLICY DEVELOPMENT

This refined Conservative social vision consequently acknowledged the British public's affinity with 'society' and community, their need for viable and good quality public services (delivered more diversely and flexibly where possible), yet fused with the principles of choice, individualism and autonomy, and contained within a streamlined model of the state. The context of such policy evolution stemmed from a growing perception among moderate Conservatives that the primarily economic policy emphasis of the 1980s had resulted in a comparative neglect of social policy, particularly relating to Thatcher's often misquoted and exaggerated claim from 1987 that 'there is no such thing as society'. The Major administration aspired to retrieve the notion of 'society', yet also mould a less 'statist' and bureaucratic governmental approach in its wake. In acknowledging the social dimension and being willing to remedy the often adverse social consequences of Thatcherite policies, this more civic-orientated Conservatism was central to Major's attempts to distinctively define his social policy programme, despite it being difficult to wholly detach himself from what had gone before, and policy connections between the two premierships certainly lingered.

The Major government's attempts to soften and redefine the Conservatives' image within the social policy sphere occurred during the second significant recession since 1979, and consequently in the early 1990s unemployment was rising, bankruptcies and house repossessions were escalating, and unerring social tensions remained. Major's government subsequently sought to regain the political initiative by translating both new and existing theoretical influences into practical policies. While specifically new policies did emerge under Major's premiership during the first part of the 1990s, the majority were certainly formulated during the Thatcher regime. In addition to this, due to short-term internal party divisions, economic and social policy-making was often disjointed in terms of cultivating a coherent and connected vision, to the detriment of a fluent and consistent social policy message. It should ultimately be noted that the practical evolution of Major's social policy agenda would occur over a prolonged timescale that in political terms he reaped only limited benefits from.

Health

As a pivotal element of UK social policy, John Major was noted for his passionate support for the NHS during the 1992 general election campaign, namely 'what it had meant to his own family [and] supporting the principles on which it was based' as evident in his own later remarks that 'when I was young my family had depended on public services. I have never forgotten ... what the National Health Service meant to my parents, or the security it gave despite all the harsh blows life dealt them.'[8] This acknowledgement of the value of such a vital social 'safety net' arguably represented an attitude 'that Mrs Thatcher could never have achieved or have wanted to',[9] with Thatcher never as publicly enthused about the social and welfare merits of the NHS, and being more inclined to be critical of its bureaucratic and centralised image. Major himself acknowledged this and remarked that some political colleagues 'saw the NHS as an embarrassing problem, ever demanding money, not as the source of national pride it is and should be'.[10] Yet despite his own personal enthusiasm for this key area of social policy, Thatcher's legacy had created significant problems within this sphere, and its focus on reducing the range and scope of the state's public service provision led to core public services, notably the NHS, experiencing difficulties in securing the required investment under Conservative rule.

The unerring financial and practical limitations generated by the apparently unlimited demands of NHS service-users put Major's administration under almost constant pressure as it sought to reform and streamline this monolithic public institution. New Labour's dynamic social policy agenda that vigorously emerged during the mid-1990s was ultimately successful, and such 'alarmist' and ruthless New Labour campaigns as '24 hours to save the NHS' appeared to strike a chord with the wider public, many of whom perceived (rightly or wrongly) a decaying public sector and under-invested social policy sphere. This was despite the fact that there was a 3.2 per cent spending increase on the NHS during the period 1979–97,[11] yet critics claimed that such an increase was inadequate to meet growing public demand and an ageing population. This debate about NHS funding haunted the Major government as it continued with the Thatcherite 'internal market' as outlined in the NHS and Community Care Act 1990, which had the primary focus of instilling enhanced competition and choice within the organisation in order to improve both efficiency and quality of service for patients. In keeping with this theme, this legislation also established GP fundholders, with individual doctors given greater financial autonomy and encouraged to compete with each other in bidding for services for their patients from different hospitals, while also creating 'NHS Trusts', which provided further budgetary freedoms and organisational autonomy for individual hospitals within the NHS framework. This series of features meant that Major could proclaim the merits of choice, competition and efficiency as a vital means of re-energising and bolstering this often cumbersome public service, yet political opponents claimed it was a smokescreen for under-investment that compromised the quality and provision of the NHS, and that principles of the marketplace were inconsistent with the provision of genuine and universalised public healthcare.

Housing

As with other aspects of social policy, public housing was an area where Major's Conservatives sought to disentangle the control of the state and create more autonomous and individualistic policies. Following the flagship and highly successful 'Right to Buy' policy of the early 1980s, Major's administration extended this theme by further reducing the state's control over the remaining public housing stock. One such innovation was 'Housing Action Trusts' (HATs) as a consequence of the 1988 Housing Act, which came into full effect after 1990 in a selection of mainly 'run-down' urban locations. Such 'HATs' had apparently positive social motives in seeking to revive deprived inner-city areas and estates (particularly those with crumbling high-rise blocks), although a condition of such funding was to detach such areas from the control and funding of local 'big city' authorities (most of which were Labour-run). Major's government therefore desired to depict itself as the Disraelian instigator of innovative public service reform within the heart of the UK's troubled inner cities, providing targeted funding and regeneration, while investing in and then removing less desirable housing stock from direct control of the state. Small yet concentrated chunks of housing stock were therefore permanently removed from local authority remit and devolved to the control of such 'arms-length' public corporations throughout the early 1990s, being eventually taken over by housing associations, while smaller-scale housing co-operatives were also encouraged.

While concerns were highlighted about long-term funding of such projects and the reduced levels of local democratic control over them (bypassing the accountability of local councillors), this further deconstruction of the state's control over public housing built on the policy momentum of the 1980s, and paved the way for the full-blown 'stock transfer' of the remaining state housing to housing associations during New Labour's first term of office. In this policy sphere the Major administration could therefore be said to have consolidated the populism of the Thatcher regime, creating a reformulated cross-party policy consensus in the process that lingered beyond his premiership.

Welfare payments

Another prominent example of the Major government's attempt to instil greater individualism and responsibility into welfare provision was the introduction of Jobseeker's Allowance (JSA), a revamped version of unemployment benefit, which from 1996 placed more focus on jobseekers taking a more pro-active and dynamic role. In a positive sense, this welfare reform could be seen as a means of incentivising and improving employment prospects, instilling greater self-reliance in those seeking work. Yet political opponents argued that it was a further underhand means of cutting welfare costs, introducing more rigorous and negative conditionality into the benefits system, which in turn reduced the generosity and 'universality' of unemployment benefit for those with genuine need, which potentially harmed their social conditions as a result. Yet this specific welfare reform has stood the test of time to the present day, and its theme of 'conditionality' and 'value for money' infused the narrative framework around which future administrations from different parties would pitch their own welfare programmes.

Broader public service reform

As more generalised areas of public service reform, prominent policy initiatives included the 'Citizen's Charter' along with the moralistic campaign of 'Back to Basics'. The Citizen's Charter was launched in 1991 and sought to practically improve the quality, choice, transparency and variety of public services within a consumerist and decentralised narrative, with Major arguing in reformist language that the 'public sector had suffered for years because it was too secretive and too ready to cover up substandard performance'.[12] Back to Basics was a more thematic political agenda launched at the 1993 Conservative Party conference, which prioritised the maintenance of traditional values and improved educational standards across society, linked to Major's 'innermost personal beliefs'.[13] Yet both initiatives were criticised within both political and media circles as being vague, nebulous, uninspiring and practically ineffective, and fuelled allegations that the Conservatives had exhausted their ideas for social policy reinvigoration. While the pursuit of improved standards and quality were admirable aspirations, the deep-rooted challenges affecting key social issues such as healthcare, benefits, housing and broader public service reform were perhaps reflective of a creaking welfare state which lacked dynamism and which faced shortages in resources, equipment and facilities. This struck at the heart of the Conservative Party's indifferent social policy record during its prolonged period in office over eighteen years, and could be seen as a factor in its 1997 general election catastrophe.

Various long-term social problems and growing poverty levels were claimed by critics to be primarily caused by post-1979 Conservative policies, and although Major ultimately retained faith in free-market values, he often sought to soften the momentum and social impact of such policies, and this marked him out as having at least a moderately revised approach to social policy in comparison to Margaret Thatcher. Indeed, a 'Heathite' awareness of the potentially negative social implications of a significantly shrunken state saw the seemingly inexorable reductions to public spending temporarily reversed during the mid-1990s as a means of strengthening and investing in some key public services in order to cushion the blow of a painful recession and rising unemployment (see Table 1), only to be again scaled back when economic growth returned. However, such fiscal flexibility and concessions to social pressures generated the further ire of Thatcherite ideologues who still lurked within the Conservative hierarchy, in particular Peter Lilley, an ardent Thatcher acolyte who remained Major's Secretary of State for Social Security throughout the period 1992–97. This role entailed a primary interest and influence over social and welfare policy-making, and he could therefore be viewed as an unerring brake on any radical detachment from the fundamentals of Thatcher's neo-liberal settlement. Lilley also absorbed and relayed the concerns and influence of loyalist Thatcherite backbenchers who feared that Major's rhetoric and advocacy of short-term spending increases (to ostensibly address political unpopularity and social tensions) consequently created the negative potential to weaken the ideological impetus of the 1980s. The further public spending reductions as a percentage of GDP by the end of Major's rule (again see Table 1) can be seen as a clear reflection of this influence.

Table 1: Public spending trends in UK as a percentage of GDP (1975–97)[14]

Year	Public Spending as % of GDP
1975–76	49.7
1978–79	45.1
1981–82	47.7
1984–85	47.5
1987–88	41.6
1990–91	39.4
1993–94	43.0
1996–97	39.9

CONCLUSION – INEFFECTIVE OR FLEXIBLE SOCIAL REFORMER?

Although Thatcher loyalists may disagree, John Major was arguably a more effective advocate than his predecessor in practically implementing a 'marketised' and diversified range of public services and social policies. This in turn consolidated the New Right ideological principles from the 1980s, and moulded them for longer-term purpose into the 1990s and beyond. Many of Thatcher's fledgling ideas therefore came to fruition during the Major years, having been delayed during much of her premiership due to her primary focus on economic matters. Under Major's rule, privatisation and deregulation accelerated (including the flagship rail privatisation), with the volume of increasingly autonomous public bodies such as NHS Trusts and housing corporations gathering momentum, alongside various streamlined and modified social welfare benefits. This continued the New Right's narrative of a 'reduced' state, and such policies had a notable social impact on the landscape of 1990s Britain.

Major could consequently be said to have maintained the impetus of Thatcherite-driven social reform, while tempering it with a remedial awareness of potentially adverse social implications, which consequently slowed down but didn't stop ongoing inequality. This indicates a modification of Thatcherite excesses, resulting in 'a process of ideological realignment ... during the Conservative leadership of John Major',[15] although a more critical view argues that it has been difficult to identify a clear and distinct social policy theme for the Major government. Indeed, if a social policy theme existed between 1990 and 1997 'it is difficult to pick out ... partly because at the end of the Thatcher period her government passed a series of very distinctive policy measures ... which it had fallen to the Major government to implement' and that any theme as such 'was not composed by Major',[16] and such a perspective features a downgrading of Major's role.

Major placed renewed emphasis on addressing a stuttering 'social mobility', and in doing so responded to claims that the Thatcher government had marginalised specific poorer social groups and undermined core public services while radically restructuring the country's economy. Major himself later remarked that during its eighteen years in power 'the public face of the Conservative Party ... allowed itself to be seen as not caring about improving the public sector',[17] and there has been much ensuing debate as to whether his socially orientated Conservatism genuinely represented a more 'moderate' and 'compassionate' variant, whether it diluted Thatcher's core principles and rebuked her ideology, or whether he continued her radical political momentum with a modified policy agenda more suited to the 1990s. When Major's government was overwhelmingly ousted from power in May 1997, a root cause was undoubtedly the longevity of the Conservatives' time in office, yet more specific factors and their significance have been the cause of much subsequent debate; namely Major's small parliamentary majority, allegedly weak leadership, a divided party, ongoing social tensions, limited policy vision, or a combination of all of these. John Major would later claim that his government dragged Britain out of recession while also easing significant social tensions due to specific policy decisions made. Yet the delivery of economic growth alongside social policy innovation and legitimate social emancipation was a major challenge during the entire period between 1979 and 1997, and as Prime Minister for six and a half of those years, Major could ultimately claim to have consolidated and moulded this aspect of Conservative statecraft, although the period was generally viewed as a troubled and divisive one in political terms.

While some have argued that the Thatcher decade 'was a decisive one for social policy', it should be clarified that it was only after she had departed from office in 1990 that many of her 'distinctive legislative changes were placed on the statute book'.[18] Major's more emollient style subsequently presided over the final evolution of various social policy innovations, originally devised during the 1980s, and in their implementation he sought to be more attuned to the party's collective social conscience. Having recognised that the socio-economic policies of the previous decade were often perceived as being divisive and inflexible, Major sought to blunt and tweak some of the harsher and more negative social implications that such policies had potentially created (notably evident in his swift abandonment of the poll tax). He ultimately sought to mould a more stable model of society within an image of reassuring calm, perhaps an advisable strategy in the wake of the turbulent previous decade.

While this approach frustrated some of the ideological zealots keen to keep the torch of Thatcherism burning bright, Major and his allies addressed the perception and actual scenario that the New Right's political approach to the challenges of the 1980s had resulted in socio-economic inequalities becoming both more evident and indeed more tolerated within Britain, with 'civic society' diminished in the process. Consequently, by the mid-1990s 'the Conservative Party was perceived by the voters as indifferent or even hostile to public services',[19] despite Major having vigorously fought to reverse its negative image on social issues. He had certainly attempted to generate a more compassionate and empathetic dimension to social policy-making, yet the effectiveness of such efforts can be questioned by the evolution of the 1992–97 Parliament, when New Labour's vibrant social agenda gathered momentum and ruthlessly critiqued Conservative socio-economic policy fallings, significantly contributing to Major's comprehensive 1997 general election defeat. The Major administration therefore struggled to deal with the kind of society and subsequent social dynamics that Conservative policies had created during the entirety of its eighteen years in power, and in turn failed to articulate appropriate policy remedies to wholly appease the demanding public mood during the final phase of the party's prolonged time in office. Yet on a more positive note, Major's revived social focus within Conservative policy-making arguably laid the foundations for a more dynamic, pragmatic and compassionate form of social Conservatism in the long term, which emerged in later policy narratives such as 'The Big Society'. This indicated a revived, realigned and 'modernised' Conservative approach to social policy fit for the twenty-first century that showed a willingness to move on from the language and debates of the 1980s, and which was ultimately instigated during Major's period as Prime Minister.

ENDNOTES

1 John Major's statement in Downing Street after being invited to form a new government, 28 November 1990

2 See H. Young, *One of Us* (London: Macmillan, 1989), p.607: 'The Thatcher years saw the largest redistribution of income in favour of the well-off in modern economic history'.

3 Source: Institute of Fiscal Studies, *Living Standards, Poverty and Inequality in the UK: 2012* (London: Institute of Fiscal Studies, 2012), p.36 http://www.ifs.org.uk/comms/comm124.pdf

4 J. Major, *The Autobiography*, (London: Harper Collins, 1999), p. 246

5 See *John Major: The Movie*, 1992 Conservative Party general election broadcast, 18 March 1992 https://www.youtube.com/watch?v=xp94BNovsoo

6 John Major's speech to the Conservative Group for Europe on 22 April 1993 http://www.johnmajor.co.uk/page1086.html

7 See D. Willetts, *Modern Conservatism* (London: Penguin, 1992) and *Civic Conservatism* (London: The Social Market Foundation, 1994)

8 Major, *The Autobiography*, p. 246

9 H. Glennerster, 'Health and Social Policy' in D. Kavanagh and A. Seldon (eds.) *The Major Effect* (London: Macmillan, 1994), pp. 318–9

10 Major, *The Autobiography*, p. 246

11 R. Chote, R. Crawford, C. Emmerson and G. Tetlow, *'Public Spending under Labour'*, 2010 Election Briefing Note No.5, (London: Institute for Fiscal Studies, 2010), p.10 http://www.ifs.org.uk/bns/bn92.pdf

12 Major, *The Autobiography*, p. 250

13 Ibid. p. 387

14 Source: http://www.ukpublicspending.co.uk

15 T. Heppell and M. Hill, 'Ideological Typologies of Contemporary British Conservatism' *Political Studies Review*, Vol. 3 (2005), p. 353

16 Glennerster, 'Health and Social Policy', p. 318

17 Major, *The Autobiography*, p. 246

18 Glennerster, 'Health and Social Policy' p. 320

19 M. D'Ancona, 'Ditching their modernisation campaign was the Tories' worst strategic error since the poll tax', *Daily Telegraph* 30 December 2012 http://www.telegraph.co.uk/comment/columnists/matthewd_ancona/9770645/Ditching-their-modernisation-campaign-was-the-Tories-worst-strategic-error-since-the-poll-tax.html

13

SOCIAL MORALITY

Bruce Pilbeam

FROM THE STANDPOINT OF the early twenty-first century, it may seem remarkable how dramatically, and rapidly, public attitudes on a range of moral issues have changed since the last decades of the twentieth. Indeed, an inhabitant of the late twentieth century might well be shocked by the extent to which unmarried cohabitation, single-parent families, same-sex partnerships (even marriage) and, to a degree, transgender and 'gender-fluid' identities have become accepted within British society.[1]

Recognising this may also give us a very different perspective on recent political history. The Thatcher governments of the 1980s sought to alter, even reverse, the trajectory of post-war British society in a range of areas, from politics to economics to culture. Yet while the success of 'Thatcherism' in some of these is testified to by the fact that key ideas have latterly been embraced across the political spectrum (perhaps most notable, a renewed faith in free markets and market mechanisms), in others it is far less clear-cut. In the realm of social morality especially, Thatcher's efforts to promote so-called 'Victorian virtues' and a traditional family model – as seen, for example, in legislation such as Section 28 of the 1988 Local Government Act, which banned the promotion of homosexuality – tell a very different story. The sea-change in policy-making around gay rights in the twenty-first century illustrates this well: the age of consent was equalised at sixteen in 2001, Section 28 was repealed in 2003, civil partnerships for same-sex couples were introduced in 2004, and a law permitting same-sex marriages was passed in 2013 (the last occurring under a Conservative-led coalition government).

This brings us to the intervening Major era. Should this be understood as representing a continuation of the Thatcherite project – a perhaps last-ditch attempt to turn back the tide of the 'permissive society'? Or did it represent a break with the past, in which Conservatives sought to fashion a more caring, tolerant and compassionate brand of Conservatism? What will be shown in this chapter is that the evidence is in fact contradictory. However, this may be explained by the fact that the 1990s was a transitional period in British history, in which many of the previous certainties surrounding social morality were being eroded, but with no settled consensus around new ones having yet replaced them.

To begin an examination of the Major government's policies in relation to moral issues, it will be useful first to consider some of the key ideas that informed them.

BACK TO BASICS: FORWARD TO THE PAST?

If the Thatcher era may be described as a revolutionary one, the revolution it initiated remained very much incomplete by the period's end. In many areas, including social morality, practice far from fully matched the robust rhetoric, and many ideas were never translated into policy. For traditionalists, for example, measures like Section 28 represented very meagre efforts to reverse the advance of moral permissiveness. Nonetheless, a definite climate was fostered in the 1980s that prised certain social values (like individualism, self-reliance and entrepreneurialism) and disdained others (such as those of collectivism and 'alternative' lifestyles).

Yet the passing of the Thatcher era provoked a wave of self-reflection among Conservatives, including various attempts to address the criticism that the untrammelled market forces, unleashed in the 1980s, had in fact greatly damaged the social fabric, destroying communities and undermining the values that bound society together. Notions such as the social market and caring capitalism were advanced – supported, for example, by Chris Patten (Conservative Party Chairman from 1990–92). Possibly the most significant intellectual attempt to answer critics' charges was articulated by David Willetts (who also served in the Major government) in his notion of civic conservatism.[2] Willetts' vision sought to reconcile a commitment to free markets with a belief in the value of historic communities and a sense of social obligation.

After Major became Prime Minister, there was also a conscious effort to project a very different image to Thatcher's. Whereas Thatcher had been strident and combative, Major was presented as a more consensual, caring figure, a depiction that was strongly emphasised during the 1992 general election campaign. Major himself talked of building a 'genuinely classless society', which was intended to suggest a more inclusive and socially concerned Conservatism.[3] As such, many saw in Major a figure more in tune with the One Nation tradition of Conservatism, with its commitment to social unity and justice that had been marginalised during the aggressively individualistic Thatcher years and expected him to move the Conservative Party away from the harsh, 'unfeeling' policies of the recent past.

However, if an organising framework ever emerged for the Major government's social policies, it appeared to be one that went against these indications: 'Back to Basics'. The Back to Basics campaign was initiated by Major himself in a speech delivered at the 1993 Conservative Party conference. The launching of this campaign may be understood in various ways. It may have been an attempt to provide the administration with a coherent overall agenda that it had previously lacked (which might give substance to the idea of a 'Majorite' philosophy analogous to Thatcherism). Alternatively, it may be seen as an effort to redirect attention away from the government's various policy disasters (especially Black Wednesday and Britain's forced withdrawal from the ERM). Regardless, most commentators have interpreted it as a backwards-looking call for a return to traditional moral values, implying that any notion that Major's might be a more modern or compassionate form of Conservatism was simply untrue.

Before attending to the details of Major's speech, it is worth reflecting on the response that swiftly followed: widespread mockery and derision. This in itself may have represented a significant watershed moment in British politics. If there had ever been a time when the media and public would listen respectfully to politicians' exhortations to more moral behaviour, the scornful response to Major's speech seemed to confirm that this time had passed. At any rate, ever since, British politicians have proven highly wary of making speeches that might be viewed as promoting any sort of moral back to basics.

What appeared to undo Back to Basics almost from its inception was the miasma of 'sleaze' that soon engulfed the Major government. Following the campaign's launch, a succession of sex scandals involving Conservative MPs, including Tim Yeo, David Ashby and Michael Brown, was splashed across the front pages of tabloid and broadsheet newspapers alike. These were gleefully seized upon by critics as proof that the Back to Basics campaign entailed little more than rank hypocrisy. In particular, the Conservative Party's claim to being the party of traditional family values seemed completely undercut. Moreover, the later revelation by Edwina Currie in 2002 that she and Major had engaged in a four-year extramarital affair, while he was a whip in Margaret Thatcher's government, has cemented the view that Back to Basics was nothing but a sham.

Yet what precisely did Major say in his 1993 speech? In fact, the sections relating to moral issues are largely comprised of vague, even anodyne, statements. It was certainly no fire and brimstone condemnation of immorality (indeed, religion is invoked explicitly only once, in the gentle ridiculing of a speech by John Prescott) and nor did the speech offer much in the way of policy prescriptions. A key passage gives a flavour of its content and tone:

> The old values – neighbourliness, decency, courtesy – they're still alive, they're still the best of Britain ... It is time to return to those old core values, time to get back to basics, to self-discipline and respect for the law, to consideration for others, to accepting a responsibility for yourself and your family and not shuffling off on other people and the state.[4]

Certainly, some important traditional Conservative themes are touched on here: the importance of law and order, individual responsibility, and the centrality of the family. Moreover, in its rejection of statism, it would seem in keeping with the long Conservative tradition of anti-statist thinking and preference for devolving welfare and other responsibilities to what Burke called society's 'little platoons', as suggested by Thatcher's oft-misunderstood claim that 'there is no such thing as society' *(as a totality)*, or David Cameron's call for re-energising civil society via his notion of a 'Big Society'.

Yet what is also striking about Major's speech is the way it mixes the banal and uncontroversial (who does *not* believe in neighbourliness, decency or courtesy?) with largely abstract propositions. For example, responsibility to one's family is important ... but what *sort* of family? While some Conservatives were seemingly quite definite about what this should be – for example, both Michael Portillo and Peter Lilley delivered speeches at party conferences starkly condemning single mothers – Major himself offered no such concrete assertions about which family model should be privileged. Especially significant is that Major later protested that he had never intended for his speech to initiate a crusade about personal morality at all.[5]

In truth, the failure of Back to Basics to gain any real purchase was as much down to the fact that the Conservative Party was divided and confused about how far it was either right or possible to uphold absolutist positions on moral issues in the face of changing social realities as it was to the 'sleaziness' of its MPs.

Turning next to specific policies, an array of issues might be considered to fall within the domain of social morality, including abortion, euthanasia and 'obscenity'. However, it will be useful here to reflect in detail on three areas that saw significant debates and policy developments during the Major years: law and order; the family; and LGBT rights.

LAW AND ORDER: TOUGH ON CRIME, TOUGH ON CRIMINALS

One of the clearest areas in which continuity with the past can be identified is that of law and order. Indeed, a tough approach to criminal justice is one of the most obvious ways in which Major's government sought to realise a Back to Basics approach in policy-making, plainly rejecting modern or 'progressive' thinking.

Law and order had been a central component of Thatcher's attempt to reshape British society. Consequently, it was something of an embarrassment to Conservatives that crime rates had continued to rise throughout the 1980s and into the 1990s.[6] Between 1982 and 1992, there was an average annual increase of 6 per cent in the number of offences notified to the police in England and Wales. This meant that the number of offences recorded per 100,000 people rose from 6,580 in 1982 to 10,940 in 1992 (equalling 5.6 million offences in total in the latter year). Over the same period, the rate of offences cleared up by the police fell from 37 per cent in 1982 to 26 per cent in 1992.

The 1990s was also marked by various moral panics around crime, centred on the idea of an unruly and dangerous 'underclass' (a concept imported from the United States) and a renewed concern with juvenile delinquency. Anxieties crystallised around the case of James Bulger, a toddler abducted and murdered on Merseyside in 1993 by two young boys. This led to an outpouring not only of sadness and shock, but also finger-pointing. Rather than being viewed as an isolated, exceptional occurrence, it was widely portrayed as symptomatic of a debased, corrupted culture, with a whole range of targets apportioned blame, including: the rising number of single mothers and absentee fathers; the decline of family and school discipline; and the decay of traditional moral and religious values.

The difficulty for the Major government was that, unlike the Thatcher administration, which had been able to forward the argument that it was seeking to rectify years of overly soft, left-wing approaches to law and order, it succeeded eleven years of strong Conservative governance. During the 1980s, the police had enjoyed major increases in funding and manpower, while legislation had given them expanded powers and also allowed courts to pass tougher sentences. Yet crime rates had continued to rise. What neither the Thatcher nor Major governments cared to consider was that it may have been their *own* policies, principally their economic ones, that might be at the heart of the problem: by creating a more divided and unequal Britain, with unemployment and alienation especially prevalent among the young, Conservatives themselves might be culpable for the rising tide of crime.

In part, the Major government's response was to put the blame on the police. Following the 1993 Sheehy Report on the structure, remuneration and conditions of service of the police, the government considered various market-style reforms to improve its effectiveness, including performance-related pay, compulsory redundancies, fixed-term contracts and the abolition of some ranks. There were also to be cuts in allowances and pension rights, and a reduction in starting salaries. These proposals were, unsurprisingly, met with great hostility from the police, and Home Secretaries Kenneth Clarke and Michael Howard both faced concerted resistance at meetings and conferences. In the end, many of the initial proposals were dropped, but nonetheless, for the supposed party of law and order, such open tensions between the Conservative Party and the police were unprecedented and damaging.

However, at the heart of the government's approach was its policies targeting criminals. After some early flirtations with more liberal ideas in areas like prison reform, the stance that came to dominate during the Major years was a doubling down on the tough approach to crime. This was clearly signalled by Michael Howard in his speech at the 1993 Conservative Party conference, in which he set out a 27-point plan for law and order. Arguing that the 'silent majority' had become the 'angry majority', and that the balance in the criminal justice system had shifted too far in favour of the criminal, he promised to embark upon the most comprehensive programme of action ever launched against crime. As part of his effort to rally traditionalists, he (in)famously declared: 'Prison works.'

Many of the measures Howard outlined were incorporated in the 1994 Criminal Justice and Public Order Act, including the abolition of the right to silence without judges being allowed to make adverse comments about the implication of guilt, extending the Attorney General's right of appeal against lenient sentences to all serious violent and sexual offences, faster court procedures for evicting squatters, greater restrictions on hunt saboteurs, controls on 'rave' parties, the introduction of secure centres for 12–14-year-old persistent offenders, and doubling the maximum sentence in young offender institutions to two years. The 1997 Crime (Sentences) Act offered a further toughening of the law by requiring minimum sentences for certain categories of repeat offences.

Whether or not prison works, the effect of these changes was to increase the size of the prison population considerably. It rose from 44,552 in 1993 to 61,114 in 1997, an increase of 37 per cent in the space of four years.[7] However, to critics, the government's law and order measures represented a worrying extension of state power, if not outright authoritarianism. In particular, they appeared to erode many important historic rights and freedoms, such as the rights to silence and protest, as well as unfairly targeting particular groups (like young people). Others questioned the efficacy of the approach, arguing that while tougher policing and sentencing might suppress, if only temporarily, social disorder, they can never truly solve it because they do not tackle its underlying social and economic causes.

Yet this last style of criticism is also mirrored in conservative analyses, even if they reject liberal and left-wing social and economic explanations. For those who believe, as many traditional conservatives do, that social disorder is essentially the result of moral failings, a law and order strategy can never provide the ultimate solution. Arguing just so, conservative sociologist Christie Davies points out that spending more money on police and putting more people in jail may be misguided responses since, as fundamentally the problem is not amenable to conventional law and order policies: the reason most people do not commit crime, he argues, is not because they fear punishment, but because they understand that it is wrong.[8] In other words, tackling crime may require a whole-scale 'remoralisation' of society, a task that is the responsibility not only (or even mainly) of the criminal justice system, but of schools, churches and other key social institutions. One of these, of course, is the family, to which we shall turn next.

THE FAMILY: SUPPORTING OR UNDERMINING?

The Conservative Party has long proclaimed itself to be the party of the family and did so loudly during the Thatcher era. As an institution, it is important to Conservatives because it is believed to establish and maintain crucial links between generations, be a 'natural' source of values like stability, order and continuity, and act as a key mechanism for inculcating virtue.

Until recently, it would have been unnecessary even to ask the question what Conservatives mean by the family. The answer was always very simple: the traditional nuclear family, constituted by a monogamous, heterosexual married couple living with their children. Yet the assumptions behind the dominance of this model have increasingly come under scrutiny and the reality of British society has come to look decreasingly less like the preferred image of many traditional Conservatives.

The truth of this was becoming readily apparent by the 1990s.[9] In 1990, approximately 26 per cent of British households were one-person households – a figure which had more than doubled since 1961, when it was only 12 per cent. Particularly worrying for many traditionalists was that the number of lone-parent families as a proportion of the total had risen to 19 per cent, compared to only 8 per cent in 1971. In part, this reflected a (relatively small) decline in the number of marriages taking place, but even more significant was the increase in the number of divorces. There were 58,000 fewer marriages in 1989 than 1971, while over the same period divorces more than doubled to over 150,000. Similarly significant for defenders of the nuclear family, the proportion of births occurring outside of marriage had also risen sharply – from under 11 per cent in 1979 to nearly 28 per cent in 1990. With increasing levels of unmarried cohabitation as well, the proportion of people living in traditional families (those comprised of a married couple with dependent children) had fallen from 52 to 41 per cent between 1961 and 1990.

The concerns of the Major government with these developments were both ideological (the threat they posed to the predominance of the nuclear family) and financial (especially the rising cost of income support for single-parent families).

To address the 'problem' of lone-parent families, the 1991 Child Support Act was passed, a key provision of which was the creation of a new body, the Child Support Agency (CSA), which was tasked with pursuing absent fathers for child maintenance payments. This reflected Major's demand that individuals accept responsibility for their own families and not 'shuffle' it off on to the state.

However, the CSA was bedevilled by problems from the start, with subsequent reviews revealing catalogues of errors, delays and severe management shortcomings. The agency managed to weather the storms of criticism for the duration of the Major government, but continued to face them afterwards, and was finally abolished in 2013.

Yet the case of the CSA revealed more than just failings of implementation. What it also demonstrated was the conflict between economic and social concerns. Even to the extent that the CSA succeeded in saving taxpayers money, it did so by fostering divisions and enflaming conflict within some of the most fragile families in the country. Many lone parents wanted nothing to do with the errant fathers of their children – men who may have been abusive, even violent, figures in their lives – but were forced to do so by the agency. Being made to pay for their children's welfare, men whom it might have been far better to have had no connection with their biological offspring were much more likely to expect greater contact in return. Yet even in cases where fathers were not unwanted presences, pitting parents against each other over their respective financial responsibilities was hardly a recipe for creating strong or happy families.

This also illustrates another key issue. While Conservatives claim to value the family because of its independence from the state – viewing it even as a possible bulwark against state expansionism – this seems to be contradicted by their frequent reliance upon state mechanisms to support it. A successful CSA might, indeed, have been more problematic for Conservative principles, as this might suggest that families are not truly autonomous entities and do not simply flourish spontaneously, but require state agencies to prop them up.

The creation of the CSA was an idea inherited from the Thatcher government. Yet one area in which Major's government seemed to depart from his predecessor's was child benefit. This had come under increasing threat in the 1980s. Having previously risen largely in line with inflation, child benefit was frozen from 1988 to 1990; furthermore, under Thatcher, there had been much discussion about changing it from a universal to a means-tested benefit. Yet Major avowed strong support for child benefit and during his tenure it remained a universal benefit and rose again with inflation. Moreover, from 1991 onwards, a higher payment was introduced for a family's first child.

Yet in other areas, government policy was viewed with great consternation by pro-family campaigners. For example, the introduction of independent tax assessment for husbands and wives in 1990 – recognising, only some six decades after women had won equal voting rights, that married women might be separate economic actors from their husbands – and a Married Couple's Allowance that was steadily decreased in value, began the process whereby the recognition of marriage in the tax system would be finally abolished (which occurred under the following Labour government, though a very modest tax allowance for married couples was reintroduced in 2015). Moreover, the 1996 Family Law Act introduced the concept of 'no fault' divorces (on the proviso that couples participate in compulsory information meetings). This part of the Act was never implemented, but it nonetheless outraged religious and other campaigners on the grounds that it would make divorce too easy and in their view further undermine the institution of the family.

Regardless, none of the trends relating to British families identified at the beginning of this section (including rates of divorce, out-of-wedlock births and single-parent families) were reversed by the Major government and a landscape of increasingly diverse family models has continued into the twenty-first century. A useful recognition of the perhaps futility for Conservatives in continuing to fight these changes is provided by Michael Portillo, who upon losing his seat at the 1997 election appeared to undergo a Damascene conversion from hard-line Thatcherite to compassionate conservative. As the former critic of single parents wrote:

> [W]e admire those many people who are doing an excellent job raising children on their own ... Our society has changed. For good or ill, many people nowadays do not marry and yet head stable families with children. For a younger generation, in particular, old taboos have given way to less judgemental attitudes to the span of human relationships ... The Tory party is conservative and not given to political correctness. Still the party never rejects the world that is. Tolerance is a part of the Tory tradition.[10]

Whether learned through a sincere reflection on principles, or simply the rude awakening of electoral defeat, the lasting lesson of the Major era for Conservatives in relation to the family, may be that it is, indeed, impossible to reject the world as it is, however they might prefer it to be.

LGBT RIGHTS: RIGHT OR WRONG?

'Children who need to be taught to respect traditional moral values are being taught that they have an inalienable right to be gay ... All of those children are being cheated of a sound start in life – yes, cheated' Margaret Thatcher, Conservative Party conference, 9 October 1987

The 1980s may be characterised as a particularly regressive time for LGBT rights – Section 28 was the first piece of explicitly anti-gay legislation in a hundred years and the climate was far from hospitable to their furtherance in many other respects. Thatcher herself was a more ambiguous figure on LGBT issues than she is sometimes portrayed – she had, after all, voted in favour of the decriminalisation of homosexuality in 1967 and was apparently tolerant of gay people individually. Nonetheless, her statement at the 1987 Conservative Party conference quoted above indicates that she regarded gay *rights* with hostility and emphatically did not believe in their promotion.

However, the issue of LGBT rights demonstrates very clearly how the 1990s was a transitional period both for Britain and the Conservative Party. On the one hand, opposition to alternative sexual lifestyles undoubtedly remained strong within and around the Conservative Party, especially among older and more traditionalist elements. For example, in 1991, Adrian Rogers, chairman of the Conservative Family Campaign (a strongly 'pro-family' organisation that supported the Conservative Party), described homosexual relationships as 'sterile, disease-ridden and God-forsaken'.[11] Furthermore, it was still considered political suicide for a Conservative MP to admit openly to being gay (not until 2002 did Alan Duncan become the first serving Conservative MP to acknowledge that he was, though he had been an MP since 1992). Moreover, there was no suggestion that the Major government would support ideas like civil partnerships for same-sex couples, let alone marriage.

Yet on the other hand, attitudes within the party and the country were undergoing major changes. Campaign groups like Stonewall UK (established in 1989) and OutRage! (formed in 1990) became more prominent, the first gay pride events occurred in Manchester in 1990 and Brighton in 1992, and a growing number of public figures and celebrities came out as gay or revealed that they were HIV positive (including DJ and comedian Kenny Everett in 1993, who had appeared at the 1983 Conservative Party conference).

One of the most significant political developments surrounded the age of consent. In 1994, Edwina Currie introduced an amendment to the Criminal Justice and Public Order Bill to lower the age of consent for homosexual men from twenty-one to sixteen, to equalise it with the heterosexual age of consent. This was defeated, though only by fourteen votes. Instead, MPs agreed to a compromise, voting 427 to 162 in favour of lowering the age to eighteen.

While this compromise did not satisfy many gay-rights campaigners, it was nonetheless notable for a number of reasons. First, in contrast to the authoritarian measures contained in the rest of the Bill, this appeared to be a comparatively 'progressive' one. Second, many Conservatives supported the age of consent being lowered to eighteen, even if not sixteen – including John Major and other Cabinet Ministers. Third, the votes revealed a generational divide, with younger Conservative MPs proving more willing to support Currie's original amendment, thus indicating that more radical change might occur in future. For example, William Hague, a government minister at the time and future party leader, voted in favour of lowering the age to sixteen. Fourth, even many of those who opposed the move to sixteen framed their arguments in very different ways to those of the past. Michael Howard, for example, argued for lowering the age of consent only to eighteen by referring to the developmental immaturity of male adolescents – in other words, using the language (if not necessarily the full evidence) of science and reason, rather than traditional anti-gay rhetoric.[12]

All this shows that the Conservative Party was – slowly, and possibly reluctantly – changing in its attitude to non-traditional sexual lifestyles. It would be a number of years, and take a number of changes of leadership, before the point would be reached when its leader might even apologise for its own discriminatory policies, as Cameron did in 2009 in reference to Section 28. Even so, the period of the Major government indicated the beginnings of this shift, as the world around it was also shifting in its beliefs.

CONCLUSION

This has been a selective survey of some of the areas in which the policies of the Major government and social morality intersected. In truth, moral questions are not restricted to the policy areas considered here, but may arise in relation to all areas of policy-making, from economics to education to foreign policy (ones dealt with in other chapters of this book). Still, what this chapter has sought to show is that Conservatives were pulled in different directions during the Major era. While some Conservatives sought to uphold very traditional conceptions of morality and institutions like the family – which found expression, for example, in very tough stances on law and order – others began to recognise that the reality of modern Britain was changing in ways that made it increasingly difficult not to be more flexible. In particular, for a party for which winning elections and holding political power have long been major priorities, more far-sighted Conservatives began to recognise that, like it or not, if the electorate was changing in its composition and values, then the party too would have to change. Ultimately, it would take much more internal wrangling, and some years in the political wilderness (during the long era of New Labour dominance) for these developments to come to fruition in the 'modernising' era of David Cameron, but some of the seeds were sown during the Major years.

ENDNOTES

1 A useful source of information in this area is the annual British Social Attitudes Survey, http://www.natcen.ac.uk
2 D. Willetts, *Civic Conservatism* (London: Social Market Foundation, 1994)
3 *Today*, 24 November 1990
4 J. Major, 'Text of Mr Major's speech to the Conservative Party Conference in Blackpool on 8 October 1993'
5 *The Guardian*, 10 January 1994
6 Home Office, *Criminal Statistics, England and Wales 1992* (London: HMSO, 1992), pp.14–15, http://www.johnmajor.co.uk/page1096.html

7 G. Allen and N. Dempsey, *Prison Population Statistics* (London: House of Commons Library, 2015), p. 25
8 C. Davies, 'Law and Order: Back to Fundamentals', in D. Anderson and G. Frost (eds) *Hubris: The Tempting of Modern Conservatives* (London: Centre for Policy Studies, 1992)
9 Office of National Statistics, *Social Trends 22* (London: HMSO, 1992), pp. 39–45
10 M. Portillo, *The Ghost of Toryism Past: The Spirit of Conservatism Future* (London: Centre for Policy Studies, 1997), pp. 18–19
11 'Obituary: Professor Peter Campbell', *Daily Telegraph,* 15 June 2005
12 For a thorough examination of these issues see M. Waites, 'Homosexuality and the New Right: The Legacy of the 1980s for New Delineations of Homophobia', *Sociological Research Online,* 5/1 (2000), http://www.socresonline.org.uk/5/1/waites.html

14

EDUCATION POLICY

Sonia Exley

INTRODUCTION

IN EDUCATION POLICY TERMS, the period during which John Major was Prime Minister is sometimes described as being one involving simply a continuation of earlier radical Thatcherite reforms which sought to advance logics of marketisation in education. The 1988 Education Reform Act (ERA) under Margaret Thatcher has long been famed for having disrupted a previous post-World War Two settlement in England and Wales wherein education was constituted as a 'national system, locally administered' – that is, run by Local Education Authorities (LEAs) with only minimal intervention from the central state. Reforms in 1988 introduced for the first time in England and Wales not only a national curriculum with national assessment, but also greater deregulated autonomy for individual schools, with some opting out of LEA planning and control altogether.

The 1988 ERA generated great momentum for change in education, but it was also in many respects lacking in policy detail. As a result, Secretaries of State for Education under Major found themselves necessarily tasked for some years post-Thatcher with much fleshing out of more complete plans for implementing what had previously been set in train. Such a situation constrained the scope for innovation,[1] and some have questioned as a result the extent to which any obvious 'Majorite' approach to education ever existed that could be identified as being distinct from Thatcherism. Others, however, have argued that Major's approach to education *was* distinct, at least in some respects. Sometimes termed 'Thatcherism with a human face'[2] (though this may not be the most accurate summary) one can, for example, point to a growing focus under Major not only on advancing classic Thatcherite liberalisations of public services, but also on using new data and ever-more detailed technologies of 'new public management' to transform those services. Majorism in education additionally took forward changing approaches to early years education and to higher education which are frequently most associated with New Labour but which clearly pre-date the 1997 general election.

MAJOR'S INHERITANCE: THE 1988 ERA IN ENGLAND AND WALES

Margaret Thatcher as Prime Minister from 1979 to 1990 did, for most of her premiership, avoid advancing substantial reforms in the realm of education. This was perhaps predictable given the bitter experiences she had had in an earlier life as Secretary of State for Education and Science from 1970 to 1974, working in what she viewed as being an obstructive, left-wing Department for Education and Science (DES). Still, such a key domain of public services as education was never going to remain out of the policy limelight forever under Thatcher, particularly in a context of high 1980s youth unemployment and when many on the right were decrying a perceived 'crisis' in education standards following the 1960s and 1970s abolition of most academically selective 'grammar' schools.

From 1981 to 1986, it is well known that Keith Joseph, as Thatcher's second Education Secretary, laid important intellectual foundations for future neo-liberal market-based reforms in English and Welsh education. However, it was not until Kenneth Baker took over at the DES in May 1986 that plans for major legislative overhaul in education really began to move forward. The 1988 ERA in England and Wales enshrined in legislation many substantial changes to the national education landscape, including for the first time the introduction of a centrally prescribed compulsory National Curriculum that would be accompanied by national testing for children at ages seven, eleven, fourteen and sixteen. As part of seeking to 'marketise' education, the ERA: 1) placed severe restrictions on LEAs' previous power to turn down parents' consumer choices of schools; 2) forced schools to compete for parents' 'business' by ensuring funding for schools more closely followed pupils and was strongly determined by student numbers; and 3) sought to decentralise much decision-making to schools in order to foster greater school diversity. City Technology Colleges (CTCs) were, in particular, introduced as a new school type to be funded by central government but at the same time privately run and managed outside LEAs' control. Existing schools could also apply to become 'Grant Maintained' (GM), 'opting out' of LEA control and being run instead by independent boards of school governors.

A CONTINUATION OF EXISTING THEMES?

Upon becoming Prime Minister in 1990, John Major did acknowledge that his own ideas on education had not yet been 'fully worked up'.[3] With Major's attention devoted heavily to the Gulf War during the early months of his premiership, in this period some initial policy on education was necessarily developed by staff within the No. 10 Policy Unit. By 1990, however, challenges arising from previous 'hasty' elements of the 1988 ERA[4] were also becoming apparent, requiring attention and detailed ironing out. Additional fears were articulated by many on the right that previous strong momentum gained in education through the 1988 Act was now being lost in the midst of civil service implementation of the Act.

Concerns outlined above led to an early decision by Major in 1990 to retain Kenneth Clarke as Secretary of State for Education and Science. Following a period at the Department of Health in which Clarke had driven through substantial reforms, he had a reputation for taking 'tough' stances with civil servants who would obstruct planned change. Clarke had been sent to the DES initially by Thatcher to 'warm up the level of activity' following an 'exceptionally calm and inactive' period that had followed the 1988 reforms under Secretary of State John MacGregor.[5] Like Thatcher, Major viewed the DES as 'complacent and bureaucratic [with] a mania for expanding its authority and influence'[6] and along with Clarke he was concerned that the 1988 reforms were gradually being subverted. As Clarke recounts: 'It was certainly very apparent when I arrived there that they didn't want these issues discussed. They didn't like grant-maintained schools. They didn't like the CTCs. They were trying to minimise the policy.'[7]

Looking overall at Major's taking forward of the ERA over time, some strong evidence of continuity with past Thatcherism can be seen. Early in his time under Major, one of Clarke's first landmark moves as Education Secretary was to reform arrangements for sixth form and further education colleges in England and Wales, 'liberating' these from LEA control and reconstituting them as autonomous, albeit publicly owned, institutions. Such reforms did strongly echo, however, previous reforms which had already been initiated by Kenneth Baker under Thatcher (again part of the 1988 ERA), wherein polytechnic colleges had been removed from LEA control. Later on, under John Patten as Education Secretary from April 1992, it may be viewed as innovative that a new Funding Agency for Schools (FAS) as set up following the 1993 Education Act. This agency was intended to constitute a channel for funding flowing from central government to GM schools, allowing for the first time a full bypassing of LEA bureaucracy.[8] FAS was also intended to plan, promote and monitor numbers of GM schools, but arguably all of these functions constituted little more than a simple and necessary streamlining of processes for increasing GM school numbers – these were, after all, always intended to be expanded over time and to be run without LEA involvement.

Under Major and all of his education secretaries – Clarke, Patten and Gillian Shephard, who took over from Patten in July 1994 – improving vocational training and education was consistently stated as being a key government priority. In 1991, training credits for school leavers and new educational qualifications – General National Vocational Qualifications (GNVQs) – were introduced following the White Paper 'Education and Training for the 21st Century'. In July 1995, under Shephard as Education Secretary, the Department for Education merged with the Department of Employment, creating the Department for Education and Employment (DfEE) and facilitating, in Shephard's view, a new and more streamlined approach to 14–19-year-old's education and training.[9] Here, it must be noted, however, that concerns about improving vocational education had long been prominent within Conservative education policy. During the early 1980s under Thatcher, Keith Joseph had been strongly influenced by unfavourable comparisons between British vocational education standards and those in countries such as Germany and Japan,[10] and vocational education emerged strongly as a theme in his 1985 White Paper 'Better Schools'. During the early 1980s, Kenneth Baker (then Minister of Industry and Information Technology) had under Thatcher been involved with both the DES and the Manpower Services Commission in setting up the £100 million Technical and Vocational Education Initiative (TVEI).[11] This influenced Baker's later ideas for CTCs, which, in keeping with their name, had a particular curricular focus on technology and on vocational skills.

Ministerial attacks on the 'education establishment' under Major – including teachers and their unions, those employing teachers in LEAs and those training teachers in universities – indicated clear continued commitment after 1990 to removing power from what were perceived as vested 'producer interests'. In 1991, under Clarke as Education Secretary, concerns became strong that Her Majesty's Inspectorate (HMI) of Schools, then an in-house part of DES, was not only carrying out insufficient numbers of school inspections but was also too close and sympathetic to the views and experiences of teachers. Such developments led Clarke to set up in 1992 a new independent inspecting body – the Office for Standards in Education (OFSTED) – that would be based outside of DES and would regularly inspect all schools in England (also LEAs after the 1996 School Inspections Act). John Major is known to have been personally strongly in favour of creating a new independent inspectorate in light of his misgivings about the DES. He lent political weight to the reform process, instructing Clarke to keep him involved throughout: 'Whitehall has a tendency to lapse into cosy relationships with the representatives of public service providers.'[12]

In the eyes of both Major and Clarke, the need for greater numbers of school inspections seemed particularly pressing given reports[13] of 'dogmatic' elements of 1960s left-wing progressivism believed still to be strongly prevalent in education. Many schools, LEA officials and other education experts were believed to be more devoted to such progressivism than they were to teaching 'the basics', and of course going 'Back to Basics' later became a key political slogan under Major. In 1991, intervening directly in new National Curriculum requirements that were being developed by experts in both history and geography, Clarke challenged such progressivism head on, removing 'quasi-political' content and issues he perceived to be 'current affairs'.[14] Under John Patten after 1992, guidelines were circulated to teachers indicating how sex education ought to be taught – ultimately with a greater focus on the importance of self-restraint, marriage, loyalty and fidelity. Patten even clashed with Conservative Department of Health Ministers over his idea that teachers should face criminal charges where they advised under-16s on contraception.[15] The above contributed further to a growing climate of traditionalism wherein Section 28 of the 1988 Local Government Act had already banned 'promotion' of 'the teaching in any maintained school of the acceptability of homosexuality as a pretended family relationship'.

Teacher training was viewed as being particularly ripe for reform as Ministers sought to tackle progressivism being taught to teachers 'at source' in university departments of education. The 1994 establishment of the Teacher Training Agency marked a very significant government policy turn – still evident today in England and Wales – towards there being more diverse routes into teaching through more workplace-centred training programmes, involving less time spent in universities and indeed minimum numbers of hours to be spent in schools.

University departments of education had, however, long been treated with deep suspicion and distrust among thinkers of the New Right, given the left-wing political views held by many inside such departments. Calls for the reform of teacher training in the name of educational standards in England and Wales began as early as the late-1970s in publications such as the 'Black Papers' and others from influential think tanks such as the Adam Smith Institute, the Hillgate Group, the Centre for Policy Studies and the Institute of Economic Affairs.[16] During his time as Education Secretary and while reforming HMI, Kenneth Clarke is said to have been particularly keen to find favour with 'No Turning Back' Thatcherite MPs[17] who within education had long been focused on removing powers from 'untrustworthy' teachers, scholars and heads of LEAs. Indeed, concerns about these groups allegedly undermining educational quality had above all else driven the initial (right-wing) case for introducing a National Curriculum.

Regarding the National Curriculum, another noteworthy development suggesting continuity with Thatcherism came in 1991 when Clarke sought replacement leaders for two key positions at the 'commanding heights of curriculum reform'.[18] David Pascall replaced Duncan Graham as head of the National Curriculum Council (NCC) and Brian Griffiths replaced Phillip Halsey as head of the School Examinations and Assessment Council (SEAC). Both new heads had strong past connections to Thatcher – Pascall had previously served in the No. 10 Policy Unit from 1982–84 and Griffiths had been Thatcher's Chief Policy Adviser. It should also be noted, however, that as early as 1993, NCC and SEAC merged to form the School Curriculum and Assessment Authority (SCAA) under the more moderate leadership of Ron Dearing. Still, one can additionally argue that eventual streamlining and 'slimming down' of the National Curriculum and its associated tests which happened under Major – though well-received by many working in education due to how overloaded and cumbersome both had become[19] – did at the same time speak to Thatcher's original neo-liberal view on a National Curriculum, namely that it ought to be parsimonious in its content.[20]

THATCHERISM WITH A HUMAN FACE?

Though many clear continuities with Thatcherism can be seen in the above, one can also argue that 'Majorism' in education was not simply a wholesale continuation of all that had gone before. In his 1999 autobiography, Major was critical of the 'conventional view of the right' during the 1980s and 1990s which suggested that public services could only ever truly be improved through contracting out of service delivery to the private sector. Although strongly in favour of many privatisations in key national areas of activity such as rail and coal mining, looking back on his time as Prime Minister, Major has argued that schools – along with hospitals – were always an area of public services he had 'no intention of permitting to be privatised'.

The extent to which the above denotes 'Thatcherism with a human face', however, or even an accurate depiction of Major's accomplishments in education, can also be considered doubtful. By the time Major left power in 1997:

- The government was in the process of doubling the size of the Assisted Places Scheme in Britain which (albeit later abolished under Labour) provided subsidies for children from less affluent backgrounds to attend private schools;
- Fifteen privately run and (to a small degree) privately funded CTCs had been set up in England, providing a key model for later 'Academies' under New Labour;

- More than 1,100 schools had opted out of LEA planning and control to become GM schools.

Although GM schools were classified as being state schools, they were nevertheless run and managed by independent boards of school governors. With regard to expansion of GM school numbers, Major did assert a need for caution here relative to Clarke (who wanted all schools to become GM, but was stalled by Major arguing that this would be 'too far ahead of public opinion').[21] However, it is also worth noting that scepticism over uncontrolled privatisation did not under Major translate into any corresponding strong increase in state spending on schools. Levels of public spending on education in England and Wales as a proportion of GDP during the early 1990s were lower than they had been even in the early 1980s, and Major's time as Prime Minister was also a period where class sizes were both large and growing at the same time as they were decreasing in other European countries.[22]

EVOLVING TECHNOLOGIES OF 'NEW PUBLIC MANAGEMENT'

Still, it nevertheless also seems inaccurate to argue, simply due to the enormity of changes introduced in 1988 in English and Welsh education, that Major's time as Prime Minister did not leave a distinctive stamp on this area of public services that might be termed 'Majorite'. The 1993 Education Act under Major is often described as being simply part of a bigger package that included and was somehow always in the shadow of the 1988 ERA. However, it was also twice the length of its predecessor[23] and although Scott has described Major's interest in education as simply being 'dutiful but distant',[24] Major himself has stated that education was always central to his vision for a 'classless society' and Seldon[25] has reinforced this view.

Major's approach to education might accurately be discerned from Thatcher's as being one which placed markedly greater emphasis than

Thatcher ever did on gaining value for money in the public sector through means such as performance monitoring, measurement and management. 'New public management' techniques were utilised for the first time in education under Major that went far beyond simple Thatcherite marketisation in the form of, for example, parental choice policies and the creation of schools outside LEA control. Growing performance management for education professionals under Major was made possible in particular by the fact that national testing (albeit instigated under Thatcher) had begun by the early 1990s to create an 'information revolution' in new types of data which were becoming available. Such data showed how well or otherwise school pupils were performing in national exams and they led to judgements (however fair or unfair) about the success or otherwise of particular schools.

Under Major's 1991 Citizen's Charter programme, new complaints procedures were introduced for users of public services, alongside 'Chartermark' awards and honours for public servants and an Office of Public Service and Science, set up to oversee the Charter Programme. All of this was intended both to reward and incentivise good public service provision in education and beyond. Within education specifically, a 1992 Parent's Charter was created, leading not only to further promotion of consumer empowerment for parents in their choosing of schools, but also a series of written promises and benchmark standards that families could expect to be upheld, with providers of education penalised – and compensation provided – where standards were not upheld.

Benchmark standards, rewards and sanctions as described above reflect in part what Le Grand has described as 'command and control' accountability in public services. Such moves in education did in many senses begin under Thatcher with the basic introduction of a National Curriculum and indeed plans for national testing to ensure teachers delivered that curriculum. However, following on from this, it was under Major that state school teachers in England and Wales became for the first time formally subject to regular appraisals (not to mention regular school inspections – see above). Under Major a Pay Review Body was set up to examine teacher pay, recommending that 'heads and governors should use appraisal information for promotions and pay increases', and here we can see the beginnings of performance-related pay in education. Such a move was strongly opposed by the National Union of Teachers during the 1990s, but it was nevertheless 'taken up enthusiastically by the Labour government at the end of the decade'.[26]

The 1993 Education Act furthermore stipulated that performance tables of school examination results and pupil attendance should be made publicly available. 'League tables' of school performance quickly gained a reputation among education professionals as having strong disciplinary effects on schools, 'naming and shaming' poorly performing institutions. Part of the effect on schools stemmed from Major's specific intention that parents should have access to performance tables. As a result, these were published in local and national newspapers, allowing data supplied to inform families' decisions on which schools they did – and did not – want their children to attend. Discipline was also felt through the 1993 creation of Education Associations – bodies set up to intervene in the management of schools wherever these were deemed to be 'failing' relative to specified targets for improvement. Where schools did not perform adequately, measures became permitted such as the removal of schools from LEA control (i.e. conversion to GM status).

John Patten has described the publication of school performance tables under Major as being 'the single most important post-war innovation' in education.[27] Trends towards published league tables and the use of these to manage performance in education under Major were originally opposed by the Labour Party.[28] But they ultimately became part of New Labour's focus on 'school effectiveness' and on 'standards not structures' in education after 1997 (albeit in a context of data evolving under Labour to include ever-more sophisticated measures of such effectiveness). Intervention in 'failing' schools to remove these from local government control can be seen very clearly today, for example in the 2016 Education and Inspections Act which has granted central government the power to convert 'coasting' schools into Academies.

FOSTERING CURRICULAR DIVERSITY BETWEEN SCHOOLS

Development of 'specialist schools' in English education – typically associated with successive Labour administrations from 1997 to 2010 – also began under John Major. Broad proposals for creating diverse state secondary schools with different sorts of curricular specialisms in order to boost parents' consumer choice had been mooted as early as 1981 by Parliamentary Under-Secretary Rhodes Boyson[29] and during the late-1980s CTCs clearly also had a 'Technology' curricular focus. However, under Major from 1990 onwards, owing to what many viewed as a failing CTC initiative (with only fifteen ever opened due to unforeseen levels of public spending required on each school), political pressure grew over time for Major to produce a more Treasury-friendly version of 'schools that specialise'. [30] In 1991, Kenneth Clarke announced a 'Technology Schools Initiative' (TSI) that would allow all GM schools to bid for extra funding in order to develop a curricular focus on technology. By 1993, TSI had funded specialisms in 220 schools[31] and had been extended so that LEA-maintained schools could also apply. From 1992, John Patten as Education Secretary developed a parallel 'Technology Colleges' programme which would give schools extra funding provided they raised a certain sum (at that point £100,000) in private sponsorship and developed a detailed three-year curriculum plan. Here was born the basic model of specialist schooling that under Labour would eventually incorporate almost 90 per cent of all secondaries in England. In 1994, specialist 'Language Colleges' and 'Sports Colleges' were announced, and in 1996 specialist 'Arts Colleges' were also announced. Specialist schools under Major were initially only open to GM schools, but in 1994 Education Secretary Gillian Shephard announced that the programme would, like TSI, be opened up so that LEA-maintained schools would also be able to bid.

Under Conservative rule the specialist schools programme in England reached approximately 250 schools. This formed a clear basis for a later New Labour decision to expand numbers of specialist schools rapidly, despite the Labour position on school choice and diversity prior to 1997 being described by Shephard as 'divided, muddled and chaotic'.[32] One key aspect of specialist schooling on which the Conservatives and Labour *might* have diverged regarded the role that academic selection ought to play. Traditional Conservatives during the 1990s had long been supporters of a past system of grammar education, which allocated pupils to differing schools on the basis of ability (and indeed during the mid-1990s Major additionally sought to reintroduce a 'grammar school in every town'). Corresponding with such support for selection, the early-1990s Conservative approach to specialist schooling included a provision that these schools could select small proportions of their students based on subject-specific 'aptitudes'. In 1996, plans were even unveiled by Shephard that, had the Conservatives won the 1997 general election, would have allowed all LEA schools to select 20 per cent of their students by either aptitude or general ability, with specialist schools selecting 30 per cent and GM schools up to 50 per cent. Labour in the mid-1990s was, by contrast, a party wherein many were strongly opposed to academic selection in schools. However, even on this issue, after 1997 it was announced that specialist schools would still be permitted to select 10 per cent of their student intakes based on aptitude.

A CHANGING APPROACH TO EARLY CHILDHOOD EDUCATION AND CARE

Under Major, one other key commitment from 1994 onwards was the goal of a universal entitlement to nursery education for all four-year-olds by 1997, with entitlement to be extended to three-year-olds thereafter, replacing a previous patchy and discretionary national early years landscape. Despite a 'ferocious battle' over resources with the Treasury and even a battle with parts of the Department for Education which 'did not see nurseries as a central priority',[33] under Gillian Shephard the 1996 Nursery Education and Grant-Maintained Schools Act in England and Wales led to a 1997 national roll-out of 'nursery vouchers' – £1,100 for families to spend either on public nurseries or on private nursery provision.

Although in 1998 the Labour government abolished nursery vouchers as part of its National Childcare Strategy, replacing these with a 'quasi-voucher' system that it was believed would promote better access to more affordable, quality provision, it is important to note that initial nursery vouchers under Major and Shephard 'set a precedent in relation to pre-school education as an entitlement.'[34] In the words of Major, 'we let some indestructible genies out of the bottle'.

INCREASING NUMBERS IN HIGHER EDUCATION

The early 1990s under Major was additionally a highly significant period in terms of being one in which access to higher education in Britain became a growing government priority and so began to expand a great deal. Though proportions of young people entering university after leaving school had grown under Thatcher – and indeed they had been rising gradually ever since the 1960s – under Major the proportion of those aged seventeen to thirty going to university rose from approximately one-fifth to one-third in just six years. 'One in three' was a target Major had set upon becoming Prime Minister and his goal was to achieve this by the year 2000 but the target was met some time before this.[35] Much higher education expansion stemmed from the 1992 Further and Higher Education Act, which abolished a historic 'binary divide' in Britain between traditional universities and polytechnic colleges, allowing the latter to apply for degree-awarding university status.

The introduction of tuition fees in UK higher education funding is a measure perhaps most often associated with New Labour and the 1998 Teaching and Higher Education Act. However, the background context to the 1997 Dearing Report, which formally recommended 'cost-sharing' in higher education between students and the government, was produced under Major. As a result of 'massification' in higher education and rising student numbers in the UK throughout the 1990s (coupled with public spending on higher education not keeping pace with those rising numbers), average per capita funding for students in universities also fell significantly during this period. Such deficits left universities 'beset with funding crises'.[36] It led to a hiatus in university expansion and ultimately caused Gillian Shephard in May 1996 to establish a National Committee of Inquiry into Higher Education.

CONCLUSION

Had Margaret Thatcher stayed in power after 1990, it is entirely possible that many or even most developments which took place in education under John Major would have happened anyway. History did, however, take a different course, and while a large number of detailed reforms building on initial neo-liberal marketisation of education under Thatcher may have been discussed and even planned while the 'Iron Lady' was still Prime Minister, in the event it is a reality that many did not come into being until they were later made to do so by John Major and his three successive Secretaries of State for Education.

Kenneth Baker himself, though the famed instigator of the 1988 ERA, has acknowledged a simple truth in politics that 'ministers are usually faced with the task of implementing what their predecessors have set in motion'.[37] With this in mind, it seems pertinent in particular to conclude by acknowledging a clear influence of the Major years in education on later agendas that were taken up and driven forward by New Labour, albeit in a context of subsequently higher public spending. If we are to avoid the term 'Majorism' in education, then should we also avoid the term 'Blairism'?

ENDNOTES

1 A. Seldon, *Major: A Political Life* (London: Phoenix, 1998), p. 184

2 K. Clarke, *Kind of Blue* (London: Pan Macmillan, 2016), p. 254

3 Seldon, *Major. A Political Life*, p. 185
4 See for example B. Simon, *Education and the Social Order: 1940–1990* (London: Lawrence and Wishart, 1991)
5 Clarke, *Kind of Blue*, p. 263
6 Major, *The Autobiography*, p. 249
7 Interview with Ken Clarke by Brian Sherratt, in P. Ribbins, B. Sherratt (eds), *Radical Educational Policies and Conservative Secretaries of State* (London: Cassell, 1997), p. 165
8 Although GM schools were always intended to be independent from LEAs, they continued to receive funding via LEAs until the creation of the FAS.
9 Interview with Gillian Shephard by Brian Sherratt, in Ribbins and Sherratt (eds) *Radical Educational Policies and Conservative Secretaries of State*, p. 212
10 See for example S. Prais and K. Wagner, 'Some Practical Aspects of Human Capital Investment: Training Standards in Five Occupations in Britain and Germany', *National Institute Economic Review*, 112 (1983) pp. 53–76
11 K. Baker, *The Turbulent Years: My Life in Politics* (London: Faber and Faber, 1993)
12 Major, *The Autobiography*, p. 262
13 See for example: R. Alexander, J. Rose and C. Woodhead, *Curriculum Organisation and Classroom Practice in Primary Schools* (London: DES, 1992), para. 118
14 M. Balen, *Kenneth Clarke* (London: Fourth Estate, 1994), p. 219
15 P. Dorey, 'The 3 Rs - Reform, Reproach and Rancour: Education Policies under John Major' in P. Dorey (ed.), *The Major Premiership: Politics and Policies under John Major, 1990–1997* (Basingstoke: Palgrave, 1999) p. 154
16 See for example: Adam Smith Institute, *The Omega File: Education Policy* (London: ASI, 1984)
17 Balen, *Kenneth Clarke*, p. 228
18 P. Scott, 'Education Policy' in D. Kavanagh and A. Seldon (eds), *The Major Effect* (London: MacMillan, 1994), p. 339
19 This led to a 1993 teacher boycott of some national tests.
20 For details see T. Taylor, 'Movers and Shakers: High Politics and the Origins of the National Curriculum', *The Curriculum Journal*, 6/2 (1995), pp. 161–184
21 Seldon, *Major. A Political Life*, p. 186
22 Dorey, 'The 3 Rs - Reform, Reproach and Rancour', p. 163
23 Ibid. p. 149
24 Scott, 'Education Policy', p. 338
25 Seldon, *Major. A Political Life*
26 S. Tomlinson, *Education in a Post-Welfare Society* (Maidenhead: Open University Press, 2011), p. 66
27 Interview with John Patten by Brian Sherratt, in Ribbins and Sherratt (eds), *Radical Educational Policies and Conservative Secretaries of State*, p. 195
28 Major, *The Autobiography*, p. 255
29 E. C. Bailey, 'The Development of the City Technology College Programme: 1980s

Conservative Ideas about English Secondary Education', PhD thesis, London School of Economics and Political Science, 2016

30 S. Exley, 'Specialist Schools and the Post-Comprehensive Era in England: Promoting Diversity or Perpetuating Social Segregation?', DPhil thesis, Oxford University, 2007

31 Hansard, 4 May 1993

32 Ibid. p. 222

33 Major, *The Autobiography*, p. 399

34 A. West, 'The Pre-school Education Market in England from 1997: Quality, Availability, Affordability and Equity', *Oxford Review of Education*, 32/3 (2006), pp. 283–301

35 H. Chowdry, et al., *Widening Participation in Higher Education Using Linked Administrative Data* (London: Institute of Fiscal Studies, 2010), p. 5. See also Major, *The Autobiography*, p. 396

36 Dorey, 'The 3 Rs - Reform, Reproach and Rancour', p. 164

37 Baker, *The Turbulent Years,* p. 164

15

SPORT AND THE ARTS

Kevin Jefferys

INTRODUCTION: MAJOR'S REFLECTIONS ON SPORT AND THE ARTS

IN HIS 1999 MEMOIRS, John Major devoted a whole chapter to his strong personal interest in sport and the arts. Both, he felt, were part of the 'sinews of society', but had been neglected by politicians ahead of his assumption of the premiership in 1990. The spotlight only fell on sport when a crisis arose – he cited the football hooliganism of the 1980s as a case in point – and there 'was no one individual who could articulate a coherent and positive strategy'. The arts, Major wrote, suffered because of the 'ravaged economy' of the 1970s and remained a Cinderella service under his predecessor. Margaret Thatcher did care about the arts and heritage, he believed, but primarily for reasons of national prestige; the only thing she had in common with the liberal-left arts establishment was 'mutual disregard'. From his own perspective, state subsidies for sport and the arts were justified as being socially useful, helping to nurture talent and widen opportunities. He therefore came to power determined to tackle two perennial problems: administrative muddle and under-funding. Arts and Libraries constituted a separate government department, but lacked a minister to speak on their behalf in the Cabinet, while responsibility for sport was frequently shunted around Whitehall. 'It was a mess', Major claimed, and contributed to the difficulties of sport and the arts competing against big spending departments such as health and education in the annual scramble for exchequer funding. 'No one really fought for them', he concluded. 'In the empires of Cabinet ministers they were regarded as lightweight responsibilities, and something of an irrelevant diversion.'[1]

BACKGROUND AND AIMS OF THE CHAPTER

Major's autobiographical account contained much truth, although he arguably underplayed the extent to which important strides had been made in policy towards sport and the arts *prior* to the 1980s. In practice, both sectors, starting from a low base, had experienced steady improvements during the 1960s and 1970s before suffering a downturn in fortunes under the Thatcher governments, of which Major was a member from 1985 onwards. As far as sport was concerned, ministers traditionally stood aloof; it was widely felt that sport and politics 'did not mix'. Pressure built up, however, for state support to subsidise elite amateurs, particularly those competing for Britain in the Olympic Games, and in an age of increasing leisure time for funding to improve outdated recreational facilities such as swimming pools and athletics tracks.

Labour's Harold Wilson was the first Prime Minister to adopt a more interventionist stance towards sport.[2] He knew it was never likely to be a front-line electoral issue, but calculated that as sport grew in cultural significance with increasing exposure on television, it did no harm to his party's image to be associated with sporting endeavour; hence he sanctioned Treasury money to help ensure the organisational success of the football World Cup in 1966 and was keen to be seen holding the Jules Rimet trophy when

England famously triumphed at Wembley. It was Wilson who appointed the energetic populist Denis Howell as the first Minister for Sport in 1964, and soon after Labour established an advisory Sports Council, charged with overseeing state aid towards community as well as elite amateur sport.

The Sports Council was granted executive status by Edward Heath's Tory administration in the early 1970s, giving it greater freedom from ministerial influence in distributing a small budget annually voted on in parliament. Despite periodic bouts of retrenchment, the Council under Wilson, Heath and Callaghan provided a sense of momentum in sports development, with an annual budget that rose to over £15 million by the end of the decade. Council pump-priming for local authority capital projects was partly responsible for notable advances such as the mushrooming across the country of multi-purpose leisure centres, up in number from just twelve in 1971 to 449 in 1981. But years of steady, unspectacular progress were abruptly interrupted as a result of Thatcher's well-documented indifference towards sport. In the cost-cutting and adversarial climate of the 1980s, sections of Conservative opinion questioned the need for either a Sports Council or a Minister for Sport, advocating a return to a 1950s-style hands-off approach. After years of progress for school sport under the terms of the 1944 Education Act, ministers anxious to reduce public spending also embarked on a policy that was later held up as a symbol of Thatcher's disregard for sport: the sale of school playing fields. Some 5,000 were lost during the 1980s to new building development, and school sport went into a period of pronounced decline.[3]

A similar pattern characterised arts policy before John Major became Prime Minister. The Arts Council had a longer pedigree than the Sports Council, having been established by Royal Charter in 1946, and directed its budget towards initiatives such as ensuring the Royal Opera House in Covent Garden became the national home for opera and ballet. As with sport, Harold Wilson provided a greater sense of urgency compared with previous post-war premiers. He appointed Jennie Lee as the first Minister for the Arts, sanctioned significant increases in Arts Council funding and issued a ground-breaking White Paper, later acknowledged as 'Britain's first expression of a national cultural policy'.[4] By the end of the 1970s the Arts Council received an annual budget in excess of £80 million, the bulk of which went on subsidising professional organisations such as the Royal Opera, Royal Ballet, the Royal Shakespeare Company and several leading orchestras. A report by the Council in 1981 acknowledged that it faced perennial tensions between the rival claims of maintaining high standards while also broadening accessibility. Although (as with the Sports Council) demand for funding always outstripped supply, and hard choices had to be made, the Arts Council remained confident it worked effectively in balancing its objectives, supporting over 250 separate organisations by the end of the 1970s.[5]

Echoing sport once more, the arts faced a far more challenging environment in the 1980s. Norman St John-Stevas, Thatcher's first Minister for the Arts, announced a significant cut in the arts budget shortly after the Conservatives came to power in 1979, and in a statement later the same year said the arts world had to realise that government policy 'has decisively tilted away from the expansion of the public to the enlargement of the private sector'.[6] In the decade that followed, leading roles on the Arts Council were determined in part by the readiness of appointees to follow the agenda of the day: aiming to increase business sponsorship of the arts (following the American example, where public subsidy had been slashed under the Reagan administration); reducing grants for experimental arts; and increasing pressure on museums to raise their own funds. After the abolition of metropolitan councils in the mid-1980s, the Arts Council received what on the surface looked like a real boon: an additional £25 million to be distributed as a 'replacement fund'. But in reality this sum was less than the defunct authorities were already spending on arts provision, leaving a large shortfall in funding and placing enormous strain on regional theatres, further exacerbated when the level of replacement subsidy declined year-on-year thereafter. Insiders had cause to complain that by the 1980s Britain found itself 'very low, if not at the bottom, of the league table of public spending on the arts by major European countries'.[7]

When compared with the advances of the 1964–79 period, the neglect and under-funding of the 1980s ensured that John Major faced a troubled inheritance in sport and the arts when he entered No. 10 in 1990. To his great credit, he was to display a stronger personal commitment to these sectors than any of his post-1945 predecessors, with the possible exception of Wilson. Major's aim on taking over from Thatcher, he wrote, was to give sport and the arts 'the higher profile they deserved'.[8] During the course of his premiership, he adopted a range of strategies aimed at fulfilling this ambition. His two key innovations were the announcement of a new department of state under a minister of Cabinet rank, designed to ensure that sport and the arts had greater political salience, and the introduction of a National Lottery which – over time – produced steep and unprecedented rises in public funding, over and above the direct funding for the two sectors already in place via the Exchequer. The net result was a focus on sport and the arts not seen before under a Conservative administration, contrasting starkly with the calculated coolness of the Thatcher years. But, as this chapter will show, there were limits to what the Prime Minister could achieve. Unlike his predecessor in her mid-1980s heyday, Major lacked real authority for much of his tenure in Downing Street. Although he received retrospective plaudits for his endeavours, at the time he was often too preoccupied fighting political fires across several fronts to devote much detailed attention to sport and the arts; his enthusiasm took several years to translate into tangible results, and he left office in 1997 with many of his aspirations only partially realised.

FALSE DAWNS: THE EARLY YEARS OF MAJOR'S PREMIERSHIP

Coming to power in late 1990 with the Conservatives trailing in the opinion polls, the new Prime Minister's energies were absorbed by restoring party morale and planning for a general election that could not be long delayed. He may have been far better-disposed than Thatcher towards sport and the arts, but both would have to wait for any significant breakthrough until Major – to the surprise of many pundits – secured a fourth successive electoral victory for the Tories in April 1992. In the meantime, sport continued to occupy an uncertain place within the machinery of government. Robert Atkins, MP for South Ribble and a personal friend of Major, continued in his post as Sports Minister after Thatcher's downfall but found that his portfolio of duties was transferred from the Department of the Environment – which had long-standing links with local authority recreation – to the Department of Education and Science (DES). Atkins remained at the lowly rank of a Parliamentary Under-Secretary, and by bolstering the role of the DES (returning to administrative arrangements that existed before the late 1960s) was not welcomed by all in the sporting world. David Pickup, the lead official at the Sports Council, felt the switch was disruptive, requiring the council to adjust to working with another department of state, possessing a different culture and traditions. Longstanding concerns over funding for sport also remained unresolved in Major's first year as Prime Minister. The trend continued of Treasury increases barely keeping rise with inflation. With a grant of around £44 million, David Pickup felt prospects ahead looked bleak; the Sports Council estimated that more than £300 million was needed annually just to keep pace with the repair and modernisation of existing publicly funded facilities, leaving aside the need for building new ones.[9]

In funding terms, the Arts Minister Tim Renton, MP for Mid-Sussex, presided over more successful negotiations on behalf of the arts in the early phase of Major's premiership. The Arts Council budget rose sharply in 1991–92, though critics felt this helped primarily to make up some of the ground lost after several years of severe downward pressure.[10] With a real step change in central government subsidy not in sight, one possible means of generating large amounts of extra cash for sport and the arts that was increasingly under consideration behind the scenes was that of a National Lottery. Many other nations already used the sale of lottery tickets to direct funding towards 'good causes', and unlike his predecessor – who opposed in principle the encouragement of any form of gambling – Major regarded this as a potentially important way forward. But when he initially floated the idea of introducing a lottery in 1991, his senior colleagues raised various objections: hypothecation of tax was not the traditional British way, and one outcome was likely to be a reduction in numbers taking part in the football pools, with an unwelcome fall in duty from that source certain to follow. Fearful for the future, the football pools companies negotiated a deal with the government under which more taxable revenue was directed towards recreation and the arts, but the Sports Council's blessing for this development turned sour when Robert Atkins used it as a pretext for a real-terms cut in the Council's budget for 1992–93. For David Pickup, all this amounted to promises of 'jam tomorrow'. Council members, he reflected, had real doubts that the nation's 'political masters' would ever provide anything in the way of inspired leadership for sport.[11]

Following his election victory in 1992, albeit with a narrow majority, Major had a full parliamentary term ahead and hence a greater chance of turning his rhetorical backing for sport and the arts into something of lasting substance. The clearest indication that meaningful change was at last taking place came with the creation after the election of the Department of National Heritage (DNH). Sport and leisure were made part of the remit of the new department, along with other areas regarded as central to Britain's cultural life, such as the arts, tourism, broadcasting and museums. Some observers felt the 'heritage' tag was backward looking, but generally the establishment of the DNH was well received: a signal that sport and the arts were being taken seriously, with the Secretary of State having a permanent place at the Cabinet table. The new department began life with a budget, taking into account its many and various responsibilities, of around £1 billion; tiny in relation to total government spending, but nevertheless illustrative of the Prime Minister's determination to forge a new path.

The extent to which sport and the arts successfully raised their profile from this moment on would be crucially influenced by the ability and predilections of individual ministers, and in this respect – in the short term at least

– the omens were good. The first Secretary of State for National Heritage, David Mellor, was Chief Secretary at the Treasury at the time when Arts Council funding was sharply increased ahead of the 1992 election. He was a close ally of Major, and spoke to the Prime Minister in private conversations about plans to give his new department real political and financial clout.[12] In his public utterances Mellor was soon announcing his intention to involve himself in sport and arts policy to a degree unprecedented in senior Conservative ranks. According to Sports Council chief David Pickup, Mellor was keen to act on his party's election manifesto pledge to introduce a national lottery; the minister had one eye on distributing the 'resultant largesse'. Mellor was also sympathetic to council complaints about its recent funding settlements; the council was pleased to see its budget for 1993–94 increased by almost £2 million, to £50.6 million. This compared favourably, Pickup reflected, with the 'niggardly award a year earlier'.[13]

The possibility of a fundamentally new era of government commitment to sport and the arts was, however, soon thwarted and once more put on hold. The economic debacle of 'Black Wednesday' in September 1992 was followed by fresh, severe cutbacks in public spending. The Arts Council budget was hit hard, and the curse of frequent ministerial changes (a feature of the Thatcher era in sport and the arts) – making continuity of policy difficult – struck again with a vengeance. After only six months in post, David Mellor, dubbed by the press as the 'Minister of Fun', was forced to resign following tabloid revelations about his private life. There were to be three further Secretaries of State at the DNH during the remainder of the parliament, none of whom (as discussed further below) matched Mellor's combative evangelism on behalf of sport and the arts. Ministers for Sport also continued to be easily dispensable. Robert Atkins was succeeded after the 1992 election by Salisbury MP Robert Key, but only a year later, to the 'bemusement' of the Sports Council, David Pickup wrote, Key was replaced by Iain Sproat, MP for Harwich. Pickup described Sproat as 'the least communicative' of the many ministers he dealt with, rarely consulting with sports administrators or attending meetings of the Sports Council.[14]

The one bright spot on the horizon around this time was that royal assent was granted to the 1993 National Lottery Act, promising to bring huge amounts of additional revenue in the years that followed. From the sale of every one pound ticket in regular lottery games, nearly a third would be devoted to deserving causes, including sporting projects as well the arts and charities. Although the legislation commanded broad approval in Parliament, there was considerable press and pressure group anxiety about the working of the Lottery. Some observers were unhappy with the choice of the Camelot group, a consortium of private companies, to run the Lottery, which was finally launched in November 1994. As well as wishing to see non-profit making oversight, critics worried about how lottery priorities were determined and the confining of bids at the outset almost exclusively to capital projects. For a long time after the launch, opinion was divided between the doubters, some of whom objected simply to the prominence given to this new form of gambling, and enthusiasts such as community arts groups, theatres and local sports clubs, submitting bids in the hope of winning funding for cherished projects. Although arguments were to rumble on for several years, the National Lottery appeared to mark a decisive turning point. Surely now, after the false dawns of 1990–93, the Prime Minister would be able to really deliver on – and reap some personal benefit from – his deep desire to improve sporting and cultural opportunities.

THE IMPACT OF THE NATIONAL LOTTERY ON ARTS POLICY

The National Lottery provided a massive windfall for the arts. By the time John Major left office in 1997 – with over 30 million people buying scratch cards and one pound tickets every week – over £3.5 billion had been raised for the arts and other 'good causes'.[15] Ministers at the time sought to present the impact of the Lottery as an unalloyed success, though looking back in his memoirs Major struck a notably defensive tone when describing the months after the Lottery first came into operation. Aside from disputes over 'fat cats' – centred on higher than expected profits garnered by the Camelot directors who ran the Lottery – Major felt those responsible for distributing funds, under pressure to cope with a surge in applications, made some unfortunate decisions. The Arts Council came under particularly heavy fire for awarding £55 million towards refurbishment of the Royal Opera House, leading to claims that the Lottery was being exploited by London elites for flagship projects while arts bodies in the provinces were neglected. In statistical terms, London received less per head of the population in lottery grants for the arts than the likes of Manchester and Merseyside, and grants in excess of £1 million constituted only 3 per cent of all awards by the Arts Council. 'These facts were ignored', Major lamented, as sections of the press sought to make headlines by focusing on a small number of controversial awards.[16]

In practice, however, responsibility for the troubled early history of lottery funding lay as much with the government as it did with those who operated the franchise or dispersed the funds. One recurring theme, Major later conceded, was 'our failure to rebut' media attacks on the Lottery during 1995–96. Hemmed in on all sides by criticism of his leadership – not least by the Eurosceptic 'bastards' in his own party – the Prime Minister had little time to focus on the minutiae of arts policy, and the importance of the loss of David Mellor as a forceful champion of the arts became increasingly apparent as the parliament unfolded. Mellor's successor as Heritage Secretary, Peter Brooke, was chosen as a safe pair of hands, but according to cultural historian Robert Hewison he 'was not ambitious for himself or for his department in the way that Mellor had been'.[17] Instead of developing into a dynamic new force with real muscle, the Department of National Heritage – amidst frequent government reshuffles aimed at reviving Major's flagging fortunes – became more a staging post for ministers on their way up or down the political ladder.

Peter Brooke was replaced in July 1994 by the upwardly aspiring Stephen Dorrell, who on arriving in office conceded privately that he was not overly familiar with the issues facing the DNH. He cut an uncomfortable figure in trying to defend some of the Arts Council's funding decisions, notably the awarding of £12.5 million of lottery money to purchase Winston Churchill's archive; a development that gave further ammunition to those who claimed it was 'the few' rather than 'the many' who benefited from the Lottery. Dorrell was relieved when after only a year as Heritage Secretary he was promoted to the Health portfolio.[18] His successor, Virginia Bottomley, herself demoted from Health, became a vociferous supporter of lottery causes, though she proved unable or unwilling to defend the arts component of the DNH budget from cutbacks as a general election came closer. The Prime Minister was always insistent when questioned that the advent of large sums of lottery money would not be used as a pretext for reducing the annual Treasury grant to the Arts Council. By 1995–96 the level of exchequer revenue was its highest ever, at £191 million. But in the 1996–97 Budget allocation – with lottery money of unexpectedly high proportions now coming on stream – the Council grant was cut by £5 million, and held at that figure for 1997–98, with further reductions pledged for subsequent years. The result was that in real terms, taking into account inflation, the Arts Council grant was £25 million less at the end of the 1992 parliament than at the beginning.[19]

Another key factor explaining the mixed feelings of the arts world in the months after the introduction of the Lottery was the insistence – maintained almost to the end of the Major administration – that funding should be restricted primarily to capital projects. The logic behind this decision appeared sound enough. There was a widely held perception that Britain's cultural infrastructure of museums, galleries and concert halls was in dire need of refurbishment. It was also intended that provision for capital projects would not get mixed up with the revenue costs of those organisations supported via direct grant-aid from the Arts Council. As far as the Prime Minister was concerned, it was important to resist Treasury pressure to use the Lottery as a source of revenue for mainstream expenditure. 'The capital rule', he reflected, 'helped to ring-fence lottery funding, and to underline the principle that it would not be used to replace existing government spending', even though this principle appeared under threat by 1997.[20]

A growing fear of arts administrators was that the prioritising of physical infrastructure over everyday running costs would result in the creation of 'white elephants'. Evidence to support this case came in examples such as the Norwich Playhouse, opened late in 1995 following a £400,000 contribution from the Lottery, bolstering the £2.5 million raised from other sources. Audience figures in the early months after opening, however, were lower than projected, in line with a broader fall in numbers going to regional theatres since the recession of the early 1990s. Unable to find sufficient additional sources of revenue, the playhouse was soon struggling to meet its operational costs. By 1997 the theatre was running a large deficit and had suspended operations; there was even talk of the building being turned into a themed pub. Eventually the Norwich Playhouse was rescued by a bank loan, though it reopened in 2000 not as a producing house but as a conference hall and touring venue.[21] As complaints intensified about the tight restrictions around capital spending, Heritage Secretary Virginia Bottomley announced that experiments would be undertaken aimed at subsidising small arts groups hitherto in receipt of no funding, thereby allowing lottery money to be used for the first time to support people and organisations as well as buildings. The government's intention was to further relax the capital spending rules after the next election. But for the moment the damage had been done. Lord Gowrie, a former Tory Minister for the Arts, complained as Chairman of the Arts Council in 1996: 'we can build shining new palaces of culture … But we cannot fund what goes on inside them.'[22]

A BREAKTHROUGH FOR SPORT?

With extra revenue for sport also coming on stream via the Lottery in the mid-1990s, the Prime Minister made concerted efforts in the second half of his premiership to counter accusations that progress in this area had hitherto been spasmodic. He promoted Iain Sproat from Parliamentary Under-Secretary to the higher rank of Minister of State: the first time a Conservative Sports Minister operated at the same level as Labour's Denis Howell had for most of his tenure in the 1960s and 1970s. Major also took a close personal interest in a glossy forty-page document published by the DNH in July 1995, 'Sport: Raising the Game', the most detailed outline of Tory policy since the party came to power in 1979. In his preface, Major described school sport as the 'highest priority', implicitly acknowledging there had been problems in this area. By 1994 the weekly average of Physical Education (PE) per pupil in state secondary schools was down to one hour. Several remedial proposals were suggested in 'Raising the Game'. PE was confirmed as one of only five subjects made compulsory throughout a child's school years, and the government encouraged all schools to work towards two hours of formal lesson time per week. In order to rebuild competitive games, schools were urged to provide opportunities outside the normal curriculum. An overhaul of teacher training would ensure there were adequate numbers of suitably qualified PE teachers and action would be taken to limit the upsurge since the 1980s in the sale of school playing fields.[23]

The main emphasis in the document, aside from schools, was on improving elite performance. One idea that grabbed newspaper attention was the promise to set up a British Academy of Sport. Modelled on successful examples overseas, notably in Australia, the new academy was envisaged as somewhere that would offer numerous benefits to top Olympic athletes, including residential accommodation, scholarships and bursaries, access to state-of-the-art facilities, high-quality coaching, sports science input and medical backup. In introducing 'Raising the Game', Sproat informed MPs that the government's ambitious agenda would be backed by appropriate funding drawn from the Lottery. Since getting under way a few months earlier, 440 sports projects across Britain had already been awarded £74.26 million of lottery money, and another £100 million of such funding was earmarked for the Academy of Sport. According to the minister, the breadth of the government's proposals – aiming to allow all ages and abilities to fulfil their sporting potential – together with unprecedented levels of funding, 'combine to make this the most important day in sport in a generation'.[24]

A year or so on from publication, the jury remained out as to whether the government had successfully 'raised the game'. The Sports Minister claimed 'significant progress' had been made on many of the recommendations contained in the document. He argued that Britain was moving towards a world-class performance programme to support talented athletes competing up to Olympic and world championship levels. Secondary schools were looking to improve PE provision and a prospectus had been published inviting bids to establish the Academy of Sport. Major claimed in his memoirs that his policy unit at Downing Street was also involved; Sproat knew that in seeking to push forward he had 'my full support'.[25] While the Labour opposition voiced qualified approval, press critics were more forthright in questioning how much meaningful action had been taken. *The Guardian* journalist Simon Edge wrote that the Prime Minister's hosting of an event to announce a new class of specialist sports colleges in July 1996 was intended to 'breathe life back into the initiative, because much of it has been ignored'. *The Times* took a more balanced view. While it was agreed that school sport remained in a 'desperate' plight, the government deserved the benefit of the doubt for going ahead with 'many overdue initiatives'. For *The Times*, the evidence suggested that at least 'the corner has been turned' in sport policy.[26]

But the notion that a corner had been turned took a hard knock when – aside from contending with continuing Tory divisions over Europe and a resurgent Labour Party under Tony Blair – even the sporting gods abandoned the Prime Minister. Not long after England exited the Euro '96 football tournament on home soil, the British team at the summer Olympics in Atlanta performed well below expectations. Britain finished with only one gold medal to its name (in rowing); the final tally of fifteen medals was the nation's lowest total since 1952. Even before the athletes returned home from the USA, a finger of blame was pointed at ministers. A *Guardian* editorial claimed that no one doubted Major's genuine interest, but it remained the case that 'the reason why sport was in such a dire state was a direct responsibility of the government'. The litany of failure included the undermining of PE in schools, the sale of playing fields and the scattergun approach to lottery funding, which meant sport policy lacked strategic focus. These criticisms were mild in comparison with some of the tabloid coverage after the official medal table showed Britain finishing in its lowest ever ranking, at number thirty-six. The *Daily Mirror* spoke of 'our Olympic shame': 'We are under-funded [and] second-rate, and no amount of excuses will camouflage that.'[27]

The Prime Minister doggedly refused to back away from his agenda, despite what happened in Atlanta. He summoned the manager of the Olympic team to Downing Street to account for such a poor showing, and he insisted improvements would follow from changes underway designed to bolster elite performance. In this he was to be vindicated in the fullness of time: Team GB's level of success rose dramatically from the Sydney Olympics of 2000 onwards. But by then, of course, Major was not on the political scene to reap any reward. He went into the 1997 election campaign trailing Labour by a wide margin, and manifesto claims about 'record investment in sport' had little resonance after Atlanta, which critics depicted as a fitting symbol of the neglect of sport in the era of Tory rule since 1979. Anxious not to be outflanked on sport, as was the case at the 1992 election, New Labour promised a range of fresh initiatives, and its leader, Tony Blair, was soon in a position to shape the cultural and sporting agenda as Major's successor in Downing Street. Labour secured a thumping majority of 179 seats, and the Conservative share of the vote fell to its lowest since 1832.

CONCLUSION

When he resigned as Prime Minister in 1976, one colleague said to Harold Wilson that history 'will treat you more kindly than your contemporaries'.[28] Much the same might be said of John Major, at least in relation to sport and the arts. When Team GB performed remarkably well at the 2016 Rio

Olympics, surpassing even its London 2012 medal haul, Major was showered with belated praise. His decision to divert lottery funding to elite sport, one journalist wrote, meant he deserved the 'main credit' for British success.[29] Although such claims were exaggerated – sports history is littered with examples of governing authorities squandering large sums of money and much hinged on the ability of bodies such as UK Sport to use lottery funding effectively – they pointed to the enhanced priority Major gave to sport policy in the mid-1990s. There can be no doubt that the lion's share of responsibility for the step change that occurred after the bleakness of the Thatcher era rested with the Prime Minister. Whereas during the Labour administrations of the 1960s and 1970s Wilson tried to create a supportive environment while leaving details largely to his trusty lieutenant Denis Howell, Major was the first incumbent of No. 10 who sought to provide active and persistent encouragement for sport.

And yet, when judged from the perspective of 1997 – rather than with the rosy glow of London–Rio Olympic hindsight – the sense persists that Major promised more than he delivered. As we have seen, the early years of his premiership were characterised by frustrations and setbacks, spending on sport remained only a tiny fraction of total government expenditure, and some of his principal commitments remained rhetorical aspirations at best when he left office; the drive to rebuild school sport was a case in point. The shortcomings of Major's record on sport were partly due to bad luck. It was unfortunate for him, given his emphasis on improving competitive sport, that his term of office coincided with a phase of abject performances by several national sporting teams. England's footballers failed to qualify for the 1994 World Cup finals (sinking to a lowly twenty-third at one point in the FIFA world rankings). And at the time of the humiliation suffered at the Atlanta Olympics, England was ranked among the lowest of the test match playing nations in Major's favourite sport, cricket. He was also unlucky to lose at a critical juncture the services of David Mellor, who had the potential to emulate the role played by Howell on behalf of Wilson in ensuring sustained delivery of shared objectives. At the same time, however, the fact that the DNH did not emerge as a tenacious proponent of sporting interests after 1992 was a damning reflection of the absence of any deep-seated commitment to sport within Conservative ranks at large. The advances of the 1990s were due less to sport securing an embedded position within Whitehall than to the personal drive of the Prime Minister, whose enthusiasm was not shared by many of those around him. According to a top official quoted by Major's biographer, his Cabinet colleagues 'were variously indifferent to, amused or irritated by, his passion for sport'.[30]

As regards the arts, a similar conclusion emerges: Major set in motion changes that produced great advances in the long term, but was never able to enjoy the fruits of his labours before he departed from office. In 2015 the Arts Council proclaimed that over the course of two decades since its introduction, National Lottery funding had transformed arts and cultural opportunities: helping to restore buildings and create new ones, facilitating the touring of exhibitions, creating jobs for young people, allowing arts organisations to plan ahead with stable revenue, and providing cultural provision in areas of the country where little previously existed.[31] Yet before 1997 the picture was very different. According to Robert Hewison, the dominant narratives of the mid-1990s – media criticism of 'unfair' funding decisions and priority given to 'highbrow' projects – though misleading, contributed to making the arts less, not more, popular, providing an excuse for 'the venting of envy and crude philistinism'.[32] As with sport policy, Major was proud of what he had set in motion on behalf of the arts, but if he hoped to garner personal and political benefit from his involvement while still at No. 10 he was gravely disappointed. In the arts, as in sport, history was to prove kinder than many of his contemporaries. In 1995 Hugh Colver, having resigned after a short spell in the press department of Conservative Central Office, reflected on the bitterness of frustrated arts bodies and posed the question: 'how can you lose on a policy which created over 100 millionaires in its first year and gave £1 billion to good causes and another £1 billion to the Treasury? It is a prize example of how to turn a public relations triumph into a disaster.'[33]

ENDNOTES

1 J. Major, *The Autobiography* (London: Harper Collins, 1999), pp. 401–5
2 See K. Jefferys, 'Sport Policy: An Unheralded Success Story' in A. S. Crines and K. Hickson (eds.) *Harold Wilson: The Unprincipled Prime Minister?* (London: Biteback, 2016)
3 See K. Jefferys, *Sport and Politics in Modern Britain: The Road to 2012* (Basingstoke, Palgrave, 2012)
4 *The Guardian*: editorial, 28 March 2016
5 Memorandum submitted by the Arts Council of Great Britain to the House of Commons Select Committee on Education, Science and the Arts, 13 May 1981
6 'The Tories and the Arts', *The Observer*, 14 October 1979
7 R. Hutchinson, *The Politics of the Arts Council* (London, Sinclair Browne, 1982), p. 11. Hutchinson worked previously as a Senior Research and Information Officer at the Council. See also J. McGuigan, *Culture and the Public Sphere* (London, Routledge: 2002 edn)
8 Major, *The Autobiography*, p. 405
9 D. Pickup, *Not Another Messiah: An Account of the Sports Council, 1988–93* (Bishop Auckland: Pentland Press, 1996), pp. 65–6
10 O. Turnbull, *Bringing Down the House: The Crisis in Britain's Regional Theatres* (Chicago: University of Chicago Press, 2008), pp. 105–6
11 Pickup, *Not Another Messiah*, pp. 70–2; Major, *The Autobiography*, p. 407
12 R. Hewison, *Culture and Consensus: England, Art and Politics since 1940* (London: Methuen, 1997 edn), p. 299
13 Pickup, *Not Another Messiah*, pp. 103 and 121
14 Ibid. p. 135
15 I. Henry, *The Politics of Leisure Policy* (Basingstoke: Palgrave, 2001 edn), pp. 91–2
16 Major, *The Autobiography*, pp. 409–11
17 Hewison, *Culture and Consensus* p.304; Major, *The Autobiography* p. 411
18 A. Seldon, *Major. A Political Life* (London, Phoenix, 1997), p. 481: 'Dorrell's appointment to a department about whose work he professed to have little knowledge was not a success.'
19 Hewison, *Culture and Consensus*, pp. 301–2
20 Major, *The Autobiography*, pp. 410–11
21 Turnbull, *Bringing Down the House*, pp. 107–8
22 Cited in Hewison, *Culture and Consensus*, p. 302
23 Department of National Heritage, 'Sport: Raising the Game' (London, DNH, 1995)
24 House of Commons Debates, 6th series, vol. 263, 14 July 1995, columns 800–3
25 Major, *The Autobiography* p. 412; House of Commons Debates, vol. 285, 21 November 1996, col. 644
26 *The Guardian*, 24 July 1996; *The Times*, 25 July 1996

27 *The Guardian*, 25 July 1996; *Daily Mirror*, 5 August 1996
28 Jim Callaghan, cited in J. Haines, *The Politics of Power* (London, Jonathan Cape, 1977), p.222
29 J. Rentoul, 'John Major gave us a golden Olympics', *The Independent*, 20 August 2016
30 Seldon, *Major. A Political Life*, p.595
31 Arts Council, 'The Arts Council's response to the PLACE report' (London, Arts Council, 2015)
32 Hewison, *Culture and Consensus*, p. 303
33 Cited in Ibid. pp. 303–4

16

FOREIGN AND DEFENCE POLICY

Mark Garnett

IN FOREIGN AND DEFENCE policy there was a marked contrast between the fortunes of the two Major governments. Between Major's accession in December 1990 and the general election of April 1992, Britain enjoyed significant success in several key policy areas. Within months of that fourth consecutive Conservative win, however, the government had begun to encounter a succession of setbacks which lasted until its departure from office. As such, foreign policy could be seen as following a more general pattern for Major and his ministers. In this area more than others, the key question is whether the government was chiefly the victim of adverse circumstances, or the author of its own misfortunes.

MAJOR AND HURD

When he replaced Margaret Thatcher in December 1990, John Major became the fifth (out of ten) post-war Prime Ministers who had previously served as Foreign Secretary. However, his tenure of that office was unusual for its short duration – less than a hundred days – and it is unlikely that any of his predecessors in that role would have felt the conflicting emotions which prompted Major's response to Margaret Thatcher's offer on 24 July 1989: 'Do you think it is a good idea?'[1]

Major had several personal and political reasons for answering his own question in the negative. He had no professional experience in foreign policy, and the process of adaptation would be demanding. Also, apart from marking Major as Thatcher's anointed heir – not a position which he coveted – his appointment was bound to be interpreted as an attempt by the Prime Minister to foist a compliant character on the Foreign and Commonwealth Office (FCO). The only explanation for her brutal ejection of Major's predecessor, Sir Geoffrey Howe, was the latter's insistence on retaining some autonomous thoughts and (on occasion) allowing his diplomatic conduct to betray traces of that sorely tried independence. Thatcher had responded by pursuing a foreign policy line of her own, aided by her special adviser Charles Powell. By July 1989 she had tired of bypassing the FCO, and decided to deal with the problem more directly by consigning the department to a creature of her own making.[2]

The plan backfired, and can be seen as the opening chapter in the story of Mrs Thatcher's downfall. Demotion from the FCO was a bitter blow to the benign Howe, who avenged himself in November 1990 with a resignation speech which invited his colleagues to topple the Prime Minister. By that time, Howe's ally, the Chancellor Nigel Lawson – irritated beyond endurance by the unseasonal intrusions of the Prime Minister's eccentric economic adviser, Sir Alan Walters – had left the government. His resignation, in October 1989, created a vacancy at the Treasury which was filled by the peripatetic John Major.

The miscalculations inherent in the 1989 reshuffle included a false assessment of Major. Far from being wholly committed to a continuation of Thatcher's legacy in foreign (and domestic) policy, the new crown prince was a pragmatist rather than an ideological crusader. His short spell as Foreign Secretary had done nothing to increase his confidence in Thatcher's judgement; and, by augmenting his ministerial CV, it made him a more plausible candidate to succeed her as 'his own man' rather than depending unduly on her endorsement.

Although Major was impatient with some elements of the ritual and routine of the FCO, he was beginning to enjoy his job when he was asked to leave it and resented the fact that he was moved before he could 'make any mark on policy, or to leave any lasting legacy'. At least he could feel that Thatcher had chosen the most suitable person to replace him.[3] Douglas Hurd had joined the Diplomatic Service in 1952, and had worked as a junior FCO minister in Mrs Thatcher's first term; the fact that Major, rather than Hurd, had been offered Geoffrey Howe's job was eloquent testimony to her suspicion both of the FCO and of Hurd himself, who had been an aide to the hated Edward Heath. Despite their contrasting social backgrounds – Hurd was the product of a relatively prosperous political family, and had been educated at Eton and Oxford – he and Major enjoyed a very good personal and professional relationship, which was cemented rather than soured by their rival campaigns to succeed Mrs Thatcher as Prime Minister. This is not to say that Hurd and Major agreed on everything, but at least between 1990 and 1995, when the former left office, the FCO and Downing Street were no longer in open conflict.

THATCHER'S LEGACY

In an adversarial system like Britain's, fundamental appraisals of foreign policy can be expected when the governing party changes, rather than when the incumbent Prime Minister is replaced by one of her or his colleagues. However, the circumstances of December 1990 suggested that a searching review would be helpful. While the poll tax and Europe were the issues which brought Thatcher down, foreign policy was another serious source of unease among those Conservative MPs who had not surrendered their judgement to media myth-making.

Back in 1987, Thatcher's government had showcased its foreign policy achievements in an election manifesto which boasted that 'from the White House through Europe to the Kremlin our voice is heard'.[4] Thatcher had certainly performed an unprecedented feat in the 1983–87 period, by adding an excellent personal rapport with a Soviet leader to her long-established amity with the US President, Ronald Reagan. Unfortunately for Thatcher, in 1989 Reagan left the White House; and although her friend Mikhail Gorbachev was still in the Kremlin, his prospects looked increasingly uncertain as he was outflanked by Russian ultranationalists on one side and doctrinaire liberals on the other. Indeed, Mrs Thatcher's role as a trusted interlocutor in both Washington and Moscow had been endangered at the Reykjavik Summit in October 1986, when Reagan seemed willing to contemplate the total elimination of nuclear weapons – an outcome to which the Thatcher governments had paid obligatory lip-service, but which (in the Prime Minister's view) would leave Western Europe exposed to the unquenchable expansionary designs of the Red Army.

Despite the failure of the Reykjavik Summit, it conveyed two unpalatable facts to Thatcher. First, despite all the post-Falklands rhetoric about Britain's reassertion of 'Great Power' status, the country's influence was minimal in the superpower struggle (the idealistic Reykjavik deal was only derailed because of Reagan's infatuation with the 'Star Wars' system of ballistic interception). Second, the summit showed that Reagan – free from the need to play up his anti-Communist credentials for electoral purposes – was prepared to look beyond ideology and seek agreement even with a regime which continued to deny basic freedoms to its citizens. Lacking either the opportunity or the inclination to exercise so much flexibility, the 'Iron Lady' looked increasingly isolated and outdated among Western leaders.

If the disappearance of a cruel but containable Soviet Union from Mrs Thatcher's Cold War landscape was not bad enough, it opened the prospect of a reunified Germany – thus activating a youthful fear which the adult Thatcher had never struggled very hard to suppress. Apart from its effect on Mrs Thatcher's attitude to Europe, this dramatic development inevitably increased American interest in Germany. George H. Bush, who had replaced Reagan in January 1989, was anxious that Germany should remain within NATO, a view which was shared by the West German Chancellor Helmut Kohl. After reunification in the month before Thatcher's downfall, it seemed that the 'Special Relationship' between Britain and the US was under serious threat – not least because Germany so obviously enjoyed more influence in Europe than the increasingly recalcitrant Britain.

In August 1990 Mrs Thatcher was handed a chance to defy these disturbing trends. When Iraqi forces invaded Kuwait at the beginning of that month she left Bush in no doubt of her determination to resist Saddam Hussein's aggression. In October 1990, when the Conservatives lost a crucial by-election at Eastbourne, one of the Prime Minister's leading critics privately expressed the view that 'only the Gulf can save her'.[5] Whether or not she would have been able to exploit the situation to lasting diplomatic advantage, she only had time to approve British troop deployments; it was left to John Major, who as Chancellor had not been appointed to her initial war Cabinet, to oversee the military action which began in January 1991.

MAJOR'S FIRST TERM

During 'Operation Desert Shield' John Major provided a contrasting model of war-leadership from the one that his predecessor had presented during the Falklands conflict of 1982. Throughout he showed a marked disinclination either for sabre-rattling or triumphalism. The change of style and tone was clearly appreciated by President Bush, and initial doubts in Washington were dispelled during Major's two-day visit to Camp David in December 1990. Unlike Reagan, Bush was not disposed to treat Thatcher's hectoring manner with an amused and affectionate tolerance; but his high regard for Major was based on something more positive than relief. Bush and Major were both 'consolidators', more concerned with addressing practical problems than with 'the vision thing' which had enticed their crusading predecessors. By the time of the Camp David meeting, the Bush administration could also feel confident of building a closer relationship with reunified Germany without alienating Britain; Major had held a constructive meeting with Helmut Kohl at the Rome European Council meeting earlier in December.[6]

The ejection of Saddam Hussein's forces from Kuwait by the end of February 1991 makes it easy to forget the anticipated hazards of an operation against a regime which was expected to throw everything into the fight, including its highly trained Republican Guard as well as chemical and biological weapons. Instead, the US-led coalition confronted conscripts who quickly succumbed when they did not have time to surrender. The ease of victory tempted some commentators to criticise the coalition forces for their failure to press home the advantage by advancing on Baghdad and toppling Saddam. As Douglas Hurd has recalled, the British were surprised by the sudden decision to cease hostilities, having prepared further strikes against the Republican Guard. However, according to Hurd no one either in London or Washington 'contemplated driving on to Baghdad and deposing Saddam Hussein'. The operation had achieved its objective: 'enlarging the purpose of the war was not an option'.[7]

However, as Hurd concedes, this decision partly reflected a hope and expectation 'that the ruin of [Saddam's] policy in Kuwait would lead to his downfall'.[8] In other words, decision-makers within the coalition assumed that opinion in Iraq would respond to Saddam's humiliation in a 'rational' manner – i.e. by disposing, in one way or another, of the regime which had always been characterised by miscalculation as well as brutality. Yet it was most unlikely that Saddam could ever have been coaxed into emulating Margaret Thatcher's tearful but bloodless departure from office. There was bound to be violent resistance of some kind; and the Republican Guard provided Saddam's best chance of survival. For all the diplomatic language of Hurd's memoir, it is possible to detect an argument which might have averted future complications; the coalition partners could have kept up the air war for a few more days, concentrating on Saddam's key military assets rather than the involuntary warriors who were retreating from Kuwait, in a way which would leave his regime even more vulnerable to subversion from within.

To his credit, Major did not avert his eyes from Iraq as soon as the invasion of Kuwait had been repulsed. Having been checked but not nullified, Saddam moved quickly to reassert his control over Iraq, slaughtering Shi'ite insurgents in the south of the country before turning his attention to the north where his regime had committed atrocities during the 1980s against the Kurdish population (with the apparent acquiescence of Western governments). Free from the burdens of office, Mrs Thatcher spoke out boldly on behalf of the Kurds. John Major, who was already well aware of the way in which such burdens obstructed decisive action, broached the idea of 'safe havens' for Kurds who had fled into the mountains of northern Iraq. His tactful diplomacy – inaugurated at an EC Council meeting – overcame the obvious reluctance of Britain's NATO ally, Turkey, which was faced with its own difficulties from Kurdish separatists, and a US attitude which was lukewarm at best. UN backing was secured thanks to the skilful diplomacy of Britain's permanent representative, David Hannay. The contrast with Thatcher's *modus operandi* was palpable.

Major could also derive considerable satisfaction from his dealings with the Soviet Union. He secured an invitation for President Gorbachev to attend meetings of the G7 summit, held in London in July 1991, and although the Soviet leader gained few economic concessions he was given every opportunity to use the visit to demonstrate his popularity in the West. However, this did little to mollify Gorbachev's domestic detractors, who staged a coup in the following month. Major was quick to express support for Boris Yeltsin who led resistance to the plotters, without seeming to abandon Gorbachev who was under house-arrest at the time. Major was the first foreign leader to visit Moscow after the collapse of the coup, and held cordial meetings with both Gorbachev and Yeltsin.[9]

By April 1992 the Conservatives had good reason to feel that the problems of Mrs Thatcher's third term had been addressed, and that an element of equilibrium in foreign policy had been restored under Major and Hurd. Indeed, the party's manifesto for the general election held in that month opened with a lengthy eulogy to Conservative achievements in this field – a notable departure from the usual practice of banishing non-domestic issues to the back. While the language was less vainglorious, the message was similar to that of the 1987 manifesto:

> Under the Conservatives, Britain has regained her rightful influence in the world. We have stood up for the values our country has always represented. We have defended Britain's interests with vigour and with success. The respect with which Britain is regarded in the world has rarely been higher…[10]

If true, this would indeed be a praiseworthy record: under Conservative guidance, Britain seemingly had simultaneously advanced its national interests and the cause of liberal democracy. The unqualified claim about Britain's prestige would have provoked interesting reactions from Winston Churchill and Pitt the Elder; but given the government's undeniable successes, it is not surprising that the party's publicists were tempted into unhistorical hyperbole. Nevertheless, there was a chance that this verbal bravado would leave hostages to fortune; and indeed, the approach had already shown a tendency to be counter-productive. In December 1991 'an over-enthusiastic press officer' had claimed that John Major had won 'game, set and match' over Britain's European partners at Maastricht.[11] With characteristic restraint, Douglas Hurd remarked that this boast 'did much more harm than good'.[12] However, within a few days Hurd produced a howler of his own, writing that, 'in recent years Britain has punched above its weight in the world. We intend to keep it that way'.[13] This seemed to pre-suppose that problems in the post-Cold War world would usually be susceptible to diplomatic resolution, in which Britain (thanks to the FCO) was sure to enjoy an influence out of proportion to its military might. In fact, although the Defence Review ('Options for Change') of 1990 did envisage a 'peace dividend' arising from significant spending cuts, there was no sign that the Major government had used the expectation of a peaceful 'New World Order' as a pretext for a truly radical economy-drive, associated with a re-think of its role in global politics.

A country which insisted on 'punching above its weight', in international affairs as in the boxing ring, could easily find itself sprawled on the canvass if it confronted a pugilist who was fully equipped to fight in a higher division. Hurd's thought-provoking phrase seems a trivial offence after the triumphalism of the Thatcher years, but even three years after the demolition of the Berlin Wall international affairs were clearly in flux, making it unusually important to avoid unforced errors. Some of the brashness of the 1992 Conservative manifesto undoubtedly reflected a confidence that at least one familiar landmark would remain in place; George Bush would be re-elected to serve a second term in the White House. Just to make sure, officials connected to the Conservative Party visited Washington to advise President Bush; and it was alleged that British civil servants were asked to examine Home Office records for evidence that the Democratic challenger, Bill Clinton, had engaged in 'unpatriotic' activities during his time as a student in Britain during the 1960s.

Ronald Reagan had never concealed his preference for Margaret Thatcher over any Labour contender; but in terms of the unequal etiquette of the 'special relationship' the Conservative backing for Bush was an example of 'punching below the belt'. Clinton's comfortable electoral college victory in November 1992 was thus a further blow to the Major government, while it was still reeling from Britain's ejection from the Exchange Rate Mechanism (ERM) of the European Monetary System (EMS).

Major's first-term successes had not been due entirely to good fortune – at worst, he could be credited for helping to make his own luck. Between April 1992 and the general election of May 1997, however, the stars turned against him in a way which made a mockery of the earlier optimism in the field of international affairs. There was, perhaps, a morsel of comfort for Major in the fact that his misfortunes in foreign policy escaped relatively unnoticed by the voters, who had more pressing reasons for deserting his party. But in turn this domestic unpopularity could only weaken Major's perceived diplomatic weight – with Clinton, and among Britain's EU partners who became understandably impatient for 'regime change' long before the 1997 general election.

SECOND TERM: BRITAIN AND THE BALKANS

The foreign policy problem which dominated Major's second term had actually begun amidst the self-congratulations of his first few months. The chain of events triggered by the erasure of the Berlin Wall included the collapse of the post-war Yugoslav state under the long-suppressed force of ethnic differences. In June 1991 Slovenia and Croatia declared their independence from the Serb-dominated Republic of Yugoslavia, which tried to prevent the move by military means. The newly unified Germany was determined to recognise Croatian independence, and despite serious misgivings Britain and France acquiesced in December 1991. A ceasefire was declared in early January 1992 – almost exactly coinciding with Hurd's claim about Britain punching above its weight.

Complex as they were, the tensions within Croatia and Slovenia were easier to resolve than the situation in Bosnia, where Muslims enjoyed a numerical advantage over Serbs and Croats, but did not constitute an overall majority of the population. Civil war between these factions erupted in April 1992 – coinciding with the British general election – and quickly assumed a character which evoked comparisons with Nazi atrocities in the Second World War.

For the newly re-elected Conservative government in Britain, this was a deeply unsettling development. Before the end of the Cold War, most Britons regarded Yugoslavia as a faraway country about which little was known, except perhaps that under Marshall Tito it had commendably extricated itself from Stalin's Iron Curtain. By 1992 the curtain had melted, and Yugoslavia was becoming a popular destination for British tourists. Even those who had not travelled there could be pardoned for thinking that Yugoslavia was the kind of place in which Britain should be able to 'punch above its weight' and take a leading role in promoting a satisfactory settlement.

However, the Major government was reluctant to get involved at all; and when it did, it restricted its intervention to the provision of humanitarian aid on what it depicted as a scrupulously impartial basis. From the government's perspective, this seemed the only appropriate response to a conflict which it could not hope to resolve. Indeed, although British troops were outnumbered by the French, even this limited deployment encountered opposition from Major's ministerial colleagues. When related to the conflict in Bosnia, at best the policy could only serve to keep civilians alive while the armed forces of the minority Serb population routed rival combatants. 'Ethnic cleansing' would thus mean deportation of peoples rather than genocide, but the difference would seem relatively unimportant to the displaced individuals. An arms embargo, which had been imposed in 1991, worked strongly in favour of Bosnian Serb groups, who could draw on the weaponry which had been accumulated by the Yugoslav state. The Clinton administration favoured more forceful measures – air strikes on the Bosnian Serbs, combined with a lifting of the arms embargo. However, the British pointed out that this would put the humanitarian effort in serious jeopardy – an argument which effectively spiked the guns of Clinton's advisers who regarded humanitarian intervention as a thinly disguised form of appeasement.[14]

This is not the place to follow the course of the Bosnian civil war in detail. From the Major government's perspective, however, Bosnia's tragedy was something akin to a 'perfect storm'. It seemed to the British that the Americans were indulging in irresponsible 'gesture politics', assuming that the 'shock and awe' tactics deployed so successfully in the Gulf could be translated to the very different topographical and political context of the Balkans, where (it was supposed) Serb aggression could only be thwarted by a massive influx of ground forces. Yet the Major government itself had undoubtedly benefited from the relatively rapid victory over Saddam, which gave rise to a popular view (in the UK as in Washington) that in the post-Cold War environment diplomatic conundrums could be resolved by surgical military strikes.

It is possible that the differences between Washington and London at this point would not have arisen if the Conservative Party had been more careful to conceal its preference for Bush over Clinton. More seriously, Hurd's opposition to a military-based solution in Bosnia seemed to give the lie to his remarks about Britain 'punching above its weight'. In hindsight, these ill-chosen words gave a licence to armchair generals to overlook the complexities of this situation and wonder why their country was deemed incapable of teaching the Serb regime of Slobodan Milošević an unforgettable lesson. After all, in advance of the Gulf War Saddam Hussein's Iraq had been portrayed as a major military power, and Serbia had never been accorded the same backhanded accolade.

In his frustration, Hurd committed fresh verbal indiscretions which played into the hands of his critics. In April 1993 he argued that lifting the arms embargo would merely introduce a 'level killing field' in Bosnia. In his memoirs, Hurd asserts that, far from acting as an advocate of the existing '*un*level killing field', he was arguing 'for an end to killing'.[15] It cannot be denied that Hurd abhorred the tendency of human beings to inflict violence on each other – even in pursuit of aims which could be described as 'rational'. Nevertheless, his attempt to warn against a 'level killing field' in Bosnia betrayed a feeling that, whatever the justice of the case, the Serbs were bound to prevail. From this perspective, Britain's objectives were to avoid genocide in Bosnia and to prevent the conflict from spreading to other parts of the region – but not necessarily in that order.

Unfortunately for Hurd, his phrase-making skills continued to master his diplomatic poise. In the House of Commons, during what was otherwise a measured defence of British policy towards the Balkans, he remarked that, 'I have never found the phrase "something must be done" to be a phrase which carries any conviction in the places such as the House or the government where people have to take decisions.'[16] Hurd was revealing a distaste for ill-informed public opinion, in keeping with the traditions of the FCO. However, since he had become Secretary of State, media coverage of the Gulf War had emboldened the 'something must be done' brigade by making punitive military action seem politically effective and relatively costless in terms of innocent human life. In this context, any recumbent British news-watcher who thoughtlessly exclaimed that 'something must be done' seemed less morally culpable than a Foreign Secretary who had already decided against anything which might defeat Serb aggression. One is tempted to think that Hurd's harsh language was prompted at least in part by his own susceptibility to the 'CNN effect', which had ensured the rapid transmission of heart-rending images of suffering people to television viewers throughout the Western world. Certainly John Major's much-vaunted intervention on behalf of the Iraqi Kurds could be regarded as a by-product of the CNN effect; as his biographers have written, Major had been 'appalled by what he read and saw' in media reports of the plight of the Kurds who were fleeing from Saddam's forces.[17]

Hurd announced his resignation from the government on 23 June 1995, the day after Major himself had vacated the Conservative Party leadership in order to confront his critics. Hurd therefore was no longer in office on 11 July, when more than 8,000 Muslim men and boys were slaughtered in Srebrenica by Bosnian Serb death squads. This atrocity, followed by a mortar attack on a market in the Bosnian capital, Sarajevo, provoked a NATO aerial onslaught on the Bosnian Serbs – a belated show of serious force which led to the signing of the Dayton Agreement in November 1995.

In retirement Major accepted his share of responsibility for the failure of Western policy in Bosnia, while attributing the 'inadequacy of the outside world's response' to the inherent complexity of a situation which could only be resolved when key factors turned in favour of a binding settlement.[18] All one can say on this point is that if Britain had really enjoyed the kind of global prestige of which the Conservatives had boasted before the 1992 general election, it would have been ideally placed to prevent the Srebrenica genocide. The Major government was therefore either guilty of misleading British voters, or of betraying the innocent victims of genocide in Bosnia – or, for that matter, in Rwanda, where the deaths of up to one million people had occurred in 1994 despite warnings from British intelligence. Along with the US, Britain obstructed attempts to send an effective UN force to Rwanda, then demanded that the inadequate force be further reduced, before denying that the slaughter should be considered as 'genocide' (since 'the G-word' would have triggered international intervention).[19]

AN END TO REALISM?

Before his departure from office, Hurd had been discomfited by a High Court judgement concerning the use of Britain's overseas aid budget. A dam on the Pergau River in Malaysia had been constructed (beginning in 1991), thanks largely to a grant of more than £200 million from Britain. The Malaysian government – not, perhaps, the most needy applicant for aid, or the most democratic regime in the world – had responded by placing lucrative arms orders with UK companies. This apparent misuse of the aid budget was particularly unfortunate since the overall record of the Major government in this respect was defensible, thanks to the efforts of the responsible minister, Lynda Chalker.

Doubts about Britain's moral status were increased by its treatment of Hong Kong, which was due to be handed over to the Chinese in 1997. For a hundred years, the British had ruled that colony, untroubled by the notion that its residents would benefit from democratic institutions. However, the increasing proximity of the unavoidable handover concentrated British minds on the long-neglected case for civic freedoms. As the last Governor of Hong Kong, Major's friend Christopher Patten probably did help to cement the idea that the former colony should enjoy a greater degree of democracy than other parts of China; but partially informed Britons, encouraged by the Conservatives to consider the remnants of Empire in post-Falklands terms, would be forgiven for regarding the whole episode with offended self-regard mingled with incomprehension.

In comparison to its travails over Europe, at least the Major government had been spared serious parliamentary embarrassment over foreign policy – until February 1996, when the judicial Scott inquiry into the provision of arms to Iraq was published. The inquiry related to the dealings of a company, Matrix Churchill, whose senior executives had been accused of exporting machine tools which could be used to manufacture arms for the Iraqi regime, in defiance of government rules. The company had defended itself on the grounds that the government had known of its activities, and that senior ministers had tried to evade exposure through the use of 'Public Immunity Certificates'. Labour's shadow Foreign Secretary, Robin Cook, demolished the government's defence, despite enjoying just two hours to digest the main findings of a report which ran to almost 2,000 pages.

In 1979, Douglas Hurd had published his reflections on the Heath government under the title *An End to Promises*.[20] He had been thinking primarily of that ill-starred government's *domestic* pledges, which in hindsight seemed unrealistic. When he published his memoirs more than two decades later there was no sign of a similar negative judgement on his general approach to foreign policy. This outlook had been shaped during the Cold War, when Britain's role as the junior participant in a 'special relationship' often demanded what scholars of international relations characterise as a 'realist' approach – a pursuit of the perceived national interest irrespective of ethical considerations.

Despite the apparent end of the Cold War the realist approach seemed as relevant as ever during the Gulf War – with the added bonus that this particular conflict did have an ethical rationale. Hence in 1992 the Conservatives felt fully entitled to exalt their foreign policy as a judicious blend of calculation and compassion. Unfortunately for Hurd and Major, even in the 'New World Order' the promptings of *realpolitik* would in many instances continue to conflict with liberal-democratic ideals, forcing British policy makers into awkward choices. Bosnia was a prime example of such dilemmas, and it demonstrated that, when in doubt, Hurd and Major would always favour the 'realist' option. The government's attitude to the Matrix

Churchill case could be seen as an example of 'realism' approaching the 'surreal', since the government was tacitly saying that it was not in the national interest for the public to know about decisions which ministers had taken in what they considered to be the national interest.

Hurd, in particular, was severely criticised for his 'realist' leanings. For example, Clinton's aide Sidney Blumenthal denounced the 'profound cynicism' of British foreign policy towards Bosnia, a view which was reinforced by the researches of the historian Brendan Simms.[21] No less damning than such accusations – which at least implied a degree of consistency – was the less polemical view that, in trying to play different tunes to different audiences at home, in Europe and beyond, the Major government had merely succeeded in producing a cacophony. Half-way through the government's second term, the astute academic observer William Wallace pronounced that it had 'no foreign policy' at all.[22]

Another eloquent verdict on the Hurd-Major years was delivered indirectly after the government's 1997 defeat, when New Labour's professed aspiration to 'an ethical dimension' in British foreign policy was interpreted by observers as a token of revolutionary reorientation – even though the incoming Foreign Secretary, Robin Cook, had placed this modest goal fourth out of six objectives in the new government's international dealings.[23] It remained to be seen whether Britain would fare better if its government, under a hyper-moralistic Prime Minister, decided that the realist/idealist dilemma should now be resolved in favour of the latter. However, probably the most telling testimony was enshrined in the 1997 Conservative Party manifesto, where foreign policy was almost the last thing to be mentioned; and even then, virtually all of the discussion was devoted to 'Europe'.

ENDNOTES

1 A. Seldon, *Major: A Political Life* (London: Weidenfeld & Nicolson, 1997), p. 86
2 Presumably on the (well-founded) assumption that Lady Thatcher's admirers will approve of her conduct towards the FCO, Charles Moore has confirmed this picture in *Margaret Thatcher: The Authorised Biography, Volume Two: Everything She Wants* (London: Allen Lane, 2015)
3 J. Major, *The Autobiography* (London: Harper Collins, 1999) p. 134
4 Conservative Party, *The Next Moves Forward* (London: Conservative Party, 1987)
5 Private information.
6 Seldon, *Major: A Political Life*, p. 165
7 D. Hurd, *Memoirs* (London: Little, Brown, 2003) pp. 412–3
8 Ibid.
9 Seldon, *Major: A Political Life*, pp. 229–31
10 Conservative Party, *The Best Future for Britain* (London: Conservative Party, 1992)
11 S. Wall, *A Stranger in Europe: Britain and the EU from Thatcher to Blair* (Oxford: Oxford University Press, 2008), p. 132
12 Hurd, *Memoirs*, p. 421
13 W. Wallace 'Foreign Policy' in D. Kavanagh and A. Seldon (eds.) *The Major Effect* (London: Macmillan, 1994), pp. 292–3
14 S. Blumenthal, *Clinton's Wars* London: Viking, 2003), p. 62
15 Hurd, *Memoirs*, p. 460
16 M. Stuart, *Douglas Hurd: The Public Servant – An Authorised Biography* (London: Mainstream, 1998), p. 329
17 Seldon, *Major: A Political Life*, p. 161
18 Major, *The Autobiography*, p. 549
19 See L. Melvern, 'The UK Government and the 1994 Genocide in Rwanda', *Genocide Studies and Prevention: An International Journal* 2/3 (2007), pp. 249–57
20 D. Hurd, *An End to Promises: Sketch of a Government 1970–74* (London: Collins, 1979)
21 Blumenthal, p. 62; B. Sims, *Unfinest Hour: Britain and the Destruction of Bosnia* (London: Allen Lane, 2001)
22 Wallace, p. 299
23 Robin Cook, speech on foreign policy, 11 May 1997 https://www.theguardian.com/world/1997/may/12/indonesia.ethicalforeignpolicy

17

JOHN MAJOR AND EUROPE: A CASE FOR REAPPRAISAL?

Gillian Peele

JOHN MAJOR'S LEADERSHIP OF the Conservative Party was indelibly scarred by European issues. While there were already signs of deep internal divisions over European policy under Mrs Thatcher, and indeed attitudes to Europe played a large part in the collapse of her leadership, it was under John Major's two administrations of 1990–92 and 1992–97 that the fault lines over British membership of the European Union became increasing public and bitter and dangerously dysfunctional. From the beginning Major as Prime Minister had to balance concern for the protection of British interests in the context of European policy with the need to maintain some semblance of unity in a party which seemed bent on its own political destruction. The prospect of an irrevocable split in the party over Europe, comparable to that over the Corn Laws in the 1840s, loomed especially large with Major. As he put it himself in his memoirs, 'the shadow of my nineteenth-century predecessor as Conservative Prime Minister Sir Robert Peel was forever at my side: in all my time at Downing Street he was never to leave it.'[1] Party management and the very survival of the government became all-absorbing and exhausting enterprises as the Conservatives, surprisingly re-elected in 1992, limped through a deeply unhappy period of crisis and electoral unpopularity until the general election of 1997 consigned them to opposition for thirteen years.

Major's premiership remains of interest for the understanding of how the Conservatives came to tread a path of self-destructive preoccupation with European issues, despite the evidence that the general public did not share the obsession. In the process, that fixation transformed a massively successful political party into one which needed substantial reform and reconstruction before it could again be an effective challenger for office. Ultimately, of course, although the Conservative Party survived, the UK's membership of the European Union did not. The period of Major's premiership thus also remains pertinent for those seeking to understand the ambiguous character of the UK's relationship with the European Union and the attitudes and values which eventually led to the referendum of 2016 and the vote to leave. To what extent was John Major personally responsible for the difficulties which he encountered? Could he have done anything which would have made a significant difference to the course of events or was he already boxed in by political events and the circumstances of his succession? Was his leadership style too weak and indecisive to handle the intra-party factionalism which emerged in Conservative ranks? Or was his consensual approach the only plausible one which a leader at that time could adopt? How should we now evaluate his premiership – especially in relation to Europe – and does the failure of subsequent leaders to prevent the party 'banging on about Europe' let us see his efforts from a different perspective?

In order to try to shed some light on these questions the chapter proceeds as follows. In the first section I outline Major's values, his basic attitude to European issues and his style of political leadership. In the second section I briefly highlight some of the key turning points in the handling of European policy between 1990, noting the increasing tensions which it generated within the Conservative Party. In the third section I look in more detail at the deepening fissures over European policy within Conservative ranks and discuss their interaction with the growth of opposition of Major's leadership. In the final section I revisit the evaluation of Major's strategy and tactics in relation to Europe and make some observations on the evolution of events after 1997.

AN ENIGMATIC POLITICIAN?

John Major's approach to European issues was of a piece with his general political stance. He was a pragmatist rather than an ideologue, focused on the practical policy issues rather than grand visions or projects. His rise to the premiership had been fast and at least one colleague, Kenneth Clarke, has noted that he was intensely ambitious.[2] His relatively humble background and lack of higher education made him unusual among the ranks of Conservative MPs and may have contributed to what some authors see as a deep insecurity.[3] Certainly they gave him an urge to improve the conditions of life for ordinary people and a socially liberal approach, which put him on the liberal wing of the party and distanced him from the groups on the right who were to become his critics over Europe. On European issues specifically, he was neither an enthusiastic Europhile in the vein of Cabinet colleagues like Douglas Hurd, Kenneth Clarke or Michael Heseltine; but nor was he a Eurosceptic. Rather, he saw the European Union as an organisation in which British interests could best be pursued if the UK exercised a strong leadership role. As Major famously put it, he wanted to see Britain 'at the heart of Europe'. However, this did not mean he endorsed the increasingly integrationist visions of European leaders such as Jacques Delors, who had become President of the European Commission in January 1985, or had any truck with federalist goals. Although his understanding of Europe acknowledged that it was much more than a trading entity, he wanted to preserve the political autonomy of its member states and their distinctive national institutions including a strong role for the British Parliament. When the issue of a common European currency came onto the agenda, he was adamant that, while the UK should not rule out membership altogether, it should be able to remain outside of the Eurozone for as long as it wished. Major was in favour of an enlarged community and on this, as on many other issues, he was at one with Foreign Office thinking. In his memoirs Major makes plain his distaste for the way in which France and Germany tried to stitch together deals at the expense of the other members and his exasperation at the way many of the EU institutions operated, not least because of the extent to which they side-stepped robust and honest debate.[4]

Major's own style was inclusive and conciliatory, seeking consensus in government where possible and eschewing the flamboyant and crusading approach of his predecessor. Certainly John Major's government operated in a very different way from Mrs Thatcher's, not least in the strengthening of Cabinet discussions and the reduction of strong and highly personal direction. It was dubbed a 'government of chums', although in some cases – such as the frosty relationship between Major and Norman Lamont, his Chancellor until 1993 – there was no close personal friendship. It was also a government which was much more reliant on, and appreciative of, official advice than Thatcher's had been, a fact that reflected both Major's own lack of ideological drive and his appreciation of expertise.

Major's government was inevitably shaped by the circumstances in which he had come to the leadership. Mrs Thatcher had not wanted to relinquish the premiership, while she and her supporters perhaps saw Major as the least bad alternative if there had to be a successor. Many of those who voted for him (and who were later to become critics) did so without enthusiasm; and there was among the Thatcher loyalists no acknowledgement of his legitimacy and a lingering sense that she had been driven from office by a cabal of Cabinet ministers who did not reflect the views of the party. Her own description of her ousting as 'treachery with a smile on its face' chimed with the views of some in the parliamentary party and it was associated especially in some quarters with pro-European views.

Mrs Thatcher herself had become increasingly hostile to the process of European developments over the course of her administration. She had signed the Single European Act (SEA) in 1986, which was the first major revision of the Rome Treaty, though she later claimed that she was misled about its significance. The SEA was a means of achieving two major changes in the European Economic Community. It provided a framework for the closer working of European trade relationships – the single market which came into effect in 1992 – through removing a range of internal barriers to the free movement of goods, services, people and capital. Conservatives and businesses were generally in favour of this development but much less supportive of concomitant efforts to forge a common social policy and rights for workers across Europe. The drive to create a single market also precipitated changes in the European decision-making process, including the introduction of Qualified Majority Voting (QMV) instead of unanimity. While justifiable in terms of speeding the taking of decisions, the move threated the interests of nation states which might find themselves in a minority position.

Under the impetus of the Delors presidency of the Commission, the late 1980s thus saw a new momentum injected into European affairs which was unsettling for the UK. Mrs Thatcher herself became increasingly strident on European issues, notably through speeches such as the one she delivered at Bruges in September 1988, in which she argued that the UK had not rolled back the frontiers of the state at home, only to see them reimposed at a European level with a European super-state exercising a new dominance from Brussels.[5] Her increasing opposition to the European Union and all its works continued after her premiership. From the beginning of Major's entry into Downing Street it became apparent that Mrs Thatcher would seek to influence Conservative policy, especially on European issues, and that she was more than willing to fan the fires of disunity. Although she herself had suffered from public criticisms from her predecessor, Edward Heath, there were increasingly explicit attacks on Major's policies and on Major's leadership both from Thatcher herself and from close allies such as Lord Tebbit and Lord Baker and later from Major's former Cabinet ministers, such as Norman Lamont.

Of course any new Conservative leader in 1990 would have inherited a difficult position. By that stage the Conservatives had been in power for eleven years and there was inevitably a public weariness with their policies and their personalities. The vigour of the early Thatcher years had waned and by 1990 the government had lost some of the key architects of Conservative policy, notably Geoffrey Howe and Nigel Lawson, as a result of internal disputes with Mrs Thatcher, many of them over European policy. The poll tax had proved a policy fiasco and the economy was in the doldrums. Not surprisingly public support for the government had declined and Conservative backbenchers were fearful of the party's prospects at a general election which had to be called by July 1992. But the conjunction of Mrs Thatcher's forced exit from Downing Street and the escalation of the debate about European policy added uniquely inflammatory elements to the situation.

A CHANGING EUROPEAN AGENDA

Major's first experience as Prime Minister with the capacity of European issues to produce intense headaches for the UK occurred in the negotiations over what was to become the Maastricht Treaty. Legislating the Maastricht Treaty dominated the first year of Major's second administration and its passage saw the Conservatives divided almost to the point of destroying their own government. The original negotiations over Maastricht among the EU members saw the UK adamantly and successfully defending its position on two key issues which reflected the different visions of the UK and much of the rest of the EU. On economic and monetary union, the UK was determined to reserve its ability to opt out and to retain the pound rather than adopt the single currency. Equally, the UK was adamantly opposed to including in the treaty the so-called Social Chapter which enshrined the 1989 Social Charter and which expanded the scope for potential European intervention in regulation of working conditions and social policy generally. Given that the Conservatives since 1979 had been keen to create a freer market and to roll back the corporatism of previous years, this initiative was very unwelcome. Major was unwilling to allow the Social Chapter to be included in the treaty at all, even if there was an opt-out for the UK and in the end, at Britain's insistence, the Social Chapter was removed from the formal treaty but added as a protocol to it. Thus the UK came out of the Maastricht negotiations very well, having achieved its key demands. Although the press was to become increasingly hostile to Major and his government, something which he was very sensitive about, on this occasion the media reception of the outcome of the summit was extremely positive.

Beneath the surface, however, Major recognised that the road ahead – to implementing the treaty and for dealing with subsequent developments on the EU agenda – would be rocky. The determination of some EU leaders to press ahead with a vision of Europe far removed from Britain's was unlikely to be deflected and meant that any Conservative leader would be perpetually fighting off unwelcome initiatives. Certainly the dynamics of European Union politics seemed likely to make for increasingly turbulent politics within the Conservative Party as backbenchers mobilised around European issues and other policy divisions.

Shortly after the successful Maastricht negotiations Major called and won a general election. The election victory of April 1992 was unexpected and owed much at home to the Conservatives' successful exploitation of Labour's tax and spending policies. As Major himself points out, the Conservative performance at the election was very good; but it yielded only a majority of twenty-one seats. A majority of twenty-one might have been adequate in normal circumstances although inevitably vulnerable to erosion by unforeseen factors such as deaths and resignations. But it was to prove deeply fragile in an environment where European issues were regularly on the parliamentary agenda and where there was an increasingly determined band of dissenters keen to flex their muscle. The increasing incidence of dissent on the backbenches since the 1970s has been well-documented.[6] Governments had not, until Major's 1992 administration, felt their very existence threated by increased willingness to defy the party line because until that point the issues generating intra-party disagreement had generally been diverse and the rebellious MPs had been disorganised.

Major encountered a very different situation in the House of Commons elected in 1992: the European issue was fast becoming not merely divisive within the party ranks but one which some MPs thought involved such high matters of constitutional principle that they trumped the normal demands of party loyalty. It was also true that the parliamentary party had been changing and becoming more faction ridden, with groups such as the Thatcherite 92 Group organising to advance their own agenda and slates of candidates for party committees. The 92 Group became the focus for much opposition to Major's leadership and some of its most prominent members were the 'bastards' whom Major saw as destabilising party policy. Major himself noted the shift towards a more careerist style of politician and the loss in 1992 of a large number of MPs who had been stalwart loyalists. Equally importantly were the long years of Conservative government which had created a pool of MPs who had either been dismissed from office or never offered it in the first place. Thus, although the reduced majority of 1992 gave the Conservative rebels leverage, the changed character of the Conservative backbenches (and indeed of parliamentarians generally) created a difficult environment for Major and made the party more difficult to manage.

It should be noted at this stage that Major's experience in the Whips' Office was at once a help and a hindrance. Major has been described as 'one of nature's whips' and one who was highly sensitive to the mood of his own backbenchers.[7] But as a former whip he was also heavily focused on the tactics and strategies necessary to deliver votes and perhaps less willing than he should have been to confront rebellious backbenchers or provide clear and principled leadership.

The challenge of securing the Maastricht Treaty through parliamentary legislation presented itself immediately after the 1992 election. The treaty could have been implemented before the 1992 election but this would have disrupted the parliamentary timetable and been an unhelpful backcloth to an election campaign. Major therefore thought delay until a new parliament was sensible, although the reduced majority was to prove problematic for Maastricht's passage and the government's knife-edge control of Parliament seriously diminished its authority and image.

The extraordinary struggle to get the Maastricht Treaty implemented by Parliament has been well chronicled elsewhere.[8] However three points should be made here. The first is that, despite the enormous pressure put on the rebels, the group opposed to ratification maintained its opposition and grew. Secondly, as Baker, Gamble and Ludlam have underlined, the government was forced into a humiliating series of concessions and strategic ducking of votes to avoid defeat.[9] Finally, and this perhaps was the most important long-term consequence of the Maastricht episode, the tortuous passage of the Bill alienated the public and damaged the authority of the government, highlighting the extent to which exercising control over European developments had become an increasingly difficult task for Westminster.

In the course of the long-drawn-out debate over Maastricht, external events had of course played an important role. The Danish 'no' vote in the referendum of 1992 had not merely led to the postponement of the Bill's committee stage (and raised the question of whether the treaty might be lost) but it had also led to calls, echoed by Baroness Thatcher and other senior ex-ministers, for a referendum in Britain. Support for a referendum in Britain, though rejected by the government, was strong and it became increasingly difficult to see why the UK, unlike other European countries, was denied a popular vote on the issue.

The other key external event of 1992 was the forced exit – or suspension – of the UK from the European Exchange Rate Mechanism (ERM). Black Wednesday 1992, as 16 September came to be known, was in many ways a turning point for the government, although in retrospect its significance has been subject to much reinterpretation. The background to the suspension was the market pressure put on weaker European currencies over the summer of 1992. Despite Mrs Thatcher's reluctance, the UK had joined the

ERM in 1990 when Major was Chancellor, a move which, according to his biographer, he continued to regard as his greatest achievement as Chancellor and which he believed had produced economic stability.[10] However, for a variety of complex factors, not least the strength of the deutschmark, pressure on the pound on 16 September led to fears that it would sink below the minimum level prescribed by the rules (DM 2.77). Following a wave of selling sterling over the night of 15 September, the Bank of England had attempted to prop up the currency by huge use of the reserves to buy sterling. The Chancellor, Norman Lamont, and Major attempted to alleviate the situation by raising interest rates (first from 10 per cent to 12 per cent and then to 15 per cent), although Major was well aware of the impact on domestic public opinion and on Eurosceptic critics. The attempt failed and the UK was forced to suspend its membership of the ERM.

Inevitably the government was humiliated by these developments. The opposition in debate seized on the government's lack of grip on economic policy and Eurosceptic critics on the backbenches became more strident. This fact, together with increasing criticism within the government for Major's policies, (as Seldon noted, the balance of power shifted within Cabinet) created a new backdrop for the continuing debate over Europe and the fate of the Maastricht Treaty.[11] Although Major himself considered resignation after Black Wednesday, he did not do so, and Norman Lamont also stayed despite calls for his dismissal. But Major's standing and confidence were deeply damaged by Black Wednesday and his leadership came under increasing challenge.

Writing twenty years after Black Wednesday in the *Daily Telegraph*, Daniel Hannan (a long-serving Eurosceptic MEP) described the withdrawal from the ERM that day as having unshackled sterling and ended a recession but wrecked the Conservative Party.[12] Hannan points, in that article, to the consensus behind the ERM, noting that to be pro-ERM was to be 'mainstream, modern [and] cosmopolitan'. Hannan also argued that the same people who were in favour of the ERM were those most opposed to Brexit, a point which highlights the extent to which many Conservatives have come to view the European Union as a project preferred by an elite establishment.

The UK's suspension of ERM membership had substantial consequences for Major, for the economy and for the Conservative Party, although the extent to which it caused a poll drop is disputed. Despite public announcements that we would rejoin when the time was right, the ERM fiasco made it highly unlikely that any future government would contemplate joining the euro, as Gordon Brown's resistance to Blair's greater euro enthusiasm revealed after 1997.

For Lamont himself, the departure from the ERM (in which he had never really believed) was the beginning of an unhappy period of unpopularity and declining credibility. When ultimately Major sacked him in 1993 his bitter resignation speech with its attack on a government which was 'in office but not in power' signalled that he too had joined the ranks of Major's critics and underlined how far authority was draining away from the government. In 1993, at the party conference, he advocated outright withdrawal from the EU.

CONSERVATIVE EUROSCEPTICISM

Why had opinion in the Conservative Party shifted on European issues and why had a party once known for its loyalty and the priority accorded to power become not merely prone to open factional infighting but willing to risk the defeat of its own government on European issues? Why was Major's leadership suddenly so vulnerable to attack? And could anything have been done to ameliorate the situation?

A tentative answer may be given by looking at the changing character of the European Union, and looking in a little more detail at the changing nature of Conservative politics. As far as the European Union is concerned it had by 1990 become a somewhat unattractive organisation. Much of the idealism of the early years had been replaced by bureaucratic decision-making and a style of politics which Major himself admitted was dispiriting. Secondly, since the Delors presidency the European Union had obviously been travelling in a direction which was increasingly at odds with British political values and preferences, both in terms of how decisions should be made and in terms of the substance of policy where the European Union often seemed keen to promote greater rather than less state intervention and regulation. For Conservative backbenchers, and for many other observers, the world of the European Union had become a byzantine and closed community where decision-making was opaque at best and where at worst special interests and even corruption flourished.

Opposition to European Union initiatives and general activism on European issues within the Conservative Party had, as already noted, produced increased factional organisation. There was already of course a series of groupings within the parliamentary ranks reflecting divisions which had sharpened since the Thatcher era. Within the party under Major there were on the right a number of overlapping groups. As already noted, the 92 Group became a focus of opposition on European issues and to Major's leadership. But there were also other groups on the right. Thus the Conservative Way Forward and the No Turning Back groups mobilised MPs who, as self-conscious bearers of the Thatcherite flame, were likely to be critical of the government and Major on a range of issues including Europe but who were Thatcherite in their beliefs. To these groups were added the important Fresh Start group formed under Sir Michael Spicer's aegis after the tabling of two Early Day Motions, the first immediately after the Danish referendum of June 1992, which rallied opposition to the Maastricht Treaty and called for a 'Fresh Start' on economic policy. The two EDMs were signed by a diverse group of Conservative backbenchers, including some (such as David Willetts, Charles Hendry, and David Lidington MP) from the new 1992 intake. The inspiration behind the EDMs was Michael Spicer, a former minister who had resigned in 1990. A respected financial journalist with substantial clout on the backbenches (he became chairman of the 1922 Committee in 2001) Spicer was able both to organise an influential block of some forty MPs in the Fresh Start Group and to keep lines open to the party leadership and the whips.

Individual MPs such as James Cran, Bill Cash, Edward Leigh, Teresa Gorman and John Redwood, who formed the core of opposition to Major's European policy, were prominent in these organisations. But the Eurosceptic cause attracted a wider following than the 'usual suspects' who had long been vocal on European issues. Indeed the 1992 general election brought into the House a new generation of Eurosceptic MPs, thus making it difficult to dismiss Eurosceptic Conservative critics as idiosyncratic or out of touch. Some estimates suggest that over half of the new 1992 intake was of a Eurosceptic persuasion. These new Eurosceptic MPs (who included, for example, Bernard Jenkin) injected a new legitimacy into the Eurosceptic cause.

Factional organisation and a willingness to vote against the whips on European issues obviously damaged the image of the party. But they also demoralised Major as leader. Explicit criticism of Major's leadership and calls for him to go became more frequent, both from backbenchers such as Tony Marlow and Edward Leigh and from press critics. Constituency chairmen also expressed unease after 1992 as the party's popularity plummeted. The successful, if narrow, passage of the Maastricht Bill did not end parliamentary rebelliousness and the rebels continued to threaten the government's control over the legislative process. The decision in November 1994 to remove the whip from the core rebels, following a rebellion over the European Communities Finance Bill, marked a new low-point in a Conservative Party management. This group – George Gardiner, Tony Marlow, Michael Carttiss, John Wilkinson, Richard Shepherd, Teresa Gorman, Nicholas Budgen and Sir Teddy Taylor – were joined by Sir Richard Body, a long-standing foe of British membership of the European Union who resigned the whip in sympathy, and Rupert Allason who had earlier had the whip withdrawn for being absent from the vote of confidence in the course of the 1993 Maastricht battle. Whether the initiative was sensible was debatable. The government by removing eight and losing ten of its supporters had reduced its majority, albeit temporarily; and the removal was worn as a badge of pride by the rebels who had little to fear either from the party leadership or from their constituencies. Inevitably the whip was restored in due course although the relationship between party managers and the erstwhile rebels could not be rebuilt.

The declining morale and vicious in-fighting within the party and perpetual speculation about the future of the leadership led Major to take the extraordinary course of resigning the leadership in July 1995 and daring his opponents to 'put up or shut up'. Again, opinion was divided on whether this was a wise decision. In the event, only one challenger, John Redwood, a long standing critic of Major's approach from within the Cabinet, came forward to create a contest. Although Major succeeded in his re-election bid, the result – with eighty-nine votes for Redwood, eight abstentions, four spoiled ballots and two non-votes – underlined how seriously the party was divided. Roughly one-third of the parliamentary party did not back Major.

Within the Cabinet itself there had been increasing speculation about the attitudes of the known Eurosceptics, notably Michael Portillo, Michael Howard, Peter Lilley and of course John Redwood. In 1993 Major, when asked why he had not sacked rebels within the Cabinet, had been accidentally overheard commenting on them as 'bastards', a label which was taken up with relish by the determined Eurosceptics within the wider party. With his re-election secured in 1995, Major was able to replace Redwood with William Hague and move two key pro-European figures (Michael Heseltine and Malcolm Rifkind) into the deputy premiership and the Foreign Office while giving Portillo the defence department.

By that stage of course Conservative prospects of winning the next election were already gloomy. The 1997 Labour landslide ushered in a period of further internal turmoil for the Conservatives. John Major immediately resigned and the subsequent period saw a succession of leaders trying to reunite a party shattered over its strategy. Europe – the issue which had been so prominent a factor in the party's internal strife – remained a millstone around its neck. Not until David Cameron called the referendum that finally took the UK out of the European Union did any kind of resolution seem on the horizon – at a cost.

John Major regarded the passage of the Maastricht Treaty as one of his government's most important achievements. Yet he recognised the damage which Europe had done to his party and to him. As he told the Oxford Union in a speech in 2016 Europe had divided the Conservative Party and wrecked many of his ambitions as Prime Minister, and Major recognised that public opinion in the UK made its remaining in the European Union far from certain.[13] Nevertheless, he continued to advocate the continuation of British membership arguing for example in the 2016 Palliser lecture that remaining in the EU was in Britain's economic and political interest and that the Brexiteers' arguments were misguided.[14] The decision to leave the European Union was undoubtedly not one he favoured.

CONCLUSION

John Major's approach to European issues was always shaped by the dual need to keep his party together and to defend what he and the official establishment identified as being in the UK's national interest. To a large extent he succeeded in defending that national interest, although the process often involved compromises and concession which were difficult to explain to the party, let alone the public at large. He kept the party together – just – but again as a result of tactics which often seemed less than heroic. Perhaps he failed to explain clearly and courageously the case for European membership and to provide strong leadership. But politics, as he knew, is the art of the possible and many factors, not least the changing character of the Conservative Party and the realities of European politics, required pragmatic and cautious handling. The political dynamics he had to manage as Prime Minister after 1990 substantially constrained his freedom of action. That his government was able to deliver a fourth successive election victory and take Britain forward for a time on a European path of its choosing is testimony to Major's leadership qualities.

ENDNOTES

1 J. Major, *The Autobiography* (London: Harper Collins, 1999) p. 202
2 K. Clarke, *Kind of Blue: A Political Memoir*, (London: Pan Macmillan, 2016)
3 A. Seldon, *Major: A Political Life* (London: Weidenfeld & Nicholson, 1997); A. Seldon and M. Davies, 'John Major' in C. Clarke, T. James, T. Bale and P. Diamond (eds) *British Conservative Leaders* (London, Biteback, 2015)
4 Major, *The Autobiography*
5 M. Thatcher, 'Speech to the College of Europe' (The Bruges Speech), 20 September 1988, in R. Harris (ed.) *Margaret Thatcher: The Collected Speeches* (London: Harper Collin, 1997)
6 P. Norton, *Dissension in the House of Commons, 1974–1979* (Oxford: Oxford University Press, 1980); P. Cowley, *Revolts and Rebellions: Parliamentary Voting Under Blair* (London, Politico's, 2002)
7 P. Riddell, 'Major and Parliament' in D. Kavanagh and A. Seldon (eds) *The Major Effect* (London: Macmillan, 1994)
8 D. Baker, A. Gamble and S. Ludlam, 'The Parliamentary Siege of Maastricht' *Parliamentary Affairs*, (1994) 47/1
9 Ibid.
10 Seldon, *Major: A Political Life*; Major, *The Autobiography*
11 Seldon, *Major: A Political Life*
12 D. Hannan, 'Black Wednesday: Britain was Free, but We Tories were done for,' *Daily Telegraph*, 11 September 2012
13 J. Major, 'Speech at the Oxford Union on the UK's membership of the European Union,' 13 May 2016, johnmajor.co.uk/speeches.html
14 J. Major, 'Palliser Lecture' 15 June 2016, johnmajor.co.uk/speeches.html

PART FOUR

PERSPECTIVES

18

THE VIEW FROM THE RIGHT

John Redwood MP

I WAS SAD THAT SO many colleagues pushed for the removal of Margaret Thatcher. Once the leadership election got underway to replace her, I decided to back John Major. He was the only candidate who appeared Eurosceptic, and his personal story seemed best suited for modern politics. In the early days of his premiership I was an enthusiastic supporter. I encouraged him to tackle the problems of poor quality public services through a range of initiatives, which he came to call the Citizen's Charter. With Francis Maude I helped the Prime Minister launch the original programme and did some of the policy work behind the scenes on what we might do.

There was, however, a fundamental problem with John's premiership which was a shadow over his appointment, and became a cause of friction within the party. John was a keen advocate of the European Exchange Rate Mechanism (ERM). I had written a pamphlet explaining its dangers just before entering the government, and had from within kept up opposition to it. I had always been assured by Margaret Thatcher that if my fears of its dangers started to come true they would leave. When John took over as

Prime Minister there was the possibility that this policy would shift, and he would be obstinate about leaving a mechanism that he had recommended but which could not work for the interests of the UK. I hoped that in the top job he would change his mind and could be persuaded that the ERM was a potentially very damaging device. My hopes floundered on the reality.

The 1992 election was not a comfortable one for me. As a Minister I could not openly attack the ERM policy, but nor would I give it any public support as it had the smell of death about it. Privately I continued to recommend early exit to spare us the grief that was to follow. It was clear our early days of shadowing the DM and then in the ERM had caused a nasty inflation. We had to keep the value of our currency down, which meant we created far too much money and credit to do so. We needed low interest rates and had to keep creating money to sell across the exchanges, to buy up foreign currencies. The next phase became higher interest rates followed by a recession. The process reversed as foreign currency was sold across the exchanges to try to keep the value of the pound up. As the UK bought up pounds so rates had to rise and money and credit were destroyed. It was a madness bound to produce a boom/bust cycle. The PM, the Treasury and the Bank of England remained optimistic and thought the ERM was the cure, not the disease. In the autumn of 1992 after the election win, pressures in the markets became too great and the UK was forced out of the system.

This was the defining moment of John Major's premiership and of the Conservative Party for two decades. The destruction of its main economic policy meant defeat in the next election was highly likely. It didn't matter that Labour, the Lib Dems, the CBI and the TUC had all recommended this approach. It was a Conservative government that had actually done it. The Conservative Party's reputation for economic competence was badly damaged. It meant thirteen years out of office and eighteen years without a majority. It took the worse disaster of the 2008 banking crash to change perceptions of the economic competence of the Conservatives relative to Labour.

Because the ERM did so much damage to the Conservatives' poll position and because the new government had such a small majority, it proved to be a difficult Parliament. I stayed in government and tried to help John. I was one of a select group of Cabinet ministers that did not brief against him or sound out colleagues to mount a leadership bid. The press regularly ran stories that there would be a leadership battle ere long, between Michael Portillo and Michael Heseltine as the likely front runners from a long field. My main concern was to see that the UK was not dragged into the euro, the next step of the EU in its battle to take over economic policy from member states. Having seen the enormous economic damage the ERM had done, I could not understand why anyone sensible would want to inflict the euro on us. That would be the ERM we could not easily get out of. It too would mean a boom/bust ride for those members entering that were not already fully aligned with the German currency and economy.

The disagreements became most pronounced over the Treaty of Maastricht and the legislation needed to implement it. John Major had very wisely negotiated an opt-out for us from the single currency. That allowed me to stay in the government and back the opt-out vociferously. It meant a very contentious Treaty that many Conservatives did not want to put into UK law. It did nonetheless allow us as a country to opt out of its main foolish proposal. I tried to persuade the Prime Minister to allow the Conservative Party a free vote on the legislation, which would have made it much easier. He refused and the party entered a bruising contest.

It was when the Prime Minister refused to rule out joining the euro that I decided I could no longer support him. What was the point of negotiating an opt-out from a dangerous proposal if there was doubt about using it? Why couldn't he see the damage the ERM had done, and see that the euro would do the same all over again? It did of course later give a violent boom/bust cycle to countries like Ireland and Spain just as I feared. John Major said he was fed up with the Cabinet colleagues who had been allowing or encouraging proto-leadership campaigns to build, and he was resigning to test out the position. He told us to 'put up or shut up'. I decided I could not stay in the government and shut up about the euro, as for me it was a vital matter. The euro not only spelt huge potential economic damage to the UK, but also a major transfer of governing power which I did not want.

The leadership election did no damage to the Conservative Party. We went up in the polls during it, and came back down to where we were before on John Major's win. It did produce one crucial development which made it worthwhile. Both John Major and then Labour offered a referendum before seeking to take the UK into the euro. Once we had those promises I was pretty sure we had won the battle to keep the pound. Polling showed that the voters were much more sensible than many of their MPs, and had no wish to lose their own currency. So it proved. The large majorities against the euro showed in successive polls provided the background to the decision of Tony Blair's government not to join the euro. Creating further requirements for joining, as Gordon Brown did, was worrying because it implied he still thought we might join, but it did the job of ensuring we did not do so at the most vulnerable moment. The longer we had to see the evolution of the euro scheme the clearer it became we were well out of it.

The struggles in the Conservative Party over Maastricht were principled ones. A brave group of backbenchers defied the government over implementing a much-hated treaty, and had to be welcomed back into the party. Their resistance helped create the mood hostile to the euro which informed opinion and led to the right decision not to join. Meanwhile, as I expected and feared, John Major's Conservative Party went down to a huge defeat in 1997. This had little to do with the splits over Maastricht, and everything to do with the economic catastrophe brought on by the ERM at the start of that ill-fated Parliament. Don't take my word for it – I know you won't. Just look at the polls. Conservative support plunged just after the rude exit from the ERM and the long recession it had caused. Those poll ratings never recovered.

19

A VIEW FROM THE CENTRE

Lord (Paddy) Ashdown

When the Conservatives finally decided to remove Margaret Thatcher from office I initially believed that Douglas Hurd would be her most effective successor. For while Michael Heseltine was clearly the most colourful character among the contenders, he was never going to be able to unite the party after leading the attack against Margaret. Of the three contenders, I probably knew least about John Major.

However, I came to have the utmost respect for him. He was one of the most honest, brave and sincere men to ever be Prime Minister. His treatment by Margaret and her supporters was absolutely disgraceful. He had been her chosen successor but almost immediately she said that she could no longer support him and did everything she could to undermine his premiership, claiming to be a good 'back seat driver'. At first her supporters believed that she could return; once they finally realised that would not happen they instinctively believed that nobody would match up to her. They remained infatuated with her, and her interventions before and after the 1997 election were disastrous for the party.

John's political ability was, at the time and subsequently, severely underestimated. All successful leaders know when to trust their instinct. I saw this twice during his premiership.

The first was in the 1992 general election. He was asking for a fourth successive term in office for his party, unprecedented in the democratic era. The opinion polls suggested that he was going to lose. Neil Kinnock had modernised the Labour Party. Against the wishes of his advisers John took to a very traditional form of campaigning, getting out his soap box. The contrast with Labour's slick and glitzy campaign strategy was all too clear and so-called political experts all thought he would fail. However, the scenes of him speaking at apparently spontaneous open-air rallies contrasted starkly with the triumphalism of Labour's 'Sheffield Rally' and tipped the balance. Although he deserved the credit for winning that election, his right-wing were never going to allow him that and acted like a party within a party for much of the following five years.

The second occasion was over Maastricht. Returning from the summit with opt-outs he had negotiated on the single currency and the Social Chapter John may well have expected the loyalty of his MPs, but they had other ideas. Whipped up by Margaret they acted disgracefully. Enjoying the notoriety they had created for themselves they failed to heed the wishes of the party leader. Scenting short-term political advantage Labour sided with the rebels to defeat the Maastricht Bill. I took the decision to support the government as I believed that it was in the long-term interests of the country. When the result of the vote was announced and it became clear that the votes of my party had got the Bill through, Labour MPs rounded on me and my colleagues. I believed then, and I still believe, that I was right to take a more principled stand and support the Maastricht Treaty.

It quickly became clear that John's main objective was to hold his party together. As I looked across the floor of the House of Commons I believed that this would be one task in which he would fail. The party was on the verge of civil war. However, to my astonishment, he did keep the party together up until the 1997 election.

There were other successes too, not least John's quiet determination to build a peace process in Northern Ireland. Although this came to fruition under Tony Blair he could not have achieved this without the heavy lifting of John's premiership and he deserves credit. Although the situation in Northern Ireland is far from perfect it is much better than when I saw active service there.

There were, of course, numerous failures. Shortly after I became the first leader of the newly merged Liberal Democrats I set out a vision for decentralising public services which would involve the state letting go of its centralised control and for people to have much more influence over things such as health, housing and education in their localities. The Citizen's Charter claimed to be doing this but Tories instinctively do not like letting go. It therefore descended into things like the 'traffic cone hotline' and was rightly lampooned by the satirists. Back to Basics was rightly criticised. Rail privatisation has been a clear example of policy failure. More generally, John's style of political communication was antiquated and he fared much worse than Tony Blair in responding to the media age, which Tony handled brilliantly.

Once the inevitable election result was announced in 1997, John took himself off to watch the cricket at Lord's. He acted with dignity then and has done so ever since. He is the very model of how a former Prime Minister should operate. His interventions have been minimal but when he has spoken out it has been when he believed that it was in the best interests of his country and his party, such as his intervention in the 2016 EU referendum. Saying that he has been a very good ex-Prime Minister may sound like a backhanded compliment but it is one of the hardest roles to fulfil. Ted Heath did to Margaret what she in turn did to John. Although I was close to Tony Blair and we tried to achieve an agreement between our respective parties which would have brought about a new progressive alliance in British politics I now have far more respect for John as an ex-Prime Minister than I do for Tony. As John's stock has increased since he ceased being Prime Minister, Tony's has decreased to the point where he is now widely, if sometimes unfairly, vilified.

John's successes as Prime Minister and subsequently deserve credit. His administrations were not a mere footnote in history between the Thatcher and Blair governments. His achievements are largely down to his character, his integrity and his political instincts. His fate was to be leader at a time when his party had been in power too long and was suffering from a spasm of matricidal guilt for its part in the political murder of their past leader.

20

THE VIEW FROM THE LEFT

Charles Clarke

THE POLITICALLY SEISMIC IMPACT of November 1990 was less John Major's entry into 10 Downing Street than Margaret Thatcher's departure.

Thatcher's leadership had been deeply polarising for the country. There was enormous opposition both to her approach and style and to many of her specific policy measures. The proposed poll tax was the last straw.

She was initially shielded from the political consequences of her unpopularity by the fact that, following the formation of the SDP–Liberal Alliance in 1981, she had been faced by an utterly divided opposition and, in 1983, by a discredited and divided Labour Party.

By 1990 those protections were gone. Labour presented a powerful and united alternative which was more credible than at any time in the preceding decade. It certainly faced an uphill struggle but it knew that it could mobilise support for Labour on the strong foundation of a widespread desire to remove her from power.

Conservative MPs were worried by Labour by-election victories in the Vale of Glamorgan and Mid Staffordshire and then the Liberal Democrat win in Eastbourne. They feared Labour success and lost confidence in Margaret Thatcher's ability to lead them to one more victory. So they dumped her and installed John Major.

Of course that decision achieved, without a general election, the change the country had been looking for – the departure of Margaret Thatcher.

Some argued about the extent to which there had been a real change or whether Major's government was simply Thatcher's by another name. But the change did make it more difficult to argue that Neil Kinnock, by 1992 Labour's leader for nine years, was the fresh post-Thatcher face the country needed.

But all of that was secondary to the new reality. Since Labour could no longer rely for support on popular opposition to Thatcher, even greater priority had to be given to demonstrating the credibility in government of its alternative.

Since 1983 Labour had already changed its position on an enormous range of policies; from unilateral nuclear disarmament to selling council houses, membership of the European Union to renationalisation of utilities, trade union laws to management of schools. Through recognition of political necessity Labour had already accepted many of Thatcher's changes, though often without enthusiasm or real conviction.

But confidence in Labour's ability to run the economy – and particularly its approach to taxation – remained the politically key and most difficult challenge. From summer 1991 onwards it was the core of Tory attacks, for example with its dishonest but effective 'Labour's Tax Bombshell' propaganda.

There were differences at the top of Labour about how to deal with this. Some thought it essential for Labour to publish its own detailed economic approach to reassure, and demonstrate clearly, what Labour would and would not do in office. Others considered that unnecessary and risked offering hostages to fortune.

The final outcome was Labour's shadow Budget, published at the beginning of the election campaign. The internal disputes had prevented it from being published earlier, so in the event it served mainly to focus attention on the subject, without giving enough time to disseminate its proposals powerfully.

Ten days before polling day, opinion surveys predicted a strong Labour win and so the final week of the campaign prioritised scrutiny of the likely Labour government. John Major, on his soapbox, reinforced this mindset by presenting himself as an outsider and oppositional figure.

In the event, Labour fell short because it had simply not done enough to convince the electorate that it could be trusted with power.

This history meant that for the rest of John Major's premiership, Labour's dominant concern was to convince the country that it could be trusted with office, while hoping to exploit Conservative failures.

The latter task was made considerably easier by the collapse of the Conservative economic case and the consequent political turmoil. On 16 September 1992 – 'Black Wednesday' – the Major government withdrew the pound from the European Exchange Rate Mechanism, so destroying its economic credibility and exposing its own internal European fault-line.

On 22 July 1993 Labour and other opposition parties combined with anti-European Union Conservatives to defeat the government on the Maastricht Treaty. Though the government won the consequent 'no confidence' vote the damage was done. The tensions between John Major and those he styled 'bastards' never disappeared. Even the leadership election he forced on 4 July 1995, which he won with 66 per cent of the vote, failed to unite his party.

John Smith, Labour leader from July 1992 until his tragically early death in May 1994, was politically astute and skilled at harrying the Conservatives and fomenting their divisions. His parliamentary tactics contributed significantly to the government's defeat over Maastricht.

However, he was less concerned about Labour's own credibility as a government-in-waiting, drawing confidence from his own personal standing and believing that internal Labour arguments about difficult policy issues were too risky.

Tony Blair, who took office on 21 July 1994, had a quite different view.

His overwhelming victory, with 57 per cent of the vote, demonstrated a Labour Party united in its view that modernisation and policy realism were the only way to show its fitness to govern.

In order to exemplify that approach Blair chose to amend Clause 4 of Labour's constitution. His proposal was hazardous, recalling as it did Hugh Gaitskell's failure to make a similar change in 1959/60. However Blair's judgement was vindicated, as two-thirds of the Labour conference in April 1995 supported the changes.

As the general election approached, Blair embodied Labour's policy approach by identifying five pledges – to cut class sizes, cut NHS waiting lists, fast-track youth justice, reduce youth unemployment and implement tight controls on government spending and borrowing. He thereby set out the ambitions and limits of what Labour would do in office.

By 1 May 1997, polling day, John Major, despite important achievements, was caught between the collapse of economic and political confidence in himself and his party, and increasing trust in the character and policies of Labour. The country decided to give the left, under Tony Blair's leadership and with his New Labour brand, the chance to govern the country.

Opinion remains divided as to whether the creation of New Labour, a conscious separation from Labour's past, was necessary for Labour to win outright.

Most Labour people believe that by 1997 the country so strongly desired a change of government that John Smith would have succeeded in winning power – though probably with a significantly smaller parliamentary majority than that achieved by Blair.

Had that been true Smith would have won without any need for the New Labour changes, which many in Labour felt uncomfortable with.

I do not share this outlook. Labour's victory in 1997 was by no means inevitable, despite the national desire for change and the low standing of John Major's government.

People would only vote to put Labour into government if they believed it would govern well and in the national interest. Labour's economic reputation in government, fairly or not, was one of failure, demonstrated by the 1931 government collapse, devaluations in 1949 and 1967, the 1976 IMF crisis and the 1978–79 Winter of Discontent.

A crucial part of New Labour was the separation from this past, combined with a strong and positive economic message. These enabled Labour to win and then, at least until 2008, to demonstrate economic competence in government.

Without the New Labour change John Major might well have been able to survive in office, and keep the left out of power for at least five more years.

21

JOHN MAJOR AND THE CLASSLESS SOCIETY

Alwyn W. Turner

When, in November 1990, John Major announced that he was a candidate for the leadership of the Conservative Party, he took the opportunity to outline his vision of Conservatism, pledging to make 'changes to produce across the whole of this country a genuinely classless society so people can rise to whatever level from whatever level they started'.[1] Meanwhile, his campaign team were suggesting that he himself was the very embodiment of this aspiration: 'classless, young, approachable, meritocratic, compassionate yet not in any sense a softie'.[2]

The personal element was also stressed by many commentators at the time; Major's talk of classlessness, it was said, sent a clear message that he was 'a working class boy made good'.[3] And that, in turn, distanced him from his Cabinet rival, the Old Etonian Douglas Hurd, though the latter was quick to stress that this was all very much common ground. 'I think we are a classless party,' Hurd protested to the press. 'Of course there may be one or two people for whom class may mean something, but they're no longer a political species, and I certainly don't belong to them.'[4] If there was something beyond character in Major's remarks, a political dimension, it was seen as being a pitch for the Norman Tebbit wing of the party, a nod that, in the words of *The Times*'s Robin Oakley, he had 'not forgotten the C2s who delivered Mrs Thatcher her election victories and who have lately been defecting in droves'.[5]

The effect, then, was to establish Major as the continuity candidate, the rightful successor to Margaret Thatcher. And indeed he was singing from the same hymn-sheet as the outgoing leader. Just the previous month, in her final conference speech as Prime Minister, she had spoken of her wish to see an 'open classless Britain', a country that allowed 'opportunity for all' and 'choice for all', one in which 'we break down barriers – barriers between workers and bosses, skilled and unskilled, tenants and owners, barriers between private and public'.[6]

Electorally, the theme of classlessness was an unqualified success for Major. He won the leadership, and employed the same tactic of stressing his personal history to secure victory in the 1992 general election. 'What does the Conservative Party offer a working class kid from Brixton?' asked a Tory poster during the latter campaign. 'They made him Prime Minister.' The message was reinforced in 'The Journey', an election broadcast directed by John Schlesinger that took the Prime Minister back to his South London roots. It was an attractive look, but translating classlessness into something deeper than mere image proved more difficult.

There was, in the first instance, some confusion over precisely what Major meant. 'I think we need a classless society, and I think we need to have what I refer to as social mobility,' he elaborated during the leadership campaign, sounding as though he had stumbled upon a hitherto unknown concept. 'And what I mean by social mobility is the capacity of everybody to have the help necessary to achieve the maximum of their ability.'[7] Or, as he put it in his first major speech as Prime Minister: 'a classless society, not in the grey sense of drab uniformity, but in the sense that we remove the artificial barriers to choice and achievement'.[8]

There was nothing here that constituted a distinguishing mark for a politician in the post-war world. In his 1954 book *British Social Mobility*, the sociologist D. V. Glass had assumed that such ambitions went without question: 'it is one of the postulates of a democratic and egalitarian society that ability, whatever its social background, shall not be denied the chance to fulfil itself'.[9] It was precisely this widespread acceptance that had prompted Michael Young's dystopian essay, warning of *The Rise of the Meritocracy* (1958).

Nor was Major's elevation from a humble background entirely unprecedented. James Callaghan, the last but one Prime Minister, had similarly not attended university, and Major was the third consecutive Tory leader to have been state-educated. In common with his predecessors, this meant he was in a minority among his senior colleagues; of his first all-male Cabinet, just two had been to state schools: Michael Howard and David Mellor. Furthermore, nine were former presidents of either the Oxford or Cambridge Union, while only four sent one or more of their own children to state school, and in three of those instances, the children were still of primary age. None of this was unusual in any way – but, by the same token, it scarcely heralded the dawning of a new egalitarian era. Likewise, the signal sent by Major's approving the award of a baronetcy to Denis Thatcher, the first to be created since 1964 and the last hereditary title handed out to date, was hardly one of classlessness.

The problem with the promise of social mobility was that – despite successive governments mouthing the words – real progress seemed to be slow in coming. This was the conclusion of every major academic study and it was accepted in political circles as well, at least in private. In 1994 a memo written by John Maples, deputy party chairman, was leaked to the press, acknowledging the failure to realise the objective thus far: 'Although in the 1980s the Conservatives seemed to promise a classless society of opportunity, the reality is now that the rich are getting richer on the backs of the rest, who are getting poorer.'[10]

Major's government, like that of Thatcher, struggled to bridge that gap between the speeches and the implementation. No one doubted the Prime

Minister's desire to see social mobility, but he found it hard to find a way to advance the cause. Perhaps the one policy that might have asserted a renewed commitment to the concept was the call for 'a grammar school in every town'.[11] That, though, was in 1996, five and a half years into Major's premiership, and it came at a time when defeat at the next election was as certain as anything in politics can be. The proposal did appear in the 1997 manifesto ('We will help schools to become grammar schools in every major town where parents want that choice'), but no one believed that Major would still be in Downing Street to enact it. In 1992, when it would have made a difference, the manifesto had spoken simply of 'protecting the right of local people to preserve their grammar schools'.

Underlying all this was still the issue of definition. Social mobility, of course, is not actually the same thing as classlessness. It implies a belief in equality of opportunity, but not the eradication of inequality itself. Indeed, by definition, social mobility demands an unequal society; it presupposes that there are strata through which one can move. As Michael Young had suggested, there is a danger that a true meritocracy would entrench inequality.

A metaphor could perhaps be found in the working of the National Lottery, one of Major's most successful legacies. 'I was concerned to ensure that a child who lived in a tower block had the same opportunity in arts and sport as the child who was the heir to rolling acres,' he said in 1998, looking back at the creation of the Lottery. 'It was part, if I may return to an old phrase, of what I thought of as a classless society.'[12] Certainly lottery funding has enabled the emergence of elite sportspeople, and has been credited with Britain's impressive performances at the 2012 and 2016 Olympic Games. A handful of athletes benefited greatly from the investment made in them, though fewer from poor backgrounds have emerged through the free market of football; 32 per cent of Olympic medal-winners in 2016 were privately educated (the same proportion as was to be found in the House of Commons). Meanwhile the Lottery itself continued to be supported disproportionately by socio-economic classes C2, D and E, and the money spent continued to be directed disproportionately to the leisure interests of those in classes A and B. As Julian Critchley once summed up the arrangement: 'The working class and the underclass are encouraged to spend in pursuit of unimaginable riches. The money raised is then spent on a series of middle-class good causes.'[13]

There was, though, another dimension to Major's classlessness agenda, beyond his talk of social mobility. 'I don't mean a society in which everyone is the same, or thinks the same, or earns the same,' he explained in his speech to the 1991 Conservative Party conference. 'But a tapestry of talents in which everyone from child to adult respects achievement; where every promotion, every certificate is respected, and each person's contribution is valued.'[14]

This was a very different proposition: the acceptance of a class society, but an insistence that all classes are worthy and essential to the running of that society: an end to snobbery and elitism. 'I want to bring into being a different kind of country,' he said, 'to bury forever old divisions in Britain between North and South, blue-collar and white-collar, polytechnic and university.'[15]

But in his response to that last mentioned division, he revealed the limitations of his thinking. Rather than seek to elevate the role of the polytechnic, to assert that it should enjoy the same standing as the university, he chose instead simply to abolish the distinction, to rebrand polytechnics as universities. And implicit in that move was a confirmation of the British prejudice in favour of the academic at the expense of the technical. This was not a celebration of diversity, but the very homogenisation to which he repeatedly declared his opposition; it declared that only one set of values really mattered. Divisions, however, remained: the abolition of polytechnic status in 1992 was followed two years later by the launch of the Russell Group, representing the self-proclaimed elite of the old universities and formalising a clear class structure in tertiary education.

If John Major failed to achieve his goal of transforming Britain into a country characterised by social mobility, he was scarcely alone. Subsequent governments have been similarly committed to the principle and similarly unsuccessful in realising it. Because the changes that are emerging – and that were apparent even during Major's premiership – have been driven not by politics, but by the democratisation of culture. The popular demand for cultural recognition was evident in the rise of the docusoap and the video diary on television in the 1990s, leading inexorably to the reality TV of the new century. It was to be seen in the nation's choice of heroes who were believed to embody 'normality', a concept so ill-defined that it stretched from Princess Diana through David Beckham to Jade Goody. And, above all else, it was to be found in the revolution of the internet that has, as yet, barely started.

A new model of class society is taking root. One that distinguishes between the elite and the ordinary. One that encourages those who have previously felt excluded to demand that their voices be heard. And one in which, whatever his background as 'a working class kid from Brixton', Sir John Major KG CH is seen as an enemy of classlessness, not its champion.

ENDNOTES

1 *The Times*, 24 November 1990
2 *The Times*, 23 November 1990
3 *The Guardian*, 24 November 1990
4 *The Sunday Times*, 25 November 1990
5 *The Times*, 24 November 1990
6 Speech delivered to Conservative Party conference, 12 October 1990
7 *The Guardian*, 28 November 1990
8 Speech delivered at QEII Conference Centre, 4 December 1990
9 D. V. Glass, *British Social Mobility* (London: Routledge and Kegan Paul, 1954)
10 J. Sopel, *Tony Blair: The Moderniser* (London: Michael Joseph, 1995)
11 *The Independent*, 29 March 1996
12 House of Commons, 7 April 1998
13 J. Critchley and M. Halcrow, *Collapse of Stout Party: The Decline and Fall of the Tories* (London: Victor Gollancz, 1997)
14 Speech delivered to Conservative Party conference, 11 October 1991
15 J. Major, *The Autobiography*, (London: Harper Collins, 1999)

22

AN OVERALL ASSESSMENT

Sir Anthony Seldon and Mark Davies

Britain is prone to be dismissive of its leaders when they are in power, and continues to be so after their fall. It is difficult for Prime Ministers to climb back up in public esteem. John Major stands out as a rare holder of the office in the last century whose standing has risen after stepping away from power. Few Prime Ministers in office have been more disparaged by the press. As his authorised biographer, my book was judged too friendly. But were the critics right? His composure in the face of relentless attacks, not least for a man without great reserves of inner security, was unusual. Major's was an important, albeit unruly, premiership at the end of the Conservative century, completing some parts of an earlier agenda while in some key respects helping to define a Conservatism for the twenty-first century.

MAJOR'S RISE TO BECOME PRIME MINISTER

For Major's leap from the Treasury to No. 10, Geoffrey Howe's devastating resignation speech came at just the right moment. Major's strong conference speech in the same month meant that his profile was at its height, and Thatcher's doubts about Major, for his lack of scepticism on Europe and his liberal domestic policy instincts, had yet to form. Some on the right alleged that Major plotted to remove Thatcher. Such a charge cannot be sustained. Indeed, following Howe's resignation on 1 November 1990, and rising speculation that Heseltine would challenge her for the leadership, Major had concluded that he had little serious hope of succeeding Mrs Thatcher, and that a leadership contest that November was likely to *worsen* his eventual chances. All the same, he had been harbouring doubts about tying his body to what he suspected was a mortally wounded carcass.

That Major wanted to become Prime Minister there can be no doubt. But this falls a long way short of him 'plotting' against Mrs Thatcher. His lack of enthusiasm for seconding her for the first ballot was because he thought she would have to go, and he was not keen on keeping her as PM. He hesitated before agreeing to second her for the second ballot because he resented her presumption without any explanation that he would be willing to back her. While all the drama was taking place from 18 to 21 November, Major was not goading colleagues, but his supporters were at work. But he himself gave no word, in public or in private, that he would stand in a second ballot. He remained loyal until she said that she was standing down. Any suggestion that his hospital stay for a dental operation between 16 and 18 November, and his subsequent convalescence at home on medical advice, was a pretext to remove him from the fray while his adjutants plotted his advance is without foundation. The operation date had been booked several weeks in advance. So the main charge – of conspiracy to bring her down – is not supported by the evidence.

There is, however, something in a second charge from the Thatcher camp – that he could have done more for her. He could certainly have been more robust defending her from Howe's assault, and spoken up more for her after Heseltine declared on 14 November. But the charge of lack of positive support, while sustainable, was a counsel of perfection, above all for one who had concluded Mrs Thatcher had outlived her usefulness.

MAJOR'S RECORD AS PRIME MINISTER

The achievements of his premiership we can now say with hindsight were underestimated by contemporaries. His government's agenda consolidated Thatcherism, succeeding in privatising coal and rail, as well as pursuing other radical policies such as the sale of the nuclear industry and traditional state organisations like HMSO. The Deregulation and Contracting Out Act 1994 produced a significant clear-out of regulations that had survived the 1980s. The government introduced welfare reforms which, for the first time since 1945, meant that welfare costs fell as a proportion of national income. The march of reform continued through institutions such as the Stock Exchange and the army, and through a mini-revolution in education.

The government had overall a solid economic record. The Major years, after the recession of 1990–92, saw consistently low inflation and steady economic growth at 2–3 per cent which showed no sign of overheating or slackening. There were unsung improvements to public services through the Citizen's Charter, and a renaissance of culture and sport through National Lottery funding, which ultimately led to Britain's considerable gold medal success at the 2012 Olympics. The key events, achievements and difficulties of Major's premiership are discussed below.

The Gulf War

Immediately upon becoming Prime Minister, Major faced the international crisis caused by Iraq's invasion of Kuwait. Charles Powell estimates that Major's most important contribution in the build-up to the international community's armed response was 'firstly his management of British public and parliamentary opinion, which he did brilliantly, and secondly his handling of our own forces.'[1] On the evening after hostilities commenced, Major made a direct television broadcast from No. 10, a ploy Thatcher had never used. It was a risk, but it was a success. His concluding remark, 'God Bless', struck a powerful chord with the families of members of the armed forces. The direct television broadcast was a formula he was to employ later in his premiership, evidence of his own satisfaction with how it went. Major provided calm, proficient and dignified leadership throughout the conflict, which was the biggest British military campaign since Korea forty years earlier. He earned the respect and confidence of the armed services. He was an equally steady and resolute leader over Bosnia. His most decisive contribution to the Gulf episode was the creation of safe havens for the Kurds, an initiative for which he was primarily responsible among international leaders. Although thousands of Kurds died at the hands of Saddam's reprisals, thousands more may have died were it not for Major's life-saving actions.

The 1992 general election

Major's achievement in securing a majority in the 1992 election was considerable. The election campaign had begun, as Michael White wrote, 'in the least favourable circumstances for a sitting government since Harold Wilson ended the last thirteen-year tenure in 1964'.[2] The country was in the middle of a recession, with the polls placing Labour 2 per cent ahead. With the party still behind in the polls midway through the campaign, Major took a dramatic step. Motivated by his failure to get through to electors in the street, he went to speak on behalf of the Conservative MP in Luton armed with a packing case and loudhailer. The packing case was to be his soapbox, from which he would harangue or charm his audience. He later explained,

> I don't like speaking to an audience on a platform ... there is no contact, no humanity, no relationship. So I was looking to get on the soapbox all the time. People kept saying "no, you mustn't do it, too dangerous, won't work, not Prime Ministerial". Eventually ... I just did it.[3]

On that soapbox, surrounded by the shouting and confusion, he felt uniquely himself and in command of his destiny. Major standing on his soapbox was to become a regular feature of the campaign.

Major showed considerable bravery with his insistence on mixing with crowds, in contrast to Neil Kinnock, who was neither an IRA target nor the subject of such venom on the streets. In Southampton, Major received his hardest direct hit from an egg, struck with such force in the face that he was nearly knocked over; for a few seconds he thought it might have been a bullet.

Major's public image was a significant factor in the eventual Conservative victory, in which they won 14 million votes, a record that still stands. The Conservatives defeated Labour by 7.5 per cent, achieving 41.9 per cent of the popular vote, an achievement even more impressive when viewed with the benefit of hindsight; in the five elections since 1992, the Conservatives have averaged only 33.5 per cent. However, the parliamentary majority of only twenty-one was a poor reward for such a convincing victory. The electoral system operated against the Conservatives because of tactical voting; if the swing had been uniform across the country, they would have won a 71-seat majority. The history of the next five years would have been different had that been the case.

Black Wednesday

Ejection from the ERM in September 1992, more than any other single event, undermined the second Major government, destroying the reputation for economic competence that the Conservatives had developed under Thatcher. Labour leader John Smith called him 'a devalued Prime Minister of a devalued government'.[4] Yet it is important to remember that entry into the ERM had been supported by Labour, the Liberal Democrats, industry, the City, the TUC and most trade unions. Major had acted on what he regarded as the best advice in the country, and had taken what he thought were the brave and right decisions. Now he found himself widely reviled.

Following the UK's departure from the ERM, stories appeared claiming that Major had cracked and lost his nerve on that fateful day. There is no truth in any of these rumours – too many witnesses testify so. Throughout the key meetings and in all the decisions, he was calm and self-possessed. Though obviously under heavy stress, he elicited opinions from everyone, asked the questions, summed up, and took the final decisions.

The world was never the same after Black Wednesday. Eurosceptic feeling would from now on be unrestrained in its attacks on the leadership. The balance of power in the Cabinet began to tilt away from Major and towards the Eurosceptic trio of Howard, Lilley and Portillo. The Tory press would never return fully to the fold. Black Wednesday cost the Conservative Party its image of managerial competence in the eyes of the electorate.

The Maastricht Treaty

The Maastricht Treaty was to cause Major great difficulty. The irony is that it was at first a personal triumph for him. He secured his twin objectives of ensuring Britain remained at the heart of European affairs while preserving freedom of action in those areas where the UK's sovereignty was deemed to be sacrosanct. Major's skills in holding his Cabinet together were rarely better displayed than over the closing phases of the Maastricht Bill. David Hunt, who was at that time Secretary of State for Employment, recorded in his contemporary notes, 'when all this is looked back on within the party, we will see that it was his determination to drive that through that enabled us to survive'.[5]

Victory was finally achieved, but at what cost? Major won plaudits for his single-mindedness and coolness under pressure. But his reliance on a confidence motion to give the Maastricht Bill the last heave through Parliament exacted a price. The rebels had developed bonds of shared adversity, and the virtual party within a party was not to be disbanded as the leadership hoped. They resented the methods that had been used against them. They went on to form a hard core of plotters, posing the threat of a leadership challenge every autumn. However, could Major have acted differently? He had staked his leadership on the Maastricht Treaty, and that meant putting it through Parliament. Bar abandoning the treaty, he had little alternative but to act as he did. If he had won a Pyrrhic victory, it was perhaps the only victory on offer.

Significant Steps towards Peace in Northern Ireland

Major's greatest initiative of his premiership came not in a purely domestic policy area, but in Northern Ireland. Progress was all the most remarkable because he had to overcome the deep-seated suspicions not just of the Unionist, Nationalist and Republican constituencies in Ireland, but also the right of his own party, which became all the harder once the government's majority began to disappear, and the right was gunning for him. Major's achievement was to carry his party, and Cabinet, with him, without the resignations and protests that followed the Anglo-Irish Declaration of 1985. The result of his efforts was that the foundation for a lasting peace in Ireland had been established by the end of his premiership.

Major's social liberalism

Major's strong social liberalism and detestation of discrimination, whether on grounds of race, gender, class or sexual preference, were rare for a Conservative Prime Minister. His sympathy for those who have been marginalised by society derived from his own personal experience of poverty during his childhood, and from his feeling that he was himself an 'outsider'. His most dramatic action in discrimination came not over race, arguably the prejudice on which he felt most strongly, but over homosexuality. His liking for thoughtful, sensitive men predisposed him to form close friendships with gays, and he had none of the hang-ups about gays that many of his generation and background had. In September 1991 he invited Sir Ian McKellen to a formal meeting at No. 10 at which McKellen raised concerns felt by gay people, including the age of consent (then set at twenty-one), police harassment of gays, homosexuality in the armed forces and abusive language in the press. McKellen found Major 'a very sympathetic listener'. Major for his part found it moving to learn more about everyday repression and harassment.[6]

The visit was a high-risk move for Major. The Conservative Family Campaign was one of several groups to go on the attack. The press response, however, was generally favourable. Several significant developments followed from the meeting: Major told his ministers to respond more positively in their departments to representations from the gay population; announcements were made about gays in the civil service; and Major agreed to hold an age of consent debate (in February 1994), albeit on an open vote, which resulted in the age of consent being lowered to eighteen. The McKellen visit gave rise to broader hopes from some that Major would develop a right-of-centre socially liberal agenda for the Conservative Party. Although Major's instincts inclined him in that direction, he did not go further because he was wary of right-wing reaction. For example, he voted to lower the age of consent to eighteen rather than bring about full legal equality by lowering it to sixteen, and he did not repeal 'Section 28'. Had his majority after the 1992 general election been bigger, he would likely have gone further in a socially liberal direction. But circumstances ran against him.

The 1997 general election

The huge defeat that the Conservatives suffered at the 1997 election happened because the country and the media were deeply bored with the Tories, and fed up with a party that seemed to have no common beliefs or loyalty to bind it together. By the end of the century, the Tories' stock of agreed policies on which the leadership could draw was running dry. There were ideas aplenty, but not ones around which all sections of the parliamentary party could unite, and with a wafer-thin and disappearing majority after 1992 all elements needed to agree if the government were to receive parliamentary endorsement for its programme.

The defeat was *not* caused because Major was not a Eurosceptic nor sufficiently Thatcherite. Politicians are fundamentally self-interested people. For most of the party's history, self-interest has dictated loyalty; in the 1990s, with the polls continually showing a huge Labour advantage and the likelihood of a heavy Tory defeat, self-interest was better served by actions other than loyally following the party leader. Coupled with that, the Tories faced Tony Blair, the most creative opposition leader in the Labour Party's history, who brilliantly exploited Tory divisions while stealing their natural voters.

THE DIFFICULT CIRCUMSTANCES OF MAJOR'S PREMIERSHIP

Many of the harsher criticisms levelled against Major's performance as Prime Minister are flawed because they have little regard for the circumstances under which Major served his premiership from 1990 to 1997. Great leaders throughout history have been made by great opportunities – war, economic depression, or a widespread shift in public mood that the leader can articulate. The historical opportunity for *any* leader who succeeded Mrs Thatcher in November 1990 was, in contrast, unusually restricting. The environment in which any historical figure acts needs to be considered under four headings: individuals, ideas, circumstances and interests.

1: The lack of scope for assertive leadership in the 1990s

The scope for assertive leadership in the 1990s was less than in the 1980s. Not only was Major a collegiate leader – and such leaders do not make the weather – but he also faced far tougher Labour leaders than did Mrs Thatcher. She served opposite James Callaghan on his way out, Michael Foot, and a young Neil Kinnock; Major faced Kinnock in his prime, John Smith, and Tony Blair, who with Alastair Campbell outclassed his lack-lustre media operation. Unlike Mrs Thatcher, Major never found a senior figure such as Whitelaw to underpin his position. Neither did Major have, like Mrs Thatcher, a coterie of sympathetic interpreters of his policies in the media and intellectual life. Instead, he had the opposite, with devastating results.

No Conservative leader in the past century has had to contend with a predecessor so overtly questioning their premiership. Thatcher and Major were both at fault for their poisoned relationship. She was perhaps the more guilty, because she saw the damage she was doing, how divided was the party, and how small the majority after 1992, and above all because she had suffered herself from similar sniping from her predecessor Edward Heath.

One of her closest friends concluded: 'She used all her political cunning to knife him and stab him and demoralise him and weaken him. Above all else she was thinking, "he is doing my job. How dare he?"'[7]

Although Major was served by some exceptional officials and able ministers, the pool of political talent at his disposal after eleven years in office, and still more so after forty-four Tories lost their seats in 1992, was restricted. The seventy former ministers on the backbenches were often bitter and unbiddable. Those who knew they would not receive jobs – including many hardened Eurosceptics – saw little reason for being loyal to Major.

2: The lack of fresh ideas on the right

The ideological background for Major in 1990 was similarly unpromising. Mrs Thatcher was able to adopt an intellectually coherent platform developed in universities and among thinkers deriving inspiration from Hayek's *Road to Serfdom* (1944) and other liberal texts, and packaged for her in the 1970s and 1980s by friendly think tanks such as the Centre for Policy Studies. A coherent body of ideas was there for her to take off the peg. By the time Major became Prime Minister, the battle for ideas had been won, as had the Cold War, and the 1990s offered fewer certainties. Blair's adoption of much of the Thatcherite agenda shows that in the 1990s fresh portmanteau ideas, certainly on the right, were not to be had.

3: Circumstances

Major served at a time when circumstances were especially difficult. Immediately upon becoming Prime Minister he was confronted by the Gulf crisis, deepening recession, the poll tax, and a party already deeply unpopular and divided over Europe. His in-tray also contained ticking bombs such as arms trading with Iraq, the Pergau Dam, and the growth of shady lobbying companies. His first years were overshadowed by the recession and the consequent problems in the public finances. His later years suffered because of a dwindling parliamentary majority at the mercy of eccentric backbenchers, and the mischance of having to steer the Maastricht Treaty through in 1993 in very different circumstances from the acclaim that had greeted his original deal in 1991.

Sleaze, neither initiated nor encouraged by Major, and which was one of the defining issues of his premiership, proved a daunting subject to confront. Major responded by establishing the Scott (1992) and Nolan (1994) enquiries, to the fury of his right, and then, when parliamentary pressures prevented him endorsing their reports to the full, he was castigated by the centre and left. The Hamilton affair, over which he had to battle with both an angry right and Hamilton's Tatton constituency, proved equally evasive of an early solution. Many more condemned Major over sleaze than came forward with practical and workable solutions. The irony remained: an honest man crippled by sleaze. He could not find the right response.

Where Heath had five years in opposition to plan, Mrs Thatcher four years and Blair three, Major had barely one month, after it seemed likely he would win in November 1990, to plan his policies and the personnel he wanted to serve him. Once in office, he again lacked the time to develop his ideas. For a cricketer, he was placed from the outset on the back foot, and only rarely did he have the chance to play forward. In electoral terms, Major suffered from the emergence of New Labour, which stole the Tories' true secret weapon, not loyalty, but adaptability. In New Labour, Major faced the supreme 'flexi-party', willing to adopt almost any policy and position to appeal to centre-ground voters.

4: Interests

Tory hegemony this century has depended in significant part on the backing of the powerful interests in the country – the City, business and the press, as well as the professions. The last was alienated by Mrs Thatcher and never fully returned. Significant elements of the first three flew away from the Tories in the 1990s. In contrast, the interests that in electoral terms had handicapped Labour since the 1970s, the trade unions, were distanced from them. There were no powerful interests for Major to slay, or the equivalent to those whose vanquishing added so greatly to Mrs Thatcher's stature – a bloated state sector, inefficient nationalised industries, over-mighty trade unions. If Major's equivalent of the Falklands War was the Gulf War, which did not end in such conclusive fashion, the equivalent of the 1980s victory in the Cold War, where the popular forces of liberal democracy triumphed over corrupt statism, was Bosnia in the 1990s, without such clear moral absolutes.

The most difficult problem of all that Major faced was that, with polls and by-elections pointing continually to the likelihood of a heavy defeat, there was little incentive for his own parliamentary party to follow his lead when an alternative – any alternative – offered the prospect of a revival in fortunes. Major did not play the hand he was dealt to best advantage. However, it would be wrong to judge a premier without balancing such factors as described above. In comparison to Major, Attlee and Thatcher both governed in favourable circumstances. With regards to Tony Blair, almost all of the factors outlined above were favourable during his time in office. Yet what did Blair achieve? Arguably less with much more.

MAJOR'S CHARACTER AND STYLE OF LEADERSHIP

Major belonged to no single school of Conservatism, had no mentors among past Tory leaders or theorists, and had no interest in redefining Toryism. He was by temperament and choice a conciliator, and had found Mrs Thatcher's style of 'macho leadership' distasteful. His chairmanship of Cabinet and Cabinet committees, in contrast, allowed ministers to express their views, and guided them to a conclusion in line with his intentions. Rather than have dissent in Cabinet, he preferred to delay decisions until he could reconcile differences. He presided over a regular and more public system of Cabinet committees, with less recourse to pressurising decisions in bilaterals than most of his predecessors. He did not have a 'kitchen Cabinet' of regular close aides and resorted to an *ad hoc* inner Cabinet only in the run-up to both general elections and during particularly difficult periods, such as late 1994. Major's consensual style made him temperamentally close to the civil service with whom he enjoyed extremely good relations. Robin Butler, Cabinet Secretary (1988–98), was his closest official.

Major's qualities of emollience, pragmatism and wanting to hold all factions together, were attracting contempt from some quarters by the end of his premiership. However, the party as a whole in 1990 had wanted a change from Thatcher to a more collegiate, inclusive and unideological leader, and that is exactly what Major proved to be. Might a Hurd, a Heseltine or a Redwood premiership have proved much more successful? Would the much-vaunted 'strong leadership' the right advocated have succeeded when the party was so fundamentally divided?

Major's consensual leadership style could be argued to have been in tune with the requirement of the times. Conservative unity on Europe, which fractured in the late 1980s, showed that Mrs Thatcher's style of leadership and negative stance on the EC was no longer tenable. Major had the difficult task of managing strong and complex trends of parliamentary and public opinion which moved decisively in a Eurosceptic direction in the 1990s. Across a range of other policy issues, his undoctrinaire approach suited the tenor of the times. Instead of, like the right, wishing that the public sector would go away or, like much of the centre-left of his party, considering it sacrosanct, he took a case-by-case approach to reform. The same applied to privatisation: rail privatisation and the Private Finance Initiative involved innovative ways of mixing public and private sectors. Major's pragmatic approach played a significant role in creating a lasting peace in Northern Ireland, which is a prime example where the accusation of Major lacking all principles or consistency falls apart. Failed leaders see little of their policy survive. This did not happen with Major, much of whose legacy was taken on board by the incoming Labour government in 1997.

A weakness in Major's character was that he never learned fully to rise above criticism, or to sift it objectively into fair comment from which he could learn. He was altogether too thin-skinned as Prime Minister, and became a much more confident figure only after he left No. 10. His inability to rise above personal criticism projected weakness; being seen to be affected emboldened those in the media who, scenting blood, wanted to go ever further in ridicule. Internalising his anger and resentment further churned him up, and did not aid his equilibrium. One can only speculate why he could not brush off the criticisms from his detractors, but his lack of deep personal security and positive self-image from childhood and adolescence clearly figured large. At Major's core was a vulnerability which no amount of success after his teens could ever remove, and which remained with him until the end of his premiership.

CONCLUSION

Despite the particularly difficult circumstances in which John Major served as Prime Minister, his achievements were not inconsiderable. His government consolidated Thatcherism, had a solid economic record, provided strong if restrained leadership upon the international stage, and helped to bring peace to Northern Ireland. These and other aspects of his government's agenda were continued by the incoming Labour government in 1997. All of this was made possible by the victory – against all odds – in the 1992 general election, a victory for which Major was much responsible, and a victory that killed off 'old Labour' until 2015. The Conservative defeat in 1997 was in part due to circumstances beyond his control, including the country's desire for change after eighteen years of Conservative rule.

Major lacked some of the robustness to be a strong Prime Minister. He did not happily assert himself nor like to be unpopular, and would sooner say 'yes' than 'no'. His track record on public spending in 1989–93, which led to the loss of the 'tax card', saw this vulnerability displayed at its most acute. His insecurity, coupled with his lack of grounding in Tory philosophy, partly explain a lack of consistency. Absence of time to prepare for office, and his disappearing parliamentary majority, prevented him from pushing ahead further with his deeply felt instincts – on constitutional reform, modernisation of his party, and reforms to help the underprivileged and dispossessed, towards whom he felt genuine personal concern.

Much of his pleasure in being Prime Minister was taken away by the barrage of criticism, and the difficulty he found in making an appropriate response. Yet he remained a dignified and polite premier, lacking arrogance in his dealings with people. He was the first Conservative premier to believe profoundly in race equality and in progress towards homosexual equality. He showed occasional political courage and a gambler's nerve, as in his defying his 'handlers' in the 1992 and 1997 general elections and in launching the 1995 leadership election. He failed to define a distinctive vision for his party, but so too did his four successors as party leader: Hague, Duncan Smith, Howard and Cameron.

In history, Major is not a towering figure like Attlee or Thatcher, but nor is he a failure like Balfour or Eden, nor a footnote in the party's evolution like Bonar Law or Douglas Home. If parliamentary circumstances had been different, Major might have been a Baldwin, presiding over a new deal between party and mass electorate. His government's enduring successes, achieved in the face of such adverse circumstances, mean from the perspective of 2017 that we can say that Major was among the more effective leaders of any party since 1945.

ENDNOTES

1 Interview, Sir Charles Powell
2 *The Guardian*, 12 March 1992
3 A. Seldon, *Major: A Political Life* (London: Weidenfeld & Nicolson, 1997) p. 279
4 House of Commons speech, 24 September 1992
5 Seldon, *Major: A Political Life*, p. 388
6 Ibid. p. 217
7 Ibid. p. 255

INDEX